The Floater's Guide

to **COLORADO**

The Floater's Guide
to **COLORADO**

by Doug Wheat

Falcon Press Publishing Co., Inc.
Billings and Helena, Montana

To Dr. Walt Blackadar—
For the memories of your laughter, courage, and infectious enthusiasm
as you paddle down the River of No Return.

Falcon Press is continually expanding its list of recreational guidebooks. All books include detailed descriptions, accurate maps, and all information necessary for enjoyable trips. You can order extra copies of this book and get information and prices for other Falconguides by writing Falcon Press, P.O. Box 1718, Helena, MT 59624, or calling toll free 1-800-582-2665. Also, please ask for a free copy of our current catalog.

Library of Congress Catalog Card Number: 83-081334
ISBN: 1-56044-371-5

Falcon Press Publishing Co., Inc.
P.O. Box 1718, Helena, MT 59624

Photos by the author unless otherwise indicated.

CAUTION:

Outdoor recreation activities are by their very nature potentially hazardous. All participants in such activities must assume the responsibility for their own actions and safety. The information contained in this guidebook cannot replace sound judgment and good decision-making skills, which help reduce risk exposure, nor does the scope of this book allow for disclosure of all the potential hazards and risks involved in such activities.

Learn as much as possible about the outdoor recreation activities you participate in, prepare for the unexpected, and be safe and cautious. The reward will be a safer and more enjoyable experience.

The Author: *When not floating rivers, author Doug Wheat teaches biology and geology. Wheat, who pioneered several of the river runs described in this book, also worked with the National Geographic Society on its new book,* America's Wild and Scenic Rivers. *He resides in Woodland Park, Colorado, with his wife and daughters.*

 Printed on recycled paper.

Acknowledgements

I would first like to thank Mr. John L.J. Hart—compatriot of Otis "Doc" Marston, Norman Nevills, Bert Loper, and other western river pioneers—for the use of his voluminous and valuable river-running files and for his helpful encouragement. I am also grateful to Tom Guerrero, Janet Baker, and Ed Madej for their help in preparation of the maps and charts. To Pristen Bird and Sanna Porte, for their useful and perceptive editing suggestions, I am most grateful. My appreciation also goes out to Carol Pickett for countless hours of assistance in preparation of the manuscript.

Many thanks to the Tutt Library at Colorado College, my alma mater, for numerous research hours spent there, and to my boating associates of the Pikes Peak Whitewater Club for their jovial companionship out on our marvelous western rivers.

I am indebted to my wife, Annetta Wheat, for her fine bird illustrations and constant support. Above all, I wish to express my gratitude to Frank Wheat, my dad, for the inspiration of his love of wilderness and wild things over the years. This book has benefitted greatly from his priceless gift of clear thinking and sense of language and by the ideas that flowed from many stimulating conversations with him.—*Doug Wheat*

How to Use This Book

Although it's difficult to reduce rivers to simple maps and charts, some of this type of generalization is necessary in such a guidebook. I have organized the chapters by river basin. A map of each basin is located on the title page, repeated as a small key map on each of the succeeding, larger-scale maps. In addition to using these maps, I urge readers to obtain the U.S. Geological Survey topographic maps for any rivers they plan to float. These can be obtained from the USGS, Federal Center, Denver, CO 80225 or at some stores.

Each chapter begins with historical and geological stories about the rivers, followed by detailed information. At the beginning of most of the descriptions of rivers or sections of rivers, I have listed pertinent data. Before using this information and the following descriptions, I recommend referring to the appendix for gradient, water level, skill, and river difficulty ratings.

The average acre-feet runoff figures offer a gage for determining the size of a river. I have listed, in most cases, sources for water level information. Check water levels before leaving, as levels constantly change.

Each hydrograph shows the runoff for typical high, low, and average water level years. For more information, I strongly suggest obtaining "Water Supply Outlook," published monthly from January to May by the Soil Conservation Service. Based on mountain snowpack and organized by river basin, these publications are extremely useful for predicting coming runoff each season. For Colorado and New Mexico, write Soil Conservation Service, P.O. Box 17107, Denver, CO 80217.

Some sections of Colorado's rivers flow across private property. Thus, river runners should always respect the rights of private landowners and be careful to exercise courtesy and consideration toward private property. This includes seeking permission to cross private land.—*Doug Wheat.*

Contents

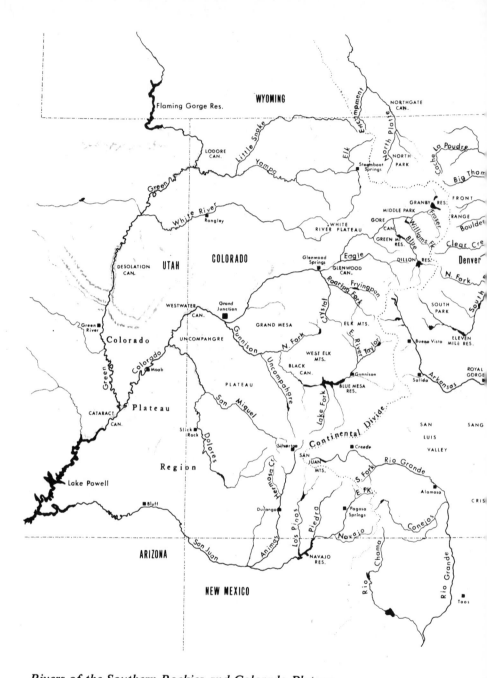

Rivers of the Southern Rockies and Colorado Plateau.

Use this general map to locate floating streams in Colorado, southern Wyoming, eastern Utah, and northern New Mexico. The table of contents in this book will direct you to more detailed maps of individual rivers.

Great

Plains

Part I
The Joy of Rivers

Black Canyon of the Gunnison.

Everybody needs beauty as well as bread,
places to play in. . .where nature may heal and cheer
and give strength to body and soul alike.
  —John Muir

Kingdom of the River Rats

The Southern Rocky Mountain country is a domain of soaring mountains and high plateaus. Beyond its steep eastern escarpment lie the Great Plains. To the north is the high desert of the Wyoming Basin. Along the southern border are the extremities of the San Juan and Sangre de Cristo ranges in New Mexico. The western margin has no clear definition. The Colorado Rockies gradually die out toward the west, blending into the high plateau country of eastern Utah. An arbitrary western limit can be located near that deep blue anomaly of the desert, Lake Powell.

Within this region flow a multitude of enchanting rivers—enough to keep any rapid-happy lover of current and canyon content for a lifetime.

Who are those who seek rivers? They can be called rafters, kayakers, boaters, paddlers, and even river rats. To them a river is not merely something to look at, but a living force to mount and ride. As eagles play on currents of air and water striders on the delicate surfaces of quiet pools, such men and women have learned to play on primordial, rushing water. They long for the tonic of wilderness on rivers that thrill their blood.

Some who seek rivers long for solitude. Others are eager for sport. Still others enjoy the adventure of exploring new territory. Their canyon haunts bear exotic names such as Royal Gorge, Black Canyon, Lodore, Split Mountain, Desolation, Slick Rock, Cataract, Animas, and Whirlpool. A canyon's tempered light suffuses the natural scene with unusual beauty. Though contained by high walls, one finds a sense of freedom in a canyon, where one is cut off from the busy outside world.

A mountain stream can be a harsh teacher. Its lore, not easily learned, can be attended by difficulty and danger. River runners must be quick, nimble, decisive. Judgement and subtlety outrank both strength and power in importance. Never opposing the river's force, they follow its lead, commanded by it rather than commanding, always accompanying it on its chosen path without the vulgar assistance of a motor.

In the winter season river runners look with delight upon dreary, snowy weather. Their spirits rise with each storm that brings the promise of enhanced animation when spring unlocks the waters.

The annual story of the Southern Rocky Mountain rivers begins in the far Pacific and the Gulf of Mexico. Saturated storm clouds are borne inland by favoring winds across coast ranges and western deserts. On reaching the Rocky Mountains, they are forced to rise. The water is squeezed out, bathing this capstone of the continent with snow. Colorado is like an immense, inverted catch basin holding the water's potential energy in winter storage.

Although spring assures the blossoming of wild rose and columbine, it does not guarantee a spring flowering for Southern Rocky Mountain rivers. Seasonal snowpacks in the Rockies can vary as much as ten-fold from year to year. Moreover, many a river has been shackled and tunneled by man. Each river has its own springtime flow pattern, responding to natural rhythms, to human design, or to both.

Melting of the snowpack usually commences early in May. Throughout May the free-flowing rivers rise, normally peaking by mid-June. From late June into July, depleting snowfields release less and less water. By August, many rivers have dropped to their lowest levels. Larger ones, and those fed by late dam releases, maintain an adequate flow for boating through August and September. The winter snowpack provides the river runner with an accurate barometer of the length of the coming season and of expected maximum river levels. Moreover, irrespective of the amount of snowpack, the regularity of yearly runoff allows advance trip planning by those who have learned seasonal rhythms.

The design of a river system is analogous to that of a tree. Their structures are arranged in much the same way—creeks for twigs, streams for branches, rivers for trunks. Both trees and rivers are fixed on the earth, yet both are vessels holding continual motion. In a tree the water flows in reverse, starting rather than culminating in the trunk, defying rather than honoring gravity. Both carry nutrients to nourish the life within them. Both are powered by the sun's energy. Both grow dormant in winter, then strengthen and blossom with the restorative radiation of spring.

Twigs to branches, branches to trunks, the waters of Colorado gather, radiating from the many ranges that occupy the central portion of the state. More major rivers rise in Colorado than in any other state outside Alaska. The North Platte crosses Colorado's northern border, the South Platte and the Arkansas flow eastward to the Mississippi, the Rio Grande courses southward to the Gulf of Mexico, and numerous branches of the Colorado trend westward, their waters eventually reaching the Pacific whence they came. With a single exception—the Green—no significant Colorado river originates in another state. On its southward course from its headwaters in the Wind River Mountains of Wyoming, this largest tributary of the mighty Colorado nicks the northwest corner of the state.

The Southern Rockies snake through central Colorado from Wyoming to New Mexico. The Continental Divide, backbone of the Rockies, separates the tributaries of the Colorado River from those rivers that terminate in the Gulf of Mexico. Several river-spawning ranges just eastward and westward form the roof of the Divide like dormer windows. In addition, many noble rivers have their sources in mountains far from the route of the Divide. The region's various ranges stand isolated by flat, intermountain "parks," islands of the Great Plains. The South Platte's youth is spent in South Park, the Colorado gathers in Middle Park, and the North Platte begins in North Park. The waters of the Rio Grande accumulate in the San Luis Valley, largest of the parks.

Not all rivers born on the flanks of the Divide found an easy way to the lowlands. In some cases their paths were blocked by smaller, granite-cored ranges. In the course of breaking through such obstacles, they have buried themselves in spectacular gorges. Fashioned in this way were Gore and Glenwood canyons of the Colorado and the Black Canyon of the Gunnison on the West Slope. On the East Slope, the process resulted in the Royal Gorge of the Arkansas, Waterton Canyon of the South Platte, and Northgate Canyon of the North Platte.

West of the Continental Divide lie high mesas, mountain ranges in themselves and the source of numerous rivers. The largest of these, the White River Plateau, is the source of the White and Yampa Rivers. To the south, lava-capped Grand Mesa spills streams into the Gunnison and Colorado. The Uncompahgre Plateau supplies water to the Dolores and San Miguel. Still further to the west lies the Colorado Plateau. Through this vast region, the Colorado River and its tributaries have carved many spectacular canyons, culminating in the greatest of all gashes in the earth's surface, the Grand Canyon.

The southwestern corner of the Rockies is dominated by the San Juan Mountains—a jagged, isolated, mostly volcanic range that has intruded into and upset the region of the plateaus. Vast quantities of snow gather in the heart of the San Juans and spawn many rivers. Radiating from the central San Juans are the Rio Grande, Animas, Piedra, San Juan, Conejos, Rio Chama, Dolores, and Uncompahgre rivers, and Lake Fork of the Gunnison River. North of the Gunnison, the Elk Mountains and West Elks are similar but smaller disturbances of the plateau region. In these mountains brew the beginnings of the Taylor and East rivers on the south face, and Roaring Fork and Crystal on the north.

East of the Continental Divide, steep mountain rivers of the Front Range of the Rockies abruptly leave their canyons, lose momentum, and drift out across the open expanse of gravel fans left by their ancestors. Such a fate awaits the Cache la Poudre, Big Thompson, South Platte, and Arkansas rivers.

Throughout the Southern Rockies, railroads and highways testify to the fact that rivers in mountainous country are the essential engineers for the arteries of human transportation. The erosive capabilities of rivers are responsible for construction of steady grades ideally suited for railroad beds. Many lines of track cling to blasted precipices in narrow canyons rather than venturing forth onto adjacent slopes. Few rivers are unaccompanied by either a railroad bed or a highway. But where river banks are high, rivers conceal themselves, and the country appears more wild and primitive to those traveling on the water than to motorists on nearby roads.

Fertile ranchlands border the rivers in slow places where floodplains were deposited. Here the rivers are bled into irrigation ditches. Most of these take small amounts of water, but some are as large as freight canals.

Cities of the Southern Rockies are located at the outlets of canyon routes into the mountains. Although greater amounts of rain and snow fall on the West Slope, the thirsty population centers are on the eastern side of the Continental Divide. For this reason, numerous storage reservoirs capture hundreds of thousands of acre-feet of water headed for the Colorado River in order to export it eastward through the Divide. The largest tunnels carry the equivalents of small rivers. (It is startling to witness a torrent pouring incongruously from a smooth mountainside.) This exportation of water enhances the volume of such East Slope rivers as the South Platte, Cache la Poudre, Arkansas, Rio Chama, and Clear Creek, and increases the length of their boating seasons. West Slope rivers, on the other hand, have been severely depleted. Smaller kayaking and canoeing rivers such as the Fraser, Fryingpan, and Navajo are nearly gone. Others, such as the Blue, Eagle, and Roaring Fork, have a moderate early season flow, but are noticeably crippled later in the year.

The history of the Southern Rocky Mountains is reflected in the names of its rivers. This was the domain of the Ute tribes before the white man's arrival. A few original Ute names such as Yampa (edible root) and Uncompahgre (hot water spring) remain. The Eagle got its name when the Utes said the river had as many tributaries as there are feathers in an eagle's tail. Spaniards were the first Europeans to probe and settle in the southern part of the region. In the south, the Dolores, San Juan, Rio Grande, Rio Chama, Piedra, and almost all other rivers retain their Spanish names. Later, those prodigious heroes of fact and fable, the mountain men, entered the region. They inspired the naming of the Encampment, Fryingpan, and Elk. The legacy of many early French fur trappers remains in the names of such rivers as the Platte ("flat") River and Cache la Poudre ("hide the powder").

Fur trappers were the first to use the rivers for transportation. Their "bull boats" were crude, round craft fashioned from hides stretched over willow frames. John Wesley Powell originated the use of wooden boats during his pioneering exploration of the Green and Colorado rivers in 1869. Various styles of wooden boats—all with watertight compartments for buoyancy in case they capsized—were employed until the invention of neoprene rubber during World War II. Not easily capsizable, resiliant against rocks, and forgiving in the event of a mistake, reinforced rubber rafts became ideal river boats. They opened up the rivers for sportsmen and adventurers in much larger numbers and remain the most popular boats for river running today.

With only a layer or two of fabric and rubber between the boater and the water, a reinforced rubber raft offers a rare closeness to river forces. It can be handled by a single oarsman or paddled by a crew. With a crew, maneuvering the raft in rough waters requires skilled teamwork and engenders a sense of camaraderie. The best rafting water is found below mountain headwaters on the larger rivers of the plateau region in western Colorado and eastern Utah.

On highly technical streams, where rafts are clumsy and uncontrollable, the kayak reigns supreme. It is a craft of great antiquity; its manufacture has been gradually perfected over centuries. Today's river kayak is constructed of practically indestructable space-age plastics and fiberglass. It is the simplest of water-borne vehicles—a watertight cylinder pinched at both ends—and draws so little water it can practically float on dew. One does not sit in a kayak—one wears it. The interior is molded to fit the shape of the user. Every movement of the lower body is transferred to the boat. The paddler and his craft are analogous to the mythical centaur—half man, half boat.

The ubiquitous open canoe, so popular in the East and Midwest, is less commonly employed on Southern Rocky Mountain rivers primarily because of their steep gradients. A watertight, decked canoe alleviates this problem. One kneels rather than sits in a decked canoe. For some boaters, kneeling is more comfortable than sitting in a kayak and has the advantage of enhancing downriver visibility. For those who enjoy the delights of traditional open canoeing, however, there are parks and open valleys in the Southern Rocky Mountains that hold many nearly undiscovered streams of a milder nature.

The recent marriage of the profit motive and the public's desire for recreation has produced the commercial rafting industry. Most guests sign onto a commercial raft for a roller coaster thrill in the rapids. However, the superior commercial operator—and there are many—stresses the wildness, beauty, and

The high brace provides stability in whitewater.

wonder of a natural river. His guests will come to see these features as more important than the thrill of a ride on a rapid. From then on, his guests will probably join the ranks of those who cherish and protect rivers.

Boating on the most popular stretches during mid-day and mid-season—such as the Colorado River near State Bridge and the Arkansas between Buena Vista and the Royal Gorge—gives the impression that Colorado rivers are overcrowded. This is emphatically not the case on most rivers. Some of the finest stretches are nearly deserted, sought only by people who desire the beauty and excitement of wildness.

No river can be accurately described by its gradient, class of difficulty, or rate of flow, just as no person can be accurately described by height, weight, or skin color. While these items of data are useful, there is much more to know. A river lives. It speaks about itself to those who listen. It will tell much more than any book can tell.

Nothing can approach a ride on a wild river for intimate contact with the elemental forces of the earth. The only requirement is a fondness for water. Such rivers evoke all the emotions—excitement, fear, enchantment, joy, peace. A wild river sings a melody that varies from piano to forte, from largo to allegro. Around each bend the river is new, one moment dashing down a cascade, the next hardly strong enough to bow the grasses in its bed.

Spend a day indoors and you may never remember it. Spend a day on a river and you'll never forget it.

Classic Southern Rocky Mountain River Runs

Wilderness Rivers

On a wilderness river, one expects insignificant cultural intrusions, although occasionally a bordering railroad track, powerline or ranch might be encountered. (See index for where in this book these runs are described in detail.)

Expert:

Animas—from Silverton to Rockwood—
   28 mi.
Colorado—through Gore Canyon—10 mi.
Colorado—through Westwater Canyon—14 mi.
Colorado—through Cataract Canyon—12 mi.
Encampment—from Colo.-Wyo. border to Encampment—20 mi.
Fraser—from Tabernash to Granby—10 mi.
Gunnison—through Black Canyon—11 mi.
Hermosa Creek—from Dutch Creek Confluence to U.S. 550—
   8 mi.
North Fork of South Platte—from Bailey to Pine—11 mi.
North Platte—from Northgate to Six Mile Gap—10 mi.
Piedra—from Piedra Rd. Bridge to Hwy. 160 Bridge—20 mi.
Rio Grande—from Lee Trail to Red River—14 mi.
Yampa—through Cross Mountain Gorge—3 mi.

Intermediate:

Arkansas—through Browns Canyon—10 mi.
Blue—from Green Mt. Dam to Spring Creek Bridge—4 mi
Dolores—through Dolores Canyon—50 mi.
Dolores—from Gateway to Colorado River—32 mi.
Green—through Lodore Canyon—35 mi.

Gunnison—through Gunnison Gorge (some expert rapids)—16 mi.
Rio Grande—from Dunn Bridge to Taos Junction—15 mi.
San Juan—from Pagosa Springs to the Rio Blanco—15 mi.
San Miguel—from Hwy. 145 Bridge to Naturita—29 mi.
Upper Rio Grande—from Rio Grande Reservoir downstream—
9 mi.
Yampa—from Deerlodge Park to the Green River (one expert
rapid)—46 mi.

Novice-Beginner:
Colorado—from Loma to Westwater—25 mi.
Colorado—from Moab to Cataract Canyon—69 mi.
Dolores—from Slick Rock to Bedrock—45 mi.
   (intermediate at high water)
Green—through Desolation Canyon—128 mi.
Green—from Green River to Cataract Canyon—121 mi.
Rio Chama—from El Vado Reservoir to Abiquiu Reservoir—
35 mi.
Rio Grande—from Lobatos Bridge to Lee Trail—23 mi.
San Juan—from Bluff to Lake Powell—84 mi.
White—from Rangely to the Green River—68 mi.

Rural Rivers

*Rural rivers are occasionally crossed by bridges and frequently bordered by
ranches, cabins, and secondary dirt roads. (See index for where in this book
these runs are described in detail.)*

Expert:
Arkansas—from Granite to Buena Vista—20 mi.
Arkansas—through Royal Gorge—8 mi.
Lake Fork—from Gateway to Blue Mesa Reservoir—
5 mi.
North Fork of South Platte—from Buffalo Creek to South Fork—10 mi.
Roaring Fork—from Aspen to Upper Woody Creek Bridge—5 mi.
Upper Crystal—from below Marble to Redstone—12 mi.
Upper San Juan—East Fork Campground to above Pagosa Springs—
7 mi.

Intermediate:
Blue River—from Silverthorne to Green Mountain
Reservoir—20 mi.
Colorado—from Pumphouse to Dotsero—58 mi.
Lake Fork of the Gunnison—from Lake City to Gateview—24 mi.
Mountain Dolores—from Rico to Dolores—37 mi.
North Platte—from Six Mile Gap to Bennet Peak Campground—
26 mi.
Rio Grande—above Creede—15 mi.
Roaring Fork—from Upper Woody Creek Bridge to Basalt—
12 mi.
Taylor—from Lodgepole Campground to Almont (some expert sec-
tions)—15 mi.

Upper Elk—from Box Canyon Campground to Glen Eden—8 mi.
Williams Fork—from Horseshoe Campground to Williams Fork Reservoir—9 mi.

Novice-Beginner:

Animas—from below Durango to Bondad Bridge—
18 mi.
Arkansas—from Canon City to Pueblo Reservoir (dangerous at high water)—25 mi.
Colorado—from end of Westwater Canyon to Moab (some intermediate rapids)—48 mi.
Lower Gunnison—from Delta to Whitewater—39 mi.
Roaring Fork—from Basalt to Glenwood Springs (some intermediate rapids)—26 mi.
San Juan—from Rio Blanco to Navajo Reservoir—30 mi.
White River—above Rangely—30 mi.
Yampa—from below Craig to Maybell (some wilderness)—49 mi.

Roadside or Urban Rivers

Numerous bridges and other structures will be encountered and the river will be bordered by an important road or highway. (See index for where in this book these runs are described in detail.)

Expert:

Clear Creek—above Golden—15 mi.
Colorado—in Glenwood Canyon from Shoshoni Powerplant to Grizzly Creek (intermediate at low water levels)—2 mi.

The alligator entrance, Black Canyon of the Gunnison.

Intermediate:

Arkansas—from Salida to Parkdale—42 mi.
Cache La Poudre—mountain canyon above Ted's Place (several expert sections)—43 mi.
Colorado—from Grizzly Creek to New Castle—18 mi.
Conejos—20 mi.
Eagle—below Dowds Junction (some expert sections)—42 mi.

Novice-Beginner

Colorado—from Rifle to Debeque Canyon—50 mi.
Dolores—Mesa Canyon above Gateway—30 mi.
Gunnison—from Almont to Blue Mesa Reservoir—18 mi.
Rio Grande—from Wagon Wheel Gap to Del Norte (several hazardous bridge abutments)—30 mi.

The Birth of Rivers:
A Geologic Odyssey

Rivers are the earth's master sculptors. They wrought the landscape we know today as the Southern Rocky Mountains. They are still digging downward, uncovering the planet's hidden structures. Their canyons are open windows into the earth's crust—showcases of lost mountain ranges, vanished Sahara-like deserts, and vast seabeds of dim ages past.

Journeying down a Southern Rocky Mountain river without some awareness of events of deep time and landform development would be like walking through an art museum without knowledge of art. The exposed strata in canyons are pages in the book of the earth's history. One can read that book while floating past. Every canyon reveals a chapter or two—but never the entire book.

Rivers recycle mountains. The stratified canyon walls themselves are the products of rivers—remains of mountains wasted by erosion, carried to the sea by long-vanished streams, and stacked neatly in horizontal beds. Regional uplift elevated these beds high above the level of adjacent seas where erosion could work its magic on them anew. Hence, canyon walls reveal the history of a series of former seabeds and highlands.

Under the primal force of water, the Rocky Mountains we know today are melting away like lumps of butter in a hot pan. The puny length of human life prevents us from perceiving such feats. We can only imagine them.

Much of the geologic spectacle we observe along the rivers of the Rockies can be understood with a degree of common sense. For example, beds with a horizontal orientation in a canyon wall are probably in the same position they were in when they were deposited, their ages being successively younger from bottom to top. One cannot assume, however, that the layers are contiguous. There may be gaps—periods when the waters receded, or for some other reason there was no sediment deposition. When beds lie tilted against granite or other crystalline rock derived from molten magma, an intrusion of granite from below probably caused the tilting.

Crystalline granite, with its associated metamorphic rock, is the foundation of the Rocky Mountain region—indeed, of the entire continent. It is the ancient, planed-down core of mountain ranges which stood in the region well over a billion years before the present mountains took their place. It formed the surface over which great seas invaded the land and deposited their beds of sediment. Its thickness has never been fathomed, but it probably extends deep into the earth's crust. Geologists call this underlying mass the *basement complex*. The rock composing it, Precambrian in age, is called basement rock. Its surface undulates beneath the beds of sedimentary strata. In places it dives, forming structural basins where the depth of overlying sediments can extend to six miles. In other places it rises close to the surface. Only in high mountain zones has the basement complex driven upward far enough that erosion could strip away its roof of sediments. This has occurred in many of the majestic ranges of the Southern Rocky Mountains; including the Sangre de Cristo, Sawatch, Gore, Park, and Front ranges.

There is another method by which the ancient basement complex can be exposed—by downcutting rivers. A canyon that crosses a structural basin—the reverse of an uplift—does not reach the basement complex. It lies too deep. But where the basement complex rises close to the surface, rivers may reveal it in their canyon walls. Canyons where the contact between basement rock and the younger sedimentary beds is most clearly exposed include the inner gorge of the Grand Canyon, Westwater Canyon, Glenwood Canyon, and Gore Canyon along the path of the Colorado; also the canyon of the upper Eagle, the Gunnison Gorge, and many others. This contact—called the Great Unconformity by geologists—stands out unmistakably because the more homogeneous quality of the basement rock provides a sharp contrast to the layered pattern of the strata above it.

Attentive river runners notice two distinct changes in the character of a canyon that cuts into an uplift of the basement complex: First, the canyon narrows and becomes more cliff-bound. Second, the river gradient steepens. These phenomena occur because granite and metamorphic rocks, as a result of tightly interlocking, crystalline texture, are far harder than the overlying sedimentary rock. The particles composing sedimentary rock are weakly cemented together. Sedimentary canyon walls usually recede from a river at a much faster rate. Gravity causes them to slump and slide. The resulting pulverized rock is eventually gobbled up by the river. The canyon widens. Of the many varieties of sedimentary rocks, only the massive sandstones—remnants of ancient dune fields—and sometimes limestones resist the weathering process and preserve some perpendicularity. Between them, weak shales, evaporites, and conglomerates constitute the sedimentary canyon's sloping terraces.

In canyons of basement rock, on the other hand, little slumping other than an occasional rock fall occurs. The result is a canyon of sheer walls close to the river's edge. Rivers flowing in canyons cut through basement rocks are almost always steeper in gradient and more boulder-clogged than their sedimentary counterparts. This is due to the increased vigor required for a river to lower its bed. When a river crossing a sedimentary basin suddenly reaches an upthrust block of granite, as do many Southern Rocky Mountain rivers, it is effectively dammed. Erosion into the softer beds above is checked as it meanders leisurely in its approach to the edge of the granite. Then it plunges precipitously through the harder basement rock, sometimes for many miles, to the next soft sedimentary basin. The gradient profile of the Colorado River, for example, looks like a staircase, steep where the river crosses resistant rocks, flat in the

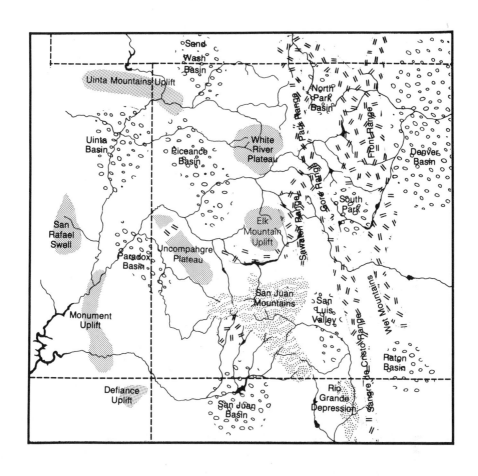

Overview of structural features of the Southern Rocky Mountain region.

sedimentary basins between. (See long profile of the Colorado River, page 45.)
Other rivers incise downward close to an uplift of basement rock, but do not
quite reach it. The Yampa came close in Juniper and Cross Mountain gorges,
as did the Green in Lodore and the Colorado in Cataract Canyon. Within
these canyons, as in canyons floored with basement rock, the gradient steepens

and the water behind them slows, owing to the damming effect of the uplift.

One might expect a river to flow placidly across the deep pile of sediments in a structural basin, unimprisoned by a canyon. This is not always the case. High plateaus, incised by deep canyons, often form the roofs of structural basins. High in the stratigraphic sequence, these canyons are walled by young strata. The more ancient beds lie far below, closer to the basement complex. Desolation and White River canyons crossing the Uinta basin and Debeque Canyon on the Piceance Basin are good examples of deep canyons walled by young strata crossing structural basins.

Other factors besides rock type help to control the character of Southern Rocky Mountain canyons. Climate is important. The amount of precipitation, a factor of elevation, plays a large role. The canyons of the arid plateau country in the western part of the region often have steeper walls than canyons in the high mountains. This is because in the plateau country, the principal agent of canyon erosion is the river itself. The torrent so outrivals the slumping and sliding of canyon walls that their cliff-bound character is preserved. In the high country to the east, where precipitation falls in abundance, canyon walls are attacked assiduously by erosive agents. Here, rivers that cut their channels into sedimentary rock often have much wider valleys than those in the drier regions to the west. The action of abundant snow and rainfall helped create wide, high-country valleys along the Little Snake, Yampa, Eagle, Roaring Fork, and East rivers.

The age of a canyon is another important factor in its declivity. Young canyons generally have steep sides, because the erosive effort has not been at work long. Older drainages, such as the Gunnison Valley and the San Juan above the Monument Uplift, are very wide and gentle.

The highest canyons in the Rocky Mountains were altered to a large extent by recently departed glaciers. The glaciers tended to widen and flatten the

Gunnison Gorge at Cable Rapids. Here the river slices into the ancient basement complex beneath sedimentary strata.

floors of these valleys and give them steeper walls. Their profiles changed from the typical V shape to a U shape. These glacial effects are most evident on higher tributary streams.

Other valleys, like that of the upper Arkansas River above Salida, were not formed in any of these ways. The Arkansas follows a fault zone. The action of water was less responsible for the formation of this valley than the faulting and displacement of masses of rock along this zone.

Almost all rivers of the plateau region at one point or another plow into tall barriers, carve spectacular gorges through them, and emerge on the other side like conquering heroes. Why do they stubbornly maintain their courses through blockading structures when easier paths through softer rocks lead around these structures? John Wesley Powell confronted this problem in June, 1869, when his party reached the Uinta Mountain uplift at the canyon he named Lodore: "...Why did not the stream turn around this great obstruction rather than pass through it?" he asked. After careful study of Lodore Canyon he arrived at the answer:

"The river had the right of way; in other words, it was running ere the mountains were formed; not before the rocks of which the mountains are composed, were deposited, but before the formations were folded, so as to make a mountain range.

"The contracting or shriveling of the earth causes the rocks near the surface to wrinkle or fold, and such a fold was started athwart the course of the river. Had it been suddenly formed, it would have been an obstruction sufficient to turn the water in a new course to the east, beyond the extension of the wrinkle; but the emergence of the fold above the general surface of the country was little or no faster than the progress of the corrasion [erosion] of the channel.

"We may say, then, that the river did not cut its way *down* through the mountains, from a height of many thousand feet above its present site, but, having an elevation differing but little, perhaps, from what it now has, as the fold was lifted, it cleared away the obstruction by cutting a canon, and the walls were thus elevated on either side. The river preserved its level, but mountains were lifted up; as the saw revolves on a fixed pivot, while the log through which it cuts is moved along. The river was the saw which cut the mountain in two."

Powell called this type of canyon, cut by a river that preceded the uplift across its path, *antecedent*. But what if a ridge of hard rock is buried by layers of sediment, and a river, in the course of deepening its canyon through such sedimentary layers, encounters the obstruction and cuts into it? Powell called the canyon through such an obstruction (the obstruction itself is often fully revealed after erosion has stripped away the overlying softer beds of rock) *superimposed*. This is how the Gunnison River carved the Black Canyon through hard basement rock even though soft sedimentary rock at a lower elevation lies barely a mile away. While cutting downward, the ancient Gunnison was held by the bounds of its sedimentary canyon walls. When it reached the buried Black Canyon Basement Complex, it could not escape sideways to the softer rocks nearby. It was trapped. Thus, it reluctantly carved one of the West's most spectacular gorges.

Powell called a third type of drainage *consequent*. In this instance, a river seeks its course through the weaker rocks, avoiding ridges and other structural barriers. Consequent drainages are directly controlled by the slope and shape of the surfaces on which they develop. If beds are buckled into folds by mountain-building activity, for example, consequent drainages will form in the bottoms of the folds (synclines) while the tops of the folds (anticlines) will become divides.

Superimposed and antecedent drainages shape the land. Consequent drainages are shaped by the land.

Examples of consequent drainages in the Southern Rocky Mountains include rivers flowing radially off the volcanic pile of the San Juan Mountains as well as the rivers that plummet down the east slope of the Front Range to the plains: the Cache la Poudre, Big Thompson, St. Vrain, and Clear Creek.

When a river carves a canyon through a ridge or other structural barrier, geologists sometimes have difficulty determining whether the barrier was superimposed during the course of the river's downcutting or antecedent to the uplift. If remnants of the beds that buried the ridge can be found, superposition can be proven. If it can be established that the course of the river predated the uplift of the ridge, antecedence can be shown. Recent evidence, however, demonstrates that canyons rarely evolve exclusively by one process alone. In the case of Lodore Canyon, later interpretations conflicted with Powell's pure antecedence theory and confused the question. Some geologists have insisted Powell was wrong, that superposition generated the canyon. But how could the entire east end of the Uinta uplift, standing over 3,000 feet above the river level, have been buried? Where did all that sediment go? Most geologists now agree that Lodore's genesis involved a combination of both canyon-making processes. The river's course was established high above its present level by superposition. Later uplifts of the Uinta Mountains deepened the canyon by antecedence. In the final analysis, Powell will probably be found to be as correct as most of his critics.

Questions of geomorphic evolution must be asked about each segment of a river separately. The headwater canyons probably originated by consequence on the high, mountainous slopes. Downriver canyons were likely to have been produced by superposition and antecedence.

The rivers of the Southern Rocky Mountains have been evolving for the past 40 to 50 million years, since the first of a series of recent crustal upheavals. Unraveling their story is a highly complex puzzle, begun by Powell and continuing today. If we could go back 20 million years, we would see an astonishingly different system of rivers. The Green and Yampa would be flowing into a huge lake in Browns Park; the course of the Colorado would be located about where the White River lies today; the Dolores would be a tributary of the San Juan; the Arkansas would drain into a lake in the San Luis Valley. Shallow lakes would also be situated behind such damming barriers as the Gore Range and Black Canyon.

What causes rivers to shift position so dramatically? The answer lies in a process called *stream piracy*, in which one river is snatched from its bed by another. Streams generally grow headward. They lengthen themselves by extending their headwaters in an upstream direction. When the upper end of one stream begins to erode the same upland surface as another stream, the stage is set for stream piracy. A larger quantity of water, a softer bed, or a steeper gradient may give one river greater eroding power than that of its neighbor. The divide between them gradually shifts in the direction of the weaker river. The stronger stream will grow headward more rapidly, eventually penetrating the latter's channel, capturing its flow into its more rapidly eroding bed.

A dry riverbed that has lost its headwaters is said to have been *beheaded*. Upland rivers, flowing sluggishly on high plateaus, are sure to get beheaded eventually by swift cataracts that eat into the plateau's flanks.

Winter in Lodore Canyon of the Green River highlights the landscape's stratified geology.

The rising structural barriers that ponded so many rivers in the Southern Rocky Mountains also halted their downcutting efforts, sometimes allowing them to be captured by swifter streams growing headward in softer rocks around the edges of the obstructions. A waterless canyon, or *wind gap*, marks the probable ancient course of the Blue River where it once joined the Colorado within granitic Gore Canyon. The uplifting block containing Gore Canyon slowed the ancestral Blue's downcutting efforts, permitting the river to be captured by a stream growing headward from the Colorado in softer rocks to the east. Today the Blue joins the Colorado just upstream from Gore Canyon. The Dolores was formerly a tributary of the San Juan. A blockading uplift allowed it to be captured by another tributary of the Colorado. Another uplift probably turned the Arkansas east, away from the San Luis Valley.

The geomorphic history of the Colorado River is filled with stories of stream piracy. All of the Colorado's river-sized tributaries upstream from the Green reach the Colorado from the south. Only short, insignificant streams join the river from the north. It is unlikely that this unusual pattern is coincidental. The courses of the ancestral Gunnison, Roaring Fork, Eagle, Blue, Williams Fork, and Fraser occupied valleys that probably continued northwestward from their present points of juncture with the Colorado. The faster downcutting, ancestral Colorado, growing headward from the southwest, in all probability captured each of these rivers in succession. In this way a number of independent, northwest-flowing rivers were merged into a single great river system and were redirected southwestward. Since the time of this piracy, the entire drainage has deepened over 3,000 feet, and the topography has been substantially altered.

Evolution of the Colorado River System By Stream Piracy

Dotted lines indicate the ancestral courses of present-day rivers. Arrows point in the direction of flow.

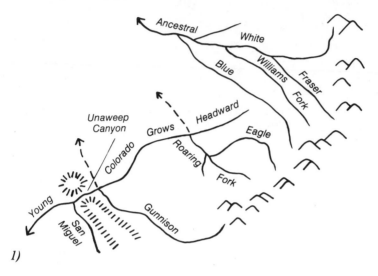

1)

Fifteen million years ago—The young Colorado has captured the Gunnison and Roaring Fork and is eroding headward toward the Blue, Williams Fork, and Fraser, which at this time comprise the headwaters of the ancestral White River.

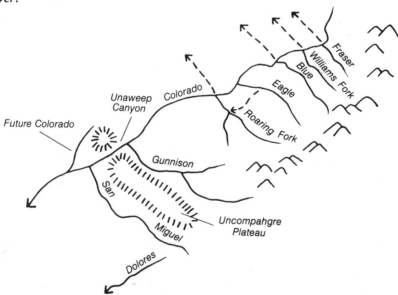

2)

Two million years ago—The Colorado has pirated the White's tributaries. The White has retreated toward the northwest. The Colorado has also pirated the Eagle from the Roaring Fork. The Dolores flows southwest into the San Juan.

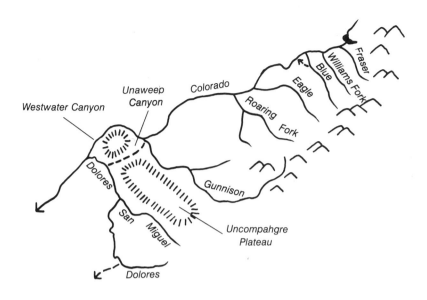

3)

Today—The Colorado, having been captured by its own tributary, has abandoned Unaweep Canyon. The Dolores now flows northward into the Colorado, having joined the San Miguel.

The most graphic example of stream piracy in the region is Unaweep Canyon—the huge abandoned canyon of the Colorado and Gunnison rivers across the Uncompahgre Plateau. A small downstream Colorado River tributary, eroding headward on an easy route in soft rocks around the northern side of the rising Uncompahgre Uplift, captured its own parent system. The capacious Unaweep Canyon was left high and dry. Further upheavals brought the Uncompahgre Plateau still higher, allowing Ruby and Westwater Canyons to be incised, by antecedence, into the northern flank of the uplift.

Most geology and geography texts show the longitudinal profile of a typical river. Such a profile resembles the side view of a ski jump—steep near the source, easing in gradient in the middle reaches, and flat as it approaches the sea. In its steep upper reaches the river is termed *youthful*. Here it dashes through a cliffbound canyon where downcutting is the dominant process. As its gradient eases in the middle reaches, the river is called *mature*. Downcutting declines, and the river's energy is directed sideward rather than downward. The valleys widen. Floodplains are deposited. The river reaches the third stage, *old age* near its ocean terminus. Here its gradient is so slight that the river wants to lengthen itself; therefore it meanders gracefully about on a broad floodplain across a mostly flat region.

This generalized pattern will not fit most Southern Rocky Moutain rivers. Near their sources, many of these rivers have already achieved old age. The Colorado, South Platte, North Platte, Rio Grande, and others meander on broad floodplains, with all the characteristics of old age, at elevations of 8,000 to 10,000 feet. In their middle reaches where, according to the model, they should be mature, they suddenly become youthful, plunging through narrow, steep canyons.

John Wesley Powell's keen mind also tackled this problem. He came up with another fundamental concept of river geology: the *base level* of erosion, or the lowest elevation to which a river can cut downward. When a river nears its base level, it usually assumes the characteristics of old age. The ultimate base level of all the earth's rivers is, of course, sea level. Thus, almost all river valleys, as they approach the sea, take on the features of old age. Why, asked Powell, should high Rocky Mountain river valleys, so far from the sea, possess these same features? He reasoned that uplifts of hard basement rock, rising across a high river's course, produce *temporary* base levels. Upstream from such a barrier, a river's downcutting action is halted; the river slows down; it deposits part of its sediment load and meanders across a broad plain above the barrier.

No barriers lie in the paths of such broad, upland river valleys as the lower Blue, East River, and Uncompahgre; yet each shows the traits of late maturity and old age. How could this happen? Since they are tributaries, their base levels are the elevations of the larger rivers into which they flow. If the master river has been affected by a structural barrier, such that its downcutting action has been halted below the confluence with its tributary and a new temporary base level established, the tributary has no choice but to conform to it. This phenomenon answers the puzzle of the lower Blue, East, and Uncompahgre rivers.

One of the most interesting valleys in the Southern Rocky Mountains is Colorado's Roaring Fork River Valley, not because of eyepopping gorges or thundering cataracts (it would be classified a mature river valley) but because of a series of lovely, sloping stream terraces that embellish its floor and flanks. Remnants of the oldest of these terraces can be found almost 800 feet above the present valley floor. From this point they descend in at least six steps to the level of the river. Some terraces are wide and covered with green pastures.

On many plateau rivers, rapids are produced by side canyon boulder fans such as this one in Desolation Canyon.

Others have been partially swept away. Each represents an ancient floodplain. Each is a remnant of a former valley floor. The river successively slashed into each of its floodplains, thereafter quieting down and creating a new floodplain at a lower level. What caused the river to engage in these repeated episodes of downcutting and stabilization? The answer is not found in the valley itself, but just upriver from its confluence with the Colorado. The Colorado, at its confluence with the Roaring Fork, has just emerged from Glenwood Canyon, a deep chasm cut into ancient strata and the resistant basement complex. As the Colorado slowly lowered itself—in fits and starts, through Glenwood's alternately softer and harder layers—so did the Roaring Fork. Each time the Colorado became relatively stabilized, floods on the Roaring Fork produced a floodplain. As the Colorado thereafter cut another bite out of Glenwood Canyon, the Roaring Fork followed suit in its own valley. Within steep-sided Glenwood Canyon there are no stream terraces, but they march up the sides of the wide Roaring Fork Valley like stairways of the gods.

Another anomalous tendency of several rivers in the region is to meander broadly, but to do so within deep canyons rather than on wide floodplains. The Green in Labyrinth and Stillwater canyons, the Dolores in Slick Rock Canyon, and the Yampa in its lower canyon perform this feat. The most famous example of all is the convoluted Great Goosenecks of the San Juan. Properly, these rivers should do their meandering on floodplains rather than in narrow, twisting canyons.

We find an answer to this puzzle in a fluvial phenomenon known as *rejuvenation*. If the base level of an old meandering river should drop for one reason or another in relation to its floodplain, its downcutting energy will be renewed, or rejuvenated. Incising with increased vigor, the stream will superimpose its meandering channel into the soft sediments of its floodplain. Before long, the meandering river will lie in a shallow trench from which it can no longer inundate the valley floor. With continued erosion, the river will incise itself still further into the underlying bedrock until it deepens to canyonlike proportions, creating *entrenched meanders*.

Water, like other physical objects, has a tendency to move in a straight line unless acted on by an outside force. Within entrenched meanders, the river water, trying to move in a straight line, is piled up against an outside force—the outer walls of the great, arching curves. These walls, continually undercut by the river, are eroded backward, enlarging the meanders. Meanwhile, in the slack water on the insides of curves, sediments are deposited. This is the familiar location of sandbars and eventually, as the canyon widens, floodplains. The canyon wall on the inside of the river's curve is generally sloping while the wall on the outside is always steep.

Along many entrenched rivers, the most circuitous curves grow close together. As their outside walls erode back, the distance between them is reduced. Sometimes the river will travel several miles before doubling back to within a few hundred feet of itself. Muleshoe Bend in Slick Rock Canyon on Dolores and Bowknot Bend in Labyrinth Canyon on the Green are two well-known examples. As its outside walls come closer together, the river will eventually breach the divide between them, and the meander will be cut off. A cutoff entrenched meander is termed a *rincon*. As the river continues to erode its bed, rincons are left high above the water level. An entrenched river tends to straighten itself out by cutting off its meanders, leaving rincons along its course. This has happened in Desolation Canyon on the Green River, where numerous rincons along the way remind river runners of a time when the canyon was twice as long as it is today. Sometime in the future, many of the entrenched meanders in Slickrock, Labyrinth, and the Great Goosenecks will be breached, thereby shortening the length of their canyons.

Most entrenched meanders in the Southern Rocky Mountain region are found on the Colorado Plateau. But rejuvenated rivers, flowing in shallow trenches, are also common up in the mountain valleys to the east. These do not meander, and their formation differs radically from that of plateau rivers. During the most recent glacial epoch—the Wisconsin—the volume of eroded rock dumped into the rivers by glacial scouring was enormous. Some rivers—those with large glaciers at their headwaters—did not have sufficient competence (energy) to transport their enormous loads of meltwater debris. Therefore, they dumped the debris in the bottoms of their valleys and, rather than meandering, *braided* across the resulting plains.

A braided river breaks into hundreds of smaller streams which unite only to divide again. The Eagle River in its valley from above Avon to below Edwards provides an example. As the meltwater sediments from the great glaciers of the Sawatch and Gore ranges spread over the Eagle Valley, the river became braided. (In Alaska, where large glaciers still exist, almost all rivers flowing from them are braided across filled valleys, as was the Eagle about 15,000 years ago.)

After the glaciers melted (only the tiniest remnants still remain), the Eagle Valley could return to normal. The river, free of its overload of rock debris, got back to work downcutting into the fill it had dumped. Today the Eagle has entrenched a shallow canyon in the outwash plain, about 30 to 60 feet deep. Boulders from the old glacial river cover its bed and provide interesting challenges for river runners. Other examples of shallow canyons cut through glacial debris are found along the mountain valleys of the Arkansas and Rio Grande rivers.

Halfway through his 1869 exploration of the Colorado River, John Wesley Powell expressed a fear felt by many river explorers:

"There are great descents yet to be made, but, if they are distributed in rapids and short falls, as they have been heretofore, we will be able to overcome them. But, maybe we shall come to a fall in these canyons which we cannot pass, where the walls rise from the water's edge, so that we cannot land, and where the water is so swift that we cannot return. Such places have been found, except that the falls were not so great but that we could run them with safety. How will it be in the future?"

Powell's trepidation was needless. No high waterfalls in the usual sense of the word exist on any major Southern Rocky Mountain rivers, except near the headwaters of the smaller streams. A few small waterfalls in the five-to-fifteen-foot range lie in the steepest canyons of the Cache la Poudre, the South Platte below Eleven Mile Reservoir, Rio Grande west of Questa, Animas below Rockwood, and Black Canyon of the Gunnison. However, river runners need never fear an approaching Niagara or Yosemite-type waterfall. The terms *falls, cataract,* and *drop* have often been attached to steep places. Lava Falls, Cataract Canyon, and the Big Drop are examples, but these would be more accurately characterized as rapids.

Why are tall waterfalls not a feature of Southern Rocky Mountain rivers? Any nonuniformity in its bed causes a river to concentrate its energy on the irregular feature. This is analogous to the example of a saw cutting wood. A hard spot such as a knot concentrates the saw's energy until it is cut through. The same can be said for planing a board. The cutting action of the plane's blade focuses on irregularities in its grade until those irregularities are reduced. Likewise, falls, over the span of ages, are reduced in stature and abruptness until they are eventually destroyed.

Many irregularities, however, punctuate river channels in this region. They originate either from surface phenomena or from the underlying geologic structure of the rocks. Surface irregularities have three sources. First are glacial moraines—piles of rock pushed ahead of the ancient valley glaciers as they advanced and left in the paths of rivers when glaciers retreated. Second are recent landslides, rock falls, and slumping of rock from adjacent canyon walls. Third are side canyon floods which poured fans of rock debris across river channels.

In higher canyons, many rapids are formed by glacial moraines and related outwash debris. A glacier can move much larger objects than a river can. Since the river's energy is insufficient to shunt them out of the way, piles of glacial boulders left in the riverbed can produce tumultuous rapids. Landslides and rock falls obstruct river channels in canyons of the narrower class. Rapids in canyons of volcanic rock are usually formed by constriction of the channel due to large-scale slumping of the lavabed walls. Almost all rapids in the semi-arid western part of the region are formed by side canyon boulder fans. Here, when a side canyon is spotted ahead, one can be reasonably certain that a rapid lies at its mouth.

Riverbed irregularities caused by the underlying structure usually result from uplifts rising across a river's path, especially when hard granitic rocks are encountered. It is safe to say that, with few exceptions, granitic canyons in the Southern Rocky Mountain region have steeper gradients than canyons in sedimentary rocks. Many rapids produced by uplifts are bolstered by landslides, rock falls, or glacial debris. Such a combination of obstructions can result in a horrendous maelstrom.

Every few years a new rapid is produced on a Southern Rocky Mountain river. In 1962, for example, a flood on a side canyon of the Yampa produced that river's most treacherous rapid, Warm Springs. A landslide from the side of the Piedra River Canyon in 1979 resulted in a rapid called Eye of the Needle. Because the water has not been scouring as long, these recently formed rapids are often more violent than older ones.

During millions of years of relentless downcutting, Southern Rocky Mountain rivers have uncovered a vast geologic story that could not be told without them. In the seams of strata exposed in canyon walls lies the long backward stretch of time, the recovery of which enhances the drama of any river trip.

The geologic story told by strata is mainly of shifting relations between water and land. When seas covered all or part of the region, the chronicle was recorded in relatively readable sedimentary deposits. Each time the seas retreated and the land reappeared, the story becomes less clear. Retreating in time to a point about 600 million years ago, the story stops abruptly and with puzzling suddenness. Although a much longer portion of earth history preceded that time, we know little about it. We call this dark age the Precambrian; its rock we call the basement complex.

We can see in the Precambrian granites and metamorphic rocks the roots of a great mountain range leveled by erosion—little else. As the earliest seas of the Paleozoic Era crept over these lowlands around 600 million years ago, the light is switched on, and the story is reasonably well recorded thereafter.

Limestone was the predominant rock deposited in the Paleozoic seas. Some call the Paleozoic the age of limestone. If limestone is the dominant rock type

GENERALIZED GEOLOGIC FORMATIONS OF THE NORTHERN HALF OF THE SOUTHERN ROCKY MOUNTAINS AND THE EASTERN COLORADO PLATEAU

Eras	Periods	Formations	
Cenozoic (60 million years ago to present)	Quaternary		Glacial deposits, terrace deposits, alluvial deposits, volcanic deposits
	Tertiary	Browns Park —	white to gray sandstone, volcanic tuff, wind deposited
		Uinta —	maroon sandstones, shales, lenses of conglomerate
		Green River —	buff to gray shales deposited in freshwater lakes, oil shale dep
		Wasatch —	reddish sandstones and shales
Mesozoic (225 million to 60 million years ago)	Cretaceous	Mesa Verde Group (central) —	sandstones, coal beds
		Mancos —	dark gray marine shale, very thick, slope former
		Frontier —	limey sandstone, some coal beds
		Mowry —	dark gray, marine shales
		Dakota —	hard beach sandstone
	Jurassic	Morrison —	thick, interbedded maroon, purple, gray sandstones and shale terrestrial origin, dinosaur fossils
		Curtis —	greenish gray, shaley sandstone at base, limestone in upper p
		Entrada —	buff to red wind deposited sandstone
		Navajo —	white to buff wind deposited
	Triassic	Wingate —	massive red sandstones
		Chinle —	red shales, slope former
		Shinarump —	coarse sandstone and conglomerate
		Moenkopi —	red, limey shale and sandstone
Paleozoic (600 million to 225 million years ago)	Permian	Maroon (central) —	coarse red conglomerates
	Pennsylvanian	Weber (western) —	white or buff cross bedded sandstone, cliff former
		Morgan —	interbedded gray limestone and red sandstone, thick, cliff form
	Mississippian	Madison —	buff to dark gray limestone and dolomite, some fossils
		Manitou —	white to buff limestone, some fossils
	Cambrian	Sawatch (central) —	beach sandstone, red to white
		Lodore (western)	coarse grained quartz sandstone
Precambrian (4.5 billion to 600 million years ago)		Uinta Mountain Group —	red, coarse grained sandstone and conglomerate
		Continental basement complex —	granite, gneiss, schist, meta-conglomerate

THE BIRTH OF RIVERS

Canyons and Valleys

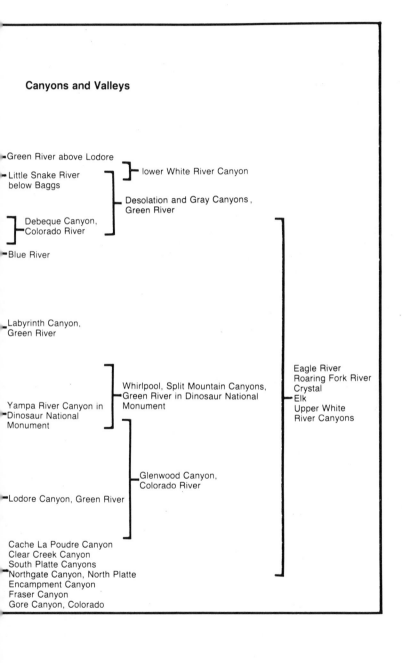

Green River above Lodore

Little Snake River below Baggs

lower White River Canyon

Desolation and Gray Canyons, Green River

Debeque Canyon, Colorado River

Blue River

Labyrinth Canyon, Green River

Whirlpool, Split Mountain Canyons, Green River in Dinosaur National Monument

Eagle River
Roaring Fork River
Crystal
Elk
Upper White
River Canyons

Yampa River Canyon in Dinosaur National Monument

Glenwood Canyon, Colorado River

Lodore Canyon, Green River

Cache La Poudre Canyon
Clear Creek Canyon
South Platte Canyons
Northgate Canyon, North Platte
Encampment Canyon
Fraser Canyon
Gore Canyon, Colorado

GENERALIZED GEOLOGIC FORMATIONS OF THE
SOUTHERN HALF OF THE SOUTHERN ROCKY MOUNTAINS
AND THE EASTERN COLORADO PLATEAU

Eras	Periods	Formations	
Cenozoic (60 million years ago to present)	Quaternary		Floodplains, landslides, glacially deposited rocks, volcanic deposits
	Tertiary	Wasatch — Animas —	reddish sandstones and shales white sandstone
Mesozoic (225 million to 60 million years ago)	Cretaceous	McDermott — Lewis — Mesa Verde Group — Mancos — Dakota —	purple conglomerate and sandstone shale sandstones, coal beds thick, dark grey to black marine shales, slope formen very hard, beach sandstone, caps plateaus
	Jurassic	Morrison — Summerville — Entrada — Carmel — Navajo — Kayenta —	thick, interbedded maroon, purple, gray sandstones and sh terrestial origin, contains dinosaur fossils shale dominant cliff former, orange to buff cross bedded sandston shale, sandstone white, cross bedded sandstone sandstone
	Triassic	Wingate — Chinle — Shinarump — Moenkopi —	massive red sandstone, forms tall cliffs red shale, slope former conglomerates shale, sandstone
Paleozoic (600 million to 225 million years ago)	Permian	Cutler Group —	often called Red Beds, mostly sandstones and arkose washed down from ancient Uncompahgre Mountains
	Pennsylvanian	Hermosa Group —	alternating beds of shale and limestone, drab in color, depo in shallow, marine environments, includes Paradox evapori
	Early Paleozoic	Leadville — Ouray — Elbert Group — Ignacio —	limestone limestone ⟩ thin layers of fossiliferous sandstone and limestone ⟩ limestone and hard sands quartzite
Precambrian (4.5 billion to 600 million years ago)		Continental basement complex —	crystalline rocks, granite, schist, gneiss

THE BIRTH OF RIVERS

Canyons and Valleys

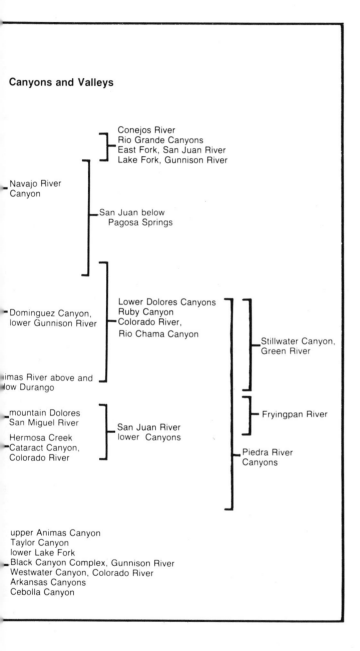

Conejos River
Rio Grande Canyons
East Fork, San Juan River
Lake Fork, Gunnison River

Navajo River
Canyon

San Juan below
Pagosa Springs

Lower Dolores Canyons
Ruby Canyon
Dominguez Canyon,
lower Gunnison River
Colorado River,
Rio Chama Canyon

Stillwater Canyon,
Green River

imas River above and
ow Durango

mountain Dolores
San Miguel River

Hermosa Creek
Cataract Canyon,
Colorado River

San Juan River
lower Canyons

Fryingpan River

Piedra River
Canyons

upper Animas Canyon
Taylor Canyon
lower Lake Fork
Black Canyon Complex, Gunnison River
Westwater Canyon, Colorado River
Arkansas Canyons
Cebolla Canyon

in a canyon, boaters can be quite sure they are traveling through strata deposited during that era.

Late in the Paleozoic Era, during what is called the Pennsylvanian Period, the first mountains rose out of the seas—the Ancestral Rocky Mountains. The erosion of these mountains left a pile of coarse conglomerates.

As the Mesozoic Era began about 225 million years ago, the land was again emerging from Paleozoic seas. This was the time of the Red Beds, when great dune-washed deserts covered the land and left colorful sandstone deposits hundreds of feet thick. Mainly terrestrial deposits remain from the early Mesozoic Era.

During the Cretaceous Period, near the close of the Mesozoic, the last great sea invaded our region. A mountain range in western Utah poured sediments into the Cretaceous Sea leaving a voluminous and detailed record of its existence. Many canyons are cut into these strata, which accumulated a thickness of two to three miles in the central Southern Rocky Mountain region.

As the Cenozoic Era opened 60 million years ago, the Cretaceous Sea had largely retreated. Water, however, still covered much of the area in the form of large freshwater lakes. But the calm was short-lived. The enormous pile of sedimentary rock from the many seas that had inundated the region for so long weighed down upon the earth's crust and threw it out of equilibrium with the molten interior. Intense heat was prevented from escaping to the surface. The unstable crust began erupting in volcanic explosions. In central Colorado the strata were bent, broken, upturned, and overturned at all angles. Displacements along fault lines raised crustal blocks thousands of feet, bringing the basement rock to the surface. Geologists call this upheaval the Laramide Revolution. It produced today's Southern Rocky Mountain ranges.

Remarkably, the Colorado Plateau to the west, although uplifted to great heights, was little disturbed by this mountain-building activity. In this region there were few volcanic eruptions. The strata was much less dislocated and bent. The Colorado Plateau is like an island of comparative calm in the midst of stormy seas.

The Laramide Revolution was active intermittently for about 40 million years. There is evidence that its last gasps may be continuing even today. It was during this time that the rivers established their present courses down from the newly formed mountains that give the crowning state of Colorado its moniker: Mother of Rivers.

River Safety

Enthusiastic as a hound in the chase, the aspiring boater spends winter evenings in preparation for summer adventure. In a heated pool he diligently perfects the bracing stroke, draw stroke, and that marvelous maneuver that brings the kayaker back from ghastly darkness—the eskimo roll.

Finally, when May sunshine brings the water up, he is ready. So is the river—ready to demonstrate that powerful natural forces cannot be taken lightly. May through June is the high water season in the Southern Rocky Mountains. The paddler will barely recognize the river that he ran so easily the previous August at low water. It is now muddy, fast, and cold—a juggernaut to the inexperienced.

With some trepidation he pulls out into the current. Quickly he realizes the river is controlling him and not vice versa. Unable to eddy-out, he finds himself in a dangerous situation. Panic overcomes training. The mistake of an upstream brace turns the boat over, and he slips into the river's grasp. He forgets even the thought of that eskimo roll so well perfected the previous winter in a quiet pool. As his life vest pulls him up he does not notice the icy water or his deathgrip on his kayak's cockpit. Fear has so mastered him he becomes incapable of thinking clearly. A large souse hole gobbles boat and boater and spits them out separately, but to his horror he is not moving downriver. The current pulls him back upriver and again into the hole. He struggles for the surface but cannot reach it. Failing and out of breath, his body relaxes. Thereupon, he quickly flushes out of the hole, gets a breath, and swims desperately for shore. He floats into a fallen tree and grasps for a branch. It breaks off in his hand. He feels rocks and tries to stand up but the strong current knocks him off his feet. With a last desperate lunge, he reaches the safety of an eddy. The cold has sapped his strength. His almost useless arms cannot pull the rest of his body out of the water. He drags himself onto shore with his elbows.

This story is true. It is repeated with variations many times each spring.

The paddler, so full of enthusiasm ten minutes before, might never enter a river again. Eager to test his newly acquired skills, he ventured forth on high water. This was his crucial mistake. High water magnifies everything dangerous about a river. It also heightens the senses and inspires a spirit of adventure. But knowledge of rivers, born of experience, is the prerequisite for high water boating. The irony of our western rivers is that boaters' enthusiasm runs highest in late spring, when rivers are in their storm season and at their most dangerous. This paddler should have waited a month or two, or found a dam-controlled river with low volume. Low water increases a boater's labor but greatly increases his safety. The velocity is less, and although obstacles are more frequent, boats are more easily controlled.

The kayaker made several mistakes that would have been much less dangerous at low water:

He failed to learn the fundamentals of self-rescue. A swimmer in a river can never depend on another paddler for rescue. One cannot crawl out of the rapids into the security of a friends's kayak. Accordingly, a strong roll technique is mandatory for those who run technically difficult whitewater. This paddler had never practiced his roll in whitewater and was unable to use it when it was needed.

Finding himself swimming, his first thought should have been to grasp a grab loop on the end of his boat, placing it and his paddle in the same hand to free the other hand for swimming. Instead, he grasped the cockpit and was therefore at the mercy of the river. Moreover, it is important, especially with canoes and rafts, to get behind the boat so as to avoid coming between it and a boulder.

When he fell into the hole, the paddler should have relaxed and allowed the current to wash him out through its bottom, instead of hopelessly battling to reach the surface. Exhaustion forced his relaxation. Should relaxation fail, diving to the bottom of the hole will almost always get a swimmer out. Removing the lifejacket, as some advocate as a last resort, might prove a bit difficult when one is being thrashed about in a violent hole. Even if successful, it would place the boater in a dangerous situation after he got out.

The paddler twice risked entrapment, the greatest threat to a lifejacketed swimmer. Entrapment occurs when one's body is pinned by the force of the current, so that self-rescue becomes impossible.

He could have been trapped in the branches of the fallen tree. Such an obstacle is called a "sweeper" when it lies in a river. One should avoid sweepers and log jams that sieve the water. These obstacles are especially common on smaller rivers. When the paddler tried to stand up, his foot could have become wedged in the rocks, with the swift current dragging him down and holding him underwater. Many cases of this type of entrapment have been reported. In swift water one should never try to stand, to slow one's downstream progress, or to push off rocks with one's feet. A foot can be caught in a crevice and a boater's career ended for good. The best procedure is to keep the legs high while swimming, standing up only in a calm eddy.

Man-made obstacles offer much higher probabilities for entrapment than natural ones. Especially dangerous are bridge abutments, strands of barbed wire across the river, and low-head dams. Rafts broach easily on bridge pilings. This is because the current drives *into* pilings rather than cushioning or "pillowing," as when deflected around the upstream side of a boulder. Extreme caution is advisable during high water periods on rivers with frequent bridges, such as the Poudre, Colorado, Eagle, or Arkansas. When striking a boulder or bridge abutment, it is best to hit it *head on*. You will avoid broaching by deflecting off the obstacle rather than wrapping around it.

Low-head dams are perhaps the most sinister of fluvial obstacles. They are commonly built at irrigation ditch intakes. Often only 3 to 6 feet high, they look innocent enough until the boater gets trapped in the artificial, hole-like hydraulic at the dam's base. These small weirs have deservedly acquired the name "drowning machines." New ones pop up every year on Southern Rocky

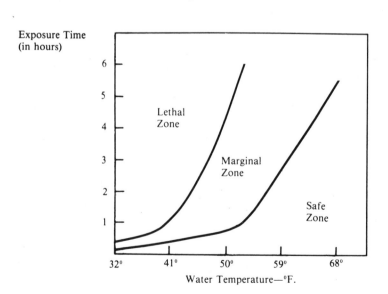

Graph depicting the average survival time for humans in varying water temperatures.

Mountain rivers. They should be scouted and almost always carried.

High water means cold water. A few hours before, it was snow and ice. Though the air temperature may be hot, the water temperature can be as low as 38 degrees F on higher mountain rivers. Humans survive only a short time in such waters. The graph on the opposite page shows the average amount of time one can expect to live in varying water temperatures.

More importantly, as cold water saps muscular strength from arms and legs they quickly become nonfunctional. It is then impossible to swim to shore. The temporarily paralyzed swimmer is at the mercy of the current. Fortunately, this threat is easily preventable. The key is proper clothing and use of a wetsuit. When the water is under 50 degrees F, at least one 100 percent wool sweater should be worn over or under the wetsuit. A waterproof paddling jacket over the sweater and wetsuit will seal much of the water out. This outfit will keep the boater comfortable whether the air temperature is hot or cold. If he must swim, it will protect him from the water's paralyzing effects and allow him time to reach shore. The wetsuit should be one-eighth or three-sixteenths inch thick. Wetsuit booties under an oversize pair of tennis shoes will protect the feet, but never use high top tennis shoes. If a foot becomes caught, these are much less likely to come off.

On a cold river, the first parts of the body to chill are hands. A pair of light neoprene gloves or pogies (wind mitts) will help alleviate this problem. Add helmet and lifejacket, and the boater is ready for the river.

A few years ago, failure to wear a lifejacket was by far the leading cause of river drownings. Lifejacket laws and general awareness have dramatically decreased this cause of death. The paddler in the previous story survived, despite many mistakes, because he wore a life vest. Today, high water and its attendant dangers are the leading cause of river fatalities. After drought years like 1977 and 1981, many neophytes in the rapidly expanding sport of river running know rivers only at their friendliest. The few tragic newspaper stories of river drownings almost always appear during May and June of high water years. Such stories have given this safe sport, enjoyed for generations by young and old, a daredevil reputation. Local sheriffs have the authority to close a river and often exercise it during its high water season. Everyone pays for the mistakes of the few as government tries to protect people who venture out unaware, without a sense for the water or knowledge of the rules of survival.

Safety is mostly common sense. Good judgement will eliminate most dangers. The experienced boater is always in control. If the unexpected appears, he can eddy-out at will. If the river drops out of sight, he will stop and carefully scout the river before proceeding. He is ever mindful that many a trap has an inviting entrance. He is bold yet cautious, determined but never reckless. He is a credit to the sport.

Of Dams and Diversions

There are few more melancholy sensations than those felt upon regarding scenes of past pleasure which have been altered or destroyed.

Accompanied by a continous chain of floating logs and trees, we entered Cataract Canyon in June 1973 with some apprehension. On a prodigious flow of 80,000 c.f.s. we knew we were in for big water. The proud Colorado roared around us as our raft leapt over the 15-foot waves. About 18 miles into the canyon we braced for mighty Gypsum Rapid. To our astonishment, we were met with a few struggling waves—and then silence. The raft nearly stopped. Drifting logs wedged around us. We had reached Lake Powell or, more appropriately Powell Reservoir. The dead silence contrasted starkly with the recent pleasures of a bustling river. The sounds of the Colorado had been stilled.

While contemplating this scene of solitude and emptiness, I was inexpressibly affected. It was a picture of mortality at which my mind trembled.

Some indulge in the river's gifts with hook and line. Others capture its energy in boats. Treating the river with respect, they mostly leave it as they found it. Still others play a destructive game with rivers. Their tools are gravel, bulldozers, cement, and dynamite.

What child hasn't delighted, on a rainy day, in stopping up a rill and diverting its flow with twigs and stones? But one who, as a child, diverted or plugged a brook, acts in matters of greater consequence as an adult. Now, he stops the fierce Colorado, pounding with the power of 100 locomotives, from carrying the Rockies to the sea. Although he appears to have provided short term benefits to his fellows—irrigation, recreation, flood control, power generation—in the long run he alters natural patterns in a most profound manner. Habitats are destroyed, the concentration of salts is increased, productive bottom-lands are eliminated, the formidable sediment flow is blocked; and many places, beautiful and sacred to those who loved them, are eliminated. These are not child's games.

A great dam, like the child's, has a limited life. It gathers and temporarily stores rock particles destined for the ocean. Lakes Mead and Powell accumulate over 200,000,000 tons of sediment in an average year. In one spring day, the chocolate Colorado carries as much as 20 million tons of silt and sand into these reservoirs. There is no possible technology that can halt or significantly decrease the filling of a large reservoir except, temporarily, another reservoir upstream. Experts give Lake Powell between one and two centuries to fill. Then a so-called reverse ooze effect will aggrade the Green and Colorado rivers upstream from the reservoir, producing miles of inner-canyon deltas. Our great-grandchildren might refer to the area as "Powell Flats," for it will resemble today's dry lake beds such as the flat desert of Utah's ancient Lake Bonneville. For a time, it might be suitable for space shuttle landings or land speed records.

It will symbolize the period when we helped ourselves to the earth. Then, as the dam finally disintegrates, a vast accumulation of mud will pour down the Colorado to the sea, destroying everything in its path.

A similar fate awaits all other reservoirs, with the exception of those at highest altitudes, which will slowly turn to bog and finally to meadow.

The Bureau of Reclamation believes that it is developing the waters of the West, but rivers live by a different clock. We cannot trick them. In due time they will wash away our grandiose dams like the tide destroys a sand castle on the beach. Once again they will roll on in their ancient canyons in primal freedom, unprovoked by man's meddling interference. Our pretentious reservoirs are ephermeral annoyances in the history of Rocky Mountain rivers.

If we are not destroying rivers by building dams, then, why be concerned?

It is possible our disruptions will have devastating consequences for mankind.

Year by year, more free-flowing streams are subtracted from the depleted supply. Measure what has already been lost: fifty miles of the upper Gunnison

River, including most of the Black Canyon; much of Flaming Gorge on the Green; scenic portions of the Colorado, Blue, Fryingpan, South Platte, San Juan, Los Pinos, and Rio Chama. Diversions have depleted the flows of several of these rivers, together with the Dolores, Roaring Fork, Fraser, Navajo, Rio Grande, Big Thompson, and Eagle. Major impoundments and diversions are under construction on the Uncompahgre, South Platte, and Dolores.

Planned water projects hover like dark clouds over treasured canyons and valleys. A series of dams and diversions planned for Poudre Canyon would impound and pipe northern Colorado's most popular clearwater fishing and kayaking river. The last large, free-flowing river in the Colorado Basin, the Yampa, is slated for the construction of storage reservoirs behind dams in strategic Juniper and Cross Mountain Canyons. Immediately south of the Yampa, beyond the Rangely oil fields, the desert wilderness of White River Canyon is the site of other planned reservoirs. Together with the Yampa, they would supply water for massive oil shale developments. The Gunnison, at present a staircase of reservoirs, is targeted for impoundment in its last flowing sections—the wild Gunnison Gorge and scenic Dominguez Canyon. If final plans materialize, much of the volume of the lower Animas will be pumped into reservoirs. Proposed projects would divert from the West Slope to the East Slope some 100,000 additional acre-feet from the Eagle, Piney, and Williams Fork rivers. Perhaps the most sinister project of all is the Denver Water Board's planned Two Forks Dam, which would bury 25 miles of the lush North and South Forks of the Platte in the mountains west of Denver.

Denver presently operates with a usable surplus of nearly 150,000 acre-feet of water. Studies have shown that employment of basic conservation techniques would extend the surplus well past the year 2000. Such studies demonstrate that water is in short supply not because of a lack of more dams and tunnels but because of waste.

On the beleagured Western Slope, problems are mounting from the incessant diverting and damming of rivers. Pure water taken from Colorado's high country to the East Slope increases the salinity of the water that remains. This situation is exacerbated by vast amounts of evaporation from existing reservoirs and leached return flow from irrigated fields, until, downstream, the Colorado is not fit for consumption or agriculture. But the Bureau of Reclamation has a solution for the damage it has created—build! Seventeen units in a six-state area are planned—some are under construction—to prevent salt from entering the Colorado or to try removing it from the river. The Bureau has poisoned the river. Now it wants to get the poison out, at the taxpayers' expense. One attempt to desalinate the Colorado is the McPhee Dam and diversion works now under construction on a major tributary of the Colorado, the Dolores River. McPhee and attendant canals will take advantage of a low divide and export the Dolores from its home of the last several million years into the San Juan Basin. Although its construction was promoted as an irrigation project, this diversion will bypass the Dolores from its bed, which crosses several influent salt basins and contributes 200,000 tons of salt per year to the already briny Colorado. The cost, in addition to hundreds of millions of dollars, will be the near-elimination of what many regard as the West's most beautiful rafting and kayaking river.

Politics plays a role. The Colorado River Compact allots more water to the state of Colorado than it can use or store. Some Coloradans believe it is in their best interests to prevent this water, born in their mountains, from escaping. The Bureau of Reclamation is glad to oblige. Dams and diversion

The old confluence of the Lake Fork (upper right) and Gunnison Rivers just above the Black Canyon. Today this area is drowned by Blue Mesa Reservoir. (Denver Public Library, photo by George L. Beam.)

works on Colorado rivers will prevent their waters from getting into the hands of Californians or Arizonans downstream.

But there is reason for hope. A decade ago there was little concern in our country for loss of individual species. Today, endangered species are protected by law. The Wilderness Act, the Clean Air Act, and the Wild and Scenic Rivers Act, all relatively recent laws, give promise of a new age which will stress preservation rather than destruction of the natural world. The Bureau of Reclamation has difficulty understanding the public's shifting attitudes. Is it possible the era is past when plugging a big river was regarded as an heroic enterprise? Is it possible we may come to recognize a duty to pass on America's wilderness river heritage to future generations rather than use it up ourselves, expending it for our own immediate needs and comforts? Contrary to popular belief, wilderness *can* be restored and rivers reestablished. Why should it not be possible to dismantle some of the more destructive monuments of an era that is over and let nature reclaim her canyons as she is reclaiming the hearts of humans?

Part II
Rivers of the West Slope

Slick Rock Canyon on the Dolores River.

Upper Colorado River Basin

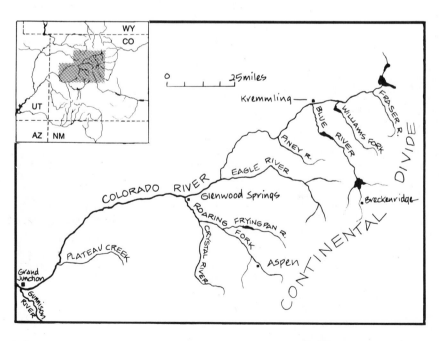

Rivers are the constant
lure to distant enterprise
and adventure. —Thoreau

"Captain" Samuel Adams
Challenges the Upper Colorado

On July 12, 1869, "Captain" Samuel Adams stood proud and anxious on the banks of the Blue River, one of the Colorado's uppermost tributaries, near Breckenridge, Colorado. He was finally ready to begin his historic voyage of discovery from Colorado to California by way of the Colorado River.

Adams had blown into town only two months before. He had told the miners and townsfolk of an Eden down the Colorado, a river corridor of vast wealth and opportunity. Adams was a man of persuasion. He easily recruited ten men for the expedition. They hastily constructed four open boats of green pine. Hundreds of pounds of flour, bacon and coffee were loaded up. Rifles, ammunition and scientific instruments were carefully packed. The largest boat, 22 feet in length, was fitted with a flag inscribed by the ladies of Breckenridge with "Western Colorado to California, Greeting!"

It was a gala sendoff. Speeches were given by Judge Silverthorne and others. Adams praised the people of Breckenridge as possessing superior intelligence and moral worthiness even at these "extreme limits of civilization."

Who was this Captain Samuel Adams and where had he come from?

In the spring of 1867, E.M. Stanton, Secretary of War, received a letter entitled "Communication from Captain (where he received title is not recorded) Samuel Adams, Relative to the Exploration of the Colorado River and its Tributaries." Stanton, apparently impressed, ordered the letter printed in the record of the 42nd Congress. In this letter Adams stressed the "great commercial importance of the Colorado of the West as being the central route between the Atlantic and Pacific Oceans."

Adams, it seems, had been kicking around the lower 350 miles of the Colorado with Captain Thomas Trueworthy of San Francisco in a small, steam-powered sternwheeler.

Several explorers, including Derby, Johnson, and Ives, had voyaged up the Colorado in steamers and told of a great central chasm—the Grand Canyon—and an impassable river beyond. In his letter to Stanton, Adams ridiculed and disparaged these accounts, insisting that "none of those dangerous obstructions which have been represented by those who may have viewed them at a distance" existed. "The Colorado must be, emphatically, to the Pacific Coast what the Mississippi is to the Atlantic." Adams implied that he was better suited than anyone to explore the river. That exploration would "have the grand result of proving the misrepresented stream to be the central route which is to connect us more firmly in the bonds of common nationality, and of reflecting honor upon your administration."

The legislators may have taken Adams with a pinch of salt. At any event, they replied in kind:

"Resolved by the House of Representatives, (the council concurring,) That the thanks of this legislature are due and hereby tendered to Hon. Samuel Adams and Captain Thomas Trueworthy for their untiring energy and indomitable enterprise as displayed by them in opening up the navigation of the Colorado River, the great natural thoroughfare of Arizona and Utah Territories."

Not quite two years later, in April 1869, Jack Sumner, Seneca and Oramel Howland, Billy Hawkins, and Bill Dunn were waiting in Green River, Wyoming to join Major John Wesley Powell, who had taken the train east to oversee construction of river boats, secure funds, and gather supplies for his exploratory voyage down the Green and Colorado rivers. As they sat around their tent drinking whiskey (about all there was to do in Green River), a fast-talking dandy jumped off the train and made himself at home at their camp. It was that pioneering proponent of the Mississippi of the West, the Honorable Captain Samuel Adams. Somehow Adams had gotten wind of Powell's plans. As this expedition fitted his imagined destiny, he rushed off to join. He arrived with the letter from Congress and various communications from Stanton to try to convince Powell that he had been ordered to accompany the expedition as a scientific advisor.

Powell's motley, inebriated crew, however, quickly caught onto Adams and made fun of him just as Congress had done two years before. Hawkins upset Adams almost to the point of his leaving when, after Adams asked why the coffee tasted so bad, Hawkins pulled a dirty sock out of the pot.

There must have been some wild storytelling during those nights beside the Green River waiting for Powell's return—Adams describing his heroic exploits on the lower Colorado and Jack Sumner telling of his first ascent of Long's Peak with Major Powell the previous August. The men must have informed Adams of their trek down the Grand River (as the Colorado above the Green River confluence was called at that time) through Middle Park, eight months before. They must have told him about the little mining town of Breckenridge up on the Blue River.

Finally, on May 11, Powell arrived with the boats. Adams, assuming the expedition was government sponsored, presented his papers. But Powell had organized the entire expedition using private funds. The letters from Congress and the Secretary of War meant nothing to him. Powell sent Captain Adams on his way.

"If you can't join'em, beat'em," Adams probably thought to himself, and scurried off to the Grand River drainage on the other side of the great Y formed by the two branches of the Colorado to put together his own expedition at Breckenridge.

Barely two months after his unsuccessful attempt to join the Powell expedition, Adams was off on the Blue River with his own band of hearty adventurers.

About eight miles below the confluence of the Blue and Ten Mile Creek, Adams and his string of crudely built boats approached Boulder Creek. "On turning a bend in the river, our real danger burst upon us, as we saw, for the first time, the white, foaming water dashing for one mile ahead of us." Chaos ensued as the boats crashed into the rocks. Although much equipment was lost, the men managed to get the boats to shore. Adams named the short stretch extending two miles below Boulder Creek "Rocky Canyon." In the next three days one of the boats broke into two pieces and was left a "complete wreck." Four men deserted.

The following day Adams named the short canyon in which Green Mountain Dam was later built "Cove Canyon." Another boat was lost there.

The men camped for a week where the Blue meets the Colorado, probably making repairs and wondering how Captain Adams managed to get them involved in this fiasco. On July 30, Adams reported, the party "started down the Grand River with our two remaining boats; ran four miles southwest to the Grand Canyon of the Grand River." It is perhaps ironic that a canyon hundreds of miles downriver, which Adams did not believe existed, was later given one of his place names. Today, the canyon he had reached is called Gore Canyon. Captain Adams had finally learned a lesson. He ascended the right wall at the head of the canyon to reconnoiter. The scene inspired a poetic flair:

"Struck by the beauty of the scenery, I this evening ascended a point above, the great chain of mountains far in the distance rising higher and still higher toward the snowy range, while Mount Lincoln, [Mount Lincoln is not visible from this point; probably he saw Eagles Nest Peak] towering far above these, bathed in the brilliant moonlight, was superbly magnificient."

Captain Adams should have stayed with philosophy and poetry. In his rapture he neglected to scrutinize the pounding fury below. Adams was a pious man. The party never traveled on the Sabbath. But no amount of piety could save them from the hell into which he was about to hurl his tiny fleet.

Fortunately, he did not try to run the boats through Gore Canyon. Carrying his heavy, unwieldy vessels, however, was an impossible task. While lowering the biggest boat through the second big drop with rope, Adams wrote, "She swung out into the current, filled with water, was held struggling an hour in the mad element, when the line parted and our best and largest boat disappeared forever. By this accident we were reduced to one boat; almost everything necessary for the trip had been lost. Here I gave the box in which I had carried my instruments to the waves. We divested ourselves of almost everything of weight, and prepared to try our fortunes in the last boat."

It took them four days to go three quarters of a mile. On the fourth day, August 7, the last boat broke loose and was dashed to bits on the rocks. Three more men deserted. Captain Adams was undaunted. He knew the river would flatten out all the way to the Gulf of California in just a few miles. Since logs in the river here were rounded and worn about the same amount as those he had observed three years before near the mouth of the Colorado, he reasoned that the river must be calm from here on.

Left with two faithful followers, Twible and Lillis, Adams began hiking downriver. The weeks of hard labor and disappointment had obviously taken their toll. He was desperate to put a few positive items, though absurdly exaggerated, into his journal:

August 11—"Built a cedar raft five by sixteen feet, and upon this we took passage, ran down the river 30 miles passing through. . .wheat we found over 6 feet in height."

Adam's next point of reference he called "Rapid Canyon." Here, he reported, "We pushed her out, and in a moment she shot like an arrow down the rapid descent. We both grabbed the cross-piece on the raft to which our provisions were lashed; she sunk four feet under the surface, but rose again in the distance of eighty yards, when in turning an abrupt angle in the river, she struck and parted. Here we lost a huge portion of our [remaining] provisions.''

Did Captain Adams quit? Not a chance. They built another raft and descended another 40 miles. The destruction of this last raft left the party with only five days' worth of flour and bacon. Captain Adams finally called it quits.

He had probably reached a point some distance above the Eagle River confluence, 150 miles down the Blue and Colorado rivers. This section has a drop of about 3,000 feet, far less than the 6,000 feet he claimed in his journal. Although no one drowned, four boats and four rafts had been sacrificed and eight of his ten men had fled. Somehow Adams rationalized that only a "narrow territory" divided him from the lower Colorado up which he and Trueworthy had driven their little steamer three years before. Again poor Adams was wrong. The most difficult portion of the route actually lay ahead in the thundering cataracts of Glenwood Canyon, the black gorge of Westwater, the graveyard of the Colorado—Cataract Canyon, and the immense depths of the Grand Canyon.

At the time Adams turned away from the river, Powell and his men were passing the junction of the Little Colorado, headed for the heart of the Grand Canyon.

Powell became the hero of the Colorado, Adams the goat. Yet Adams perservered heroically. Most men would have quit after the first disaster, far up the Blue River at Boulder Creek Rapids. If Adams had been honest in the account of his trip, entitled "Expedition of the Colorado River and its Tributaries, a Wonderful Country Opened Up"; if he had avoided condemning his adversaries; he might have found more of a place in history. In point of fact, he was the first to descend the upper Colorado, a river which still attracts hordes of river lovers each summer.

Trails and Rails on the Upper Colorado

If Captain Adams had consulted the narrative of Colonel John C. Fremont's 1843-1844 expedition, he might not have attempted his impossible journey. Fremont said of the Colorado River:

"Three hundred miles of its lower part, as it approaches the Gulf of California, is reported to be smooth and tranquil; but its upper part is manifestly broken into many falls and rapids. From many descriptions of trappers, it is probable that in its foaming course among its lofty precipices it presents many scenes of wild grandeur; and though offering many temptations, and often discussed, no trappers have been found bold enough to undertake a voyage which has so certain a prospect of a fatal termination.''

Fremont's 1844 route and the trails of trappers and Indians were abandoned with the coming of the railroads. If it had not been for David Moffat's attempt to connect Salt Lake City with Denver by a direct route through the mountains in the early 1900s, Gore Canyon and Middle Park would now be flooded by the "Great Kremmling Reservoir." The U.S. Reclamation Service had declared Gore Canyon especially well adapted for a dam, but Moffat insisted Gore Canyon was the only possible route for his railroad. In the nick of time, President Theodore Roosevelt intervened to grant right-of-way to the railroad.

Gore Canyon and Middle Park were saved from inundation.

In following years the upper Colorado and four of its major tributaries, the Fraser, Blue, Eagle, and Roaring Fork, began to be used as major transport routes into and across the Southern Rocky Mountains. Today highways, railroads, or both follow every branch of the upper Colorado Basin except the little Piney River.

Until 1921 the Colorado, from its junction with the Green to its headwaters, was called the Grand River. Since the river originated in their state, the Colorado legislature deemed it proper in that year to change its name to the Colorado. Nevertheless, many landmarks along its course retain the old designation. The river begins at Grand Lake; its upper reaches flow through Grand County; it leaves the mountains through the Grand Hogback and winds through the Grand Valley under the shadow of the Grand Mesa to Grand Junction. Later it carves the Grand Canyon, and emerges from that gorge at Grand Wash. Everything about the river and its surroundings deserves the original title. It rises in the highest mountains, carves the deepest canyons, crosses the driest deserts, and divides the widest plateaus in North America.

The upper Colorado will be defined in this book as that portion of the river above Grand Junction. Plentiful access points and a long season make this a popular boating area, but do not expect to find more than a tiny taste of pristine wilderness along the shores of any river in the upper Colorado River Basin.

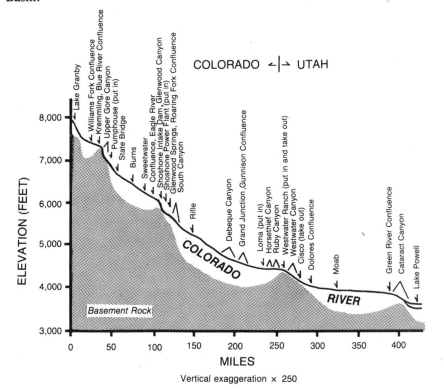

Gradient Profile of Colorado River from Lake Granby to Lake Powell. Average gradient, 12.7 ft/mile. Note sharp increases in gradient where the river meets upthrust basement rock.

Colorado River—Kremmling to Dotsero Section

The 69-mile section of the Colorado River from Kremmling to Dotsero boasts great variety. In the first 10 miles the river plunges through marginally navigable Gore Canyon. Then it moderates, winding through a series of short canyons between stretches of rural pastureland.

The 14-mile section from the mouth of Gore Canyon to State Bridge is perhaps the most popular river run in Colorado, making it a good place for non-commercial boaters to avoid, at least during peak season from mid June to early August. During this period, at least 40 commercial outfitters launch an average of 75 rafts every day. Below State Bridge the river, though still popular, is not as heavily used.

The tracks of the Denver and Rio Grande Western Railroad follow the Colorado. In addition to the tracks, a dirt road parallels the bed of the canyon next to the river much of the way. The road joins a number of tiny towns including Radium, Rancho del Rio, Bond, Burns, and Derby Junction. Most of the river runs through Bureau of Land Management (BLM) land, but a number of private ranches break up the public corridor.

Perhaps the best time to visit the upper Colorado is during May. This is high water season. Though special caution should be exercised in approaching the

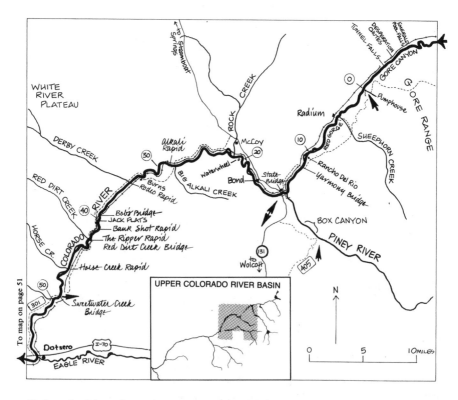

Colorado River from Gore Canyon to Eagle River confluence.

many bridge abutments, plenty of excitement can be found on big waves, and crowding is not a problem. The stretch from Pumphouse to Dotsero offers good three- and four-day raft trips with pleasant camping on public land along the route.

Colorado River: Kremmling to Pumphouse (Gore Canyon)

Physical Data: 11 mi; 350-ft drop; 32 ft/mi average gradient; 100 ft/mi maximum gradient (through Gore Canyon); 600,000 acre-ft average yearly discharge (near Kremmling).
Maps: Kremmling, Mt. Powell, and Radium USGS Quads.
Land Ownership: First 4 miles below Kremmling are private, remainder BLM.
Flow Information: Lakewood office, USGS.

If you are looking for an enjoyable raft or kayak run, Gore Canyon is not for you. Through this gorge the Colorado River resembles a cascade. Since Captain Samuel Adams's first attempt in 1869, it has swallowed up one adventurer after another. The biggest obstacle in Gore Canyon is not the Colorado's 100-foot-per-mile gradient but the unnatural presence of boulders choking the riverbed. Huge chunks of granite rolled down the canyon side during the blasting of railroad tunnels above. The resulting channel is obscured and very dangerous.

The Gore was first run without portage by the legendary kayaker Walt Blackadar in the early 1970s. On August 3, 1977, Rob Wise, with Jon Adler and Andy Reich, took the first raft through. Their craft was a 22-foot military pontoon. Wise had gained notoriety three years before as the first to raft furious Cross Mountain Gorge on the Yampa.

Despite these successes, Gore Canyon has crushed more boats and destroyed more dreams than almost any canyon in the state of Colorado.

Most of those who today attempt the Gore today are expert kayakers. They run only at low water levels and are prepared to portage four or five times past tumultuous cataracts. The first drop, Gateway Rapid, can be run, although a big hole blocks the middle. A 300-yard pool provides relief after this first drop.

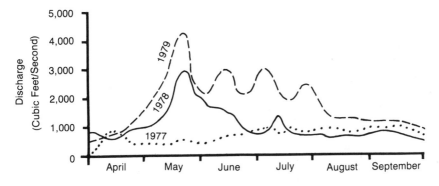

Hydrograph of Colorado River near Kremmling at upstream end of Gore Canyon.

*Rob Wise making the first-ever raft run through Gore Canyon.
(Joan Cummings photo.)*

The pool ends in a series of falls, the first being the highest. Emerald Pool Falls, Desperation Chutes, Wise Acre Falls, and Reich Gulch Rapids are all capable of raising the hair on the heads of the most intrepid storm-water fanatics. Below this first series of big falls lies another—Tunnel Falls, 15 feet high and even more frightening. Here the Colorado plummets over a vertical ledge into a frothing maelstrom with no easy recovery.

Below this biggest falls the gradient eases, though the river continues to sport class IV and V rapids for another two miles. Gore Canyon makes a much better hike than river run. It is not recommended.

Colorado River: Pumphouse to State Bridge

Physical Data: 14 mi; 200-ft drop; 14 ft/mi average gradient; 703,000 acre-ft average yearly discharge (near Pumphouse).
Maps: Radium, McCoy, and State Bridge USGS Quads.
Land Ownership: Mostly BLM; river crosses four private ranches.
Information: BLM, Kremmling Resource Area, Kremmling, Colorado 80459.

Colorado's most popular raft trip is chiefly a commercial operator's mecca, but private rafters, kayakers, and open canoeists can also enjoy the relaxing, intermediate water. The BLM has not slapped restrictions on private use, but this situation could change at any time.

The county road which leads to the Pumphouse connects State Highway 9 south of Kremmling with State Highway 131 at State Bridge. A sign on the county road points the way to the launching site. This site is nothing more than a small, grassy flat. It is justifiably referred to as a zoo during the heavy summer season. Because Pumphouse is the first good launching point on the river, it is referred to as mile zero on the Upper Colorado River Basin maps.

The fast water begins about one mile downriver at the entrance to the upper gorge. This is one of two gunsight notches which are composed of isolated chunks of ancient, hard metamorphic rock forming the nearby Gore Range. A steep drop in the middle of the gorge should be run right of the big mid-river hole. Lively water continues past the drop to the canyon's mouth. Then the country opens up as the Colorado winds past Sheephorn Creek and the Radium Bridge, a good alternate put-in. One and one-half miles below Radium is Red Gorge. Red Gorge Rapid, a big one with plenty of holes, lies in the middle of the gorge around a left turn. Easy water leads past Rancho del Rio and the Yarmony bridge beyond. The last three miles to State Bridge are punctuated with many gentle rapids. Old lava flows are visible above the river in this area. A public parking lot river-left up from the Highway 131 bridge is the usual take-out. You will probably be charged a use fee for parking here.

Colorado River: State Bridge to Dotsero

Physical Data: 44 mi; 620-ft drop; 14 ft/mi average gradient; 745,000 acre-ft average yearly discharge (near State Bridge).

Maps: State Bridge, McCoy, Blue Hill, Burns South, Sugarloaf Mountain, and Dotsero USGS Quads.

Land Ownership: Alternating private ranches and BLM land.

Information: BLM, Glenwood Springs Resource Area, Glenwood Springs, Colorado 81601.

Below State Bridge the Colorado River continues a winding course through its rural mountain valley. The railroad tracks and gravel road leave the river for short stretches and rejoin it further on. The road provides dozens of good access points in this 44-mile stretch. Rapids are interspersed with flat water. Most are easy, but a few reach class III difficulty. The numerous bridge abutments pose the greatest hazard on this part of the Colorado, especially at high water. Camping is permitted on public land, but firewood gathering has been restricted.

Several good camp spots are found river-left between State Bridge and Bond. Past Bond, a grand old waterwheel sits next to the water at mile 21 (below Pumphouse). A gravel road crosses the river at Big Alkali Creek (mile 29). Closely spaced iron abutments can make this bridge a tough one to negotiate. Here the Colorado enters a shallow, inner canyon leading to Burns. Alkali Rapid, several hundred yards below the bridge, should be scouted.

A few years ago a section of an adjoining mesa slumped into the river half a mile below Burns and about 200 yards above Derby Creek (mile 34.5). The rock debris blocked the river, producing the biggest rapid between Gore and Glenwood Canyons. Rodeo Rapid should be scouted carefully. It consists of two short, steep, boulder-studded drops.

Access is possible either at Derby Junction (permission required) or the bridge at Burns.

The next hazard obstructs the river three miles below Derby Creek at Bob's Bridge (mile 28.5). Many rafts have flipped here at high water. A large cement piling supporting the railroad bridge lies in fast water on a bend to the left. As the river sweeps around the corner above, it looks as if there is no room to get by the right side of the piling. In struggling to get to the left, many rafters have hit the huge reflex wave glancing off the piling and flipped. The correct course, not visible from above, is the easy route to the right of the piling. Bob's Bridge illustrates the benefits of judicious scouting to avoid an icy swim.

Good camping is found at Jack Flats, a mile below Bob's Bridge. Just beyond, along a cliff on the left, big waves form in what is known as Bankshot Rapid, an easy and exhilarating ride. Red Dirt Bridge, a double span, crosses the river at mile 41, just beyond Bankshot. Under it lies the Ripper, so named because of its tendency to separate rubber rafts from their floors. The Ripper is not a big rapid, but plenty of rocks and a couple of bridge pilings can cause difficulty.

In the next eight miles past Red Dirt Bridge, the Colorado crosses a series of private ranches where no landings should take place. Horse Creek Rapid, a big one, waits at mile 46. An excellent take-out is located on the left side of the river, just beyond the road bridge at mile 49.

In the next nine miles to Dotsero the Colorado passes Sweetwater and Deep creeks flowing down from the White River Plateau to the West. Here the river widens, with only a few minor rapids—including Washing Machine and Eddie's Garage.

The sides of the valley in the last 15 miles above Dotsero display the strains of immense geologic upheavals. The exposed strata, including the Red Beds, are buckled and folded at sharp angles. Lava flows cap the surrounding plateaus. At Dotsero the Colorado joins its largest tributary thus far—the Eagle River.

Colorado River—Glenwood Canyon to Grand Junction Section

In the 94-mile stretch from Glenwood Canyon to Grand Junction, the Colorado crosses the transition zone from mountains to high desert. It slices through the White River Plateau's southern shoulder in a deep gorge, then picks up the Roaring Fork in downtown Glenwood Springs and rips into South Canyon through the Grand Hogback, bisecting miles of near-vertical strata that lean against the flank of the White River Uplift and the Elk Range. At the mouth of South Canyon, the river emerges into a wide valley at the southern extension of the Piceance Basin. Bordering the valley on the north are the Roan Cliffs, capped by the oil shale-bearing Green River Formation. To the south are the lava-capped Grand and Battlement Mesas. Upriver from Grand Junction, the Colorado meets resistant beds of the Mesa Verde sandstones holding up the cliffs of DeBeque Canyon.

Below the Eagle River confluence, the Colorado begins biting into the uplift across its path, passing through increasingly older strata and boring at last into the Precambrian Basement Complex in the very heart of Glenwood Canyon. Here a small catch dam blocks the river. Taking advantage of the impervious crystalline rock at this point, engineers drilled a nearly horizontal tunnel inside the north wall of the canyon to reach the Shoshone Powerplant three miles downriver. The entire Colorado River, except during high water periods, is diverted into this tunnel. At the tunnel's end, it is hurled down the canyon wall, through penstocks, into generators, and finally back into the channel.

Between the Eagle River and the Shoshone Intake Reservoir the current is relatively calm. Several class I rapids along the 10-mile stretch build pitching haystacks at high water. This is a popular open canoe run.

Above the powerhouse the river is absent from its bed much of the year. Even when it is flowing, two enormous drops preclude boating.

Colorado River: Shoshone Powerplant to New Castle

Physical Data: 20 mi; 385-ft drop; 18.5 ft/mi average gradient; 40 ft/mi maximum gradient (powerplant to Grizzly Creek); 2,300,000 acre-ft average yearly discharge (below Glenwood Springs).

Maps: Shoshone, Glenwood Springs, Storm King Mountain and New Castle USGS Quads.

Land Ownership: Mostly BLM in Glenwood Canyon, private through Glenwood Springs, BLM through South Canyon, and private above New Castle.

Information: Glenwood Springs Chamber of Commerce.

Below the Shoshone Powerhouse the river becomes possible to boat, boasting some of the biggest water in the state—Upper and Lower Superstition, The Wall, and Tombstone Rapids—in the two miles down to Grizzly Creek. A wooden boat ramp at the powerhouse provides easy raft access. Local authorities may restrict rafting at dangerous water levels. The big rapids end at Grizzly Creek, a popular launch point. During the peak tourist season, over 100 commercial rafts put in here each day.

Rapids generally are easy through Glenwood Springs, though the big river generates powerful hydraulics during high water periods. The pace picks up past town, as the river enters the jaws of South Canyon. Two miles down,

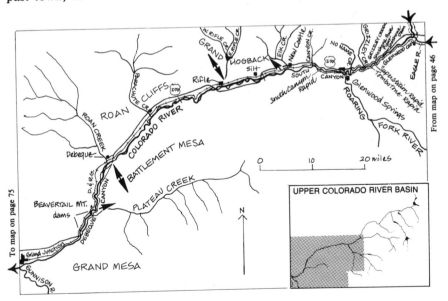

Colorado River from Eagle River confluence to Grand Junction.

under the South Canyon Creek Bridge, lies the run's eminent drop—South Canyon Rapid. The railroad bridge a mile below South Canyon Rapid is supported by dangerously spaced pilings. A wide floodplain and parking lot between the river and Interstate 70, less than a mile below New Castle, provides a good take-out. Numerous access points provide a variety of take-outs in the 20 miles between Grizzly Creek and New Castle.

At the time of publication, I-70 is under construction in narrow Glenwood Canyon. One can imagine the amount of blasted rock necessary to build a four lane road in a space barely large enough for two. Whether riverbed tampering will destroy another natural waterway remains to be seen.

Colorado River: New Castle to DeBeque Canyon

Physical Data: 64 mi; 740-ft drop; 11.5 ft/mi average gradient; 2,350,000 acre-ft average yearly discharge (below New Castle).
Maps: New Castle, Silt, Rifle, Anvil Points, Rulison, Grand Valley, Red Pinnacle, DeBeque, Wagon Track Ridge and Cameo USGS Quads.
Land Ownership: Mostly private, short stretches of public land throughout run.

In this long, gentle reach, the Colorado meanders through its wide valley then eases into DeBeque Canyon above Grand Junction. In the process of grading its channel, the river occasionally divides around large islands. Groves of cottonwoods and box elders shade the water and screen it from surrounding highways and towns. Willows choke shallower places. Thousands of geese and ducks inhabit the riverine habitat.

The run, at moderate water levels, is smooth enough to offer good open canoeing, though headgate weirs scattered through the run can present difficulties. About a dozen access points along the route accomodate any length of trip desired.

The run begins at the border between the intruded, folded, faulted mountain province to the east and the calm plateau province to the west. The valley forms the southern extention of the Piceance Basin. Low bluffs along the river are composed of the Tertiary-age Wasatch Formation. The contact between the Wasatch and overlying Green River shales sits about midway up the Roan Cliffs, which tower 3,000 feet above the river to the north.

At the contact point, the pink and reddish color of the Wasatch gives way to the dark and light grays of the Green River Formation above. Oil shale mines tunnel into the Parachute Member of the Green River Formation beneath the plateau's summit. The brownish sandstones of the Mesa Verde Formation, underlying the Wasatch, compose the cliffs of DeBeque Canyon at the end of the run. DeBeque is identical in structure and composition to Gray Canyon of the Green River 100 miles west.

The biggest rapid on the run is encountered in the first half-mile below the put-in west of New Castle. Easily seen from the highway, it rates class II and III, depending on water level. If one wishes to avoid this rapid and a steep diversion weir several miles downriver, it is possible to put in at the bridge next to Silt. Below Silt, the river divides into as many as five channels. A third good put-in is found next to the Interstate 70 rest area at Rifle. A gage on the cement jetty above the old Rifle bridge marks the water level from zero to seven feet. Above seven feet the river is at flood stage—over 25,000 c.f.s. Any level below

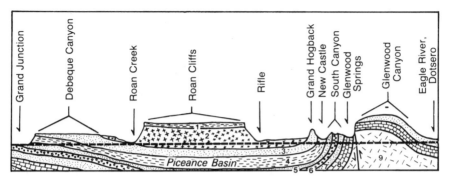

1 Green River Formation	4 Mancos Shale	7 Pennsylvanian System
2 Wasatch Formation	5 Mesozoic Formations	8 Lower Paleozoic System
3 Mesa Verde Formation	6 Maroon Formations	9 Granitic Basement Rock

Geologic profile of Colorado River from Eagle River confluence to Grand Junction (looking north).

four feet offers enjoyable canoeing and easy rafting and kayaking.

Good access is found at the Interstate 70 bridge near the town of DeBeque, 32 miles downstream from Rifle. Here you can camp and leave cars. At the time of publication, I-70 is under construction. Several bridges will span the river in this stretch, which could present bridge abutment hazards. Within De-Beque Canyon there are several roadside rest areas. A good one is located just before the river makes a wide swing around Beavertail Mountain—a tall bluff—river-right. This is the last take-out. Below Beavertail Mountain, just above Plateau Creek, lies Bureau of Reclamation's first major project on the Colorado River, the Grand Valley Diversion Dam. The river plummets 15 feet over the lip of the dam into a boiling vortex. Four miles downriver, another unnavigable diversion structure makes the lower part of DeBeque Canyon impractical for boating. Just past this second structure, DeBeque Canyon ends, and the Colorado emerges into the wide Grand Valley and the city of Grand Junction.

Fraser River

The Fraser is the highest major tributary of the Colorado. Its flow is severely depleted by extensive aqueducts and tunnels connecting the upper tributaries to each other and funneling much of their run-off eastward through the Moffat Tunnel. Today the weakened Fraser carries an adequate flow for paddling through Fraser Canyon between Tabernash and Granby only at very high water stages. U.S. Highway 40 gives the narrow canyon a wide berth, but the Denver and Rio Grande Western Railroad tracks follow it.

The Fraser cut its narrow canyon through a plug of Front Range granitic and metamorphic rock. Dense Douglas fir, lodgepole, and ponderosa forests covering the north facing walls contrast sharply with the sunny, sage-bristled southerly slopes. Water ouzels and sandpipers wing over the water while hawks soar high above. Excellent fishing and camping are found in this scenic, out-of-the-way canyon.

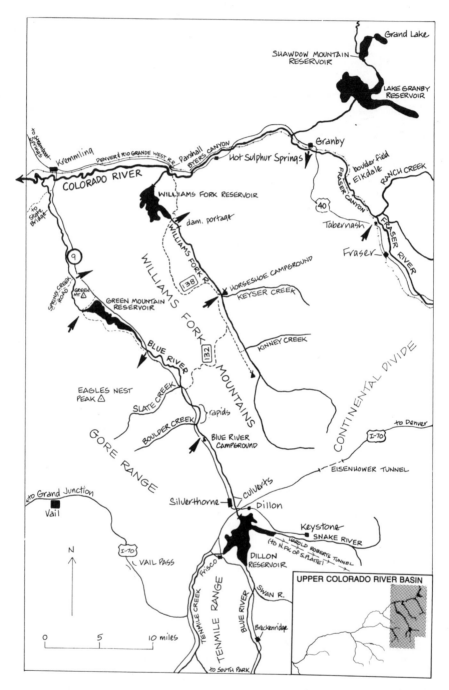

Fraser, Williams Fork, and Blue rivers.

FRASER RIVER

Fraser River Canyon: Tabernash to Granby

Physical Data: 10 mi; 360-ft drop; 36 ft/mi average gradient; 85 ft/mi maximum gradient (2nd railroad bridge to Elkdale); 70,000 acre-ft average yearly discharge (below Ranch Creek).
Maps: Fraser, Strawberry Lake, and Granby USGS Quads; Arapaho National Forest Map.
Land Ownership: Mostly BLM land; last two miles private.

The tiny Fraser is too small for rafts. However, class III to IV rapids below each of three railroad bridges offer kayakers ample excitement. The drops between the second railroad bridge and the wilderness cabins at Elkdale rate a solid class IV. A mile-long class III boulder field sits below the third railroad bridge. Caution should be exercised due to jammed logs in the narrow, alder-lined channel. Boaters must put up with flat water in the first and last two miles of the run.

To put in, walk down the tracks north of Tabernash. Ranch Creek, meeting the Fraser from the east just below Tabernash, increases the volume of the river considerably. Take out at the U.S. Highway 40 Bridge just east of Granby.

Williams Fork

The Williams Fork, the Colorado's second major tributary, is sandwiched between the Fraser and Blue rivers. Although free-flowing down to the Williams Fork Reservoir, this river is the site of a battle between conservationists and the Denver Water Board, which aims to divert its headwaters to the East Slope. Thanks to efforts of concerned people, the Williams Fork has been reprieved. Today the river is depleted by only one small diversion, the August P. Gumlick Tunnel.

From river to canyon rim, the broad slopes of the Williams Fork Valley—overspread with an unbroken cover of pine, spruce and fir—are the empire of the forest gods. The wilderness atmosphere, however, has become unsettled recently by the huge Henderson molybdenum mining and processing complex in the heart of the valley.

Williams Fork: Horseshoe Campground to Williams Fork Reservoir

Physical Data: 9 mi; 600-ft drop; 66 ft/mi average gradient; 96,000 acre-ft average yearly discharge (below Keyser Creek).
Maps: Sylvan Reservoir, Battle Mountain and Parshall USGS Quads.
Land Ownership: National Forest at top of run, then alternating BLM and private land.

A good put-in is found at Horseshoe Campground where Keyser Creek meets the Williams Fork. If the water is high enough, another put-in is available upriver opposite the Henderson Mill.

The river clips along with a steady gradient of 50 to 75 feet per mile, resulting in swift class II to IV water. Two miles downriver from Horseshoe Campground lies a rugged, three-mile-long canyon with splendid scenery and several tricky rapids.

Gliding beneath a mature evergreen forest, the little Williams Fork is a site for many log jams. Most jams can be passed, but even these can be hazardous. This is not a river for unskilled boaters. A headgate weir is located at the end of the canyon two miles upriver from the reservoir. The weir cannot be run.

County Road 138 provides a short shuttle west of the river from Horseshoe Campground over Battle Mountain to one of two bridges above the reservoir.

Blue River

The Blue, because of its crystal clear water and close proximity to Denver, is a favorite day-boating area. Its location also makes it one of the most controlled rivers in the Southern Rocky Mountains. Two reservoirs, Dillon and Green Mountain, regulate the Blue with the stringency of an irrigation system. Green Mountain was built to store water for Western Slope agricultural use. Dillon, upstream, supplies Denver via the 24-mile Roberts Tunnel through the Continental Divide. Dillon was built after an agreement that Green Mountain Reservoir would be filled each year before Denver takes water from the Blue. However, the Denver Water Board, in dry years, often balks at its agreement to release water into Green Mountain for ranchers.

What does all this mean for the Blue River? First, hoarding its water for Denver lawns results in a severe flow diminution. Second, the Water Board usually fills Green Mountain Reservoir early so it can begin routing the water into the tunnel. Releases from both dams are erratic, but high flows from Dillon usually come early in the season, while those from Green Mountain take place later. Third, the river issues from the bottom of the reservoirs, resulting in water cold as an iceberg.

Snake River and Tenmile Creek

These two large tributaries of the Blue reach Dillon Reservoir from opposite directions. Each is marginal for kayaking short distances at high water levels.

A unique attempt to reroute a stream for aesthetic purposes was undertaken on Tenmile Creek. In 1976, roadbuilders were pushing Interstate 70 near narrow Tenmile Canyon above the town of Frisco. There wasn't room for both river and highway, so the river had to go—into a pipe. The National Forest Service had a better idea. Put the stream where the highway wasn't. Using bulldozers, they dug a new trench, lined it with logs, and placed boulders in the channel. They did such a good job that many people driving down I-70 say, "Isn't it nice that the highway builders constructed the road so it didn't interfere with that pretty stream?"

The Snake River enters the Blue River Valley from the east, opposite Tenmile Creek. At high water it can be kayaked from just above the Keystone Resort to Dillon Reservoir, a distance of three miles.

Both the Snake and Tenmile Creek flow through short conduits in places, are spanned by occasional barbed wire fences, and are blocked here and there by log jams. They should be scouted carefully before putting in.

Blue River: Dillon Reservoir to Green Mountain Reservoir

Physical Data: 20 mi; 40 ft/mi average gradient; 70 ft/mi maximum gradient (for 2 miles below Boulder Creek); 134,800 acre/ft average yearly discharge (below Dillon Reservoir).
Maps: Dillon, Willow Lakes, and Squaw Creek USGS Quads.
Land Ownership: Mostly private; spotty BLM and Forest Service land.

The Blue River occupies a pastoral valley between soaring monarchs of the Gore Range to the west and the Williams Fork Mountains to the east. It is swift and cold but not overbearing, rated class I and II for most of the distance between the two reservoirs. State Highway 9 follows the river. Many rural bridges cross it; these present the main hazard on the Blue. At high water levels the river passes dangerously close to the undersides of many of these bridges, which can appear suddenly around corners.

A new kayak course was constructed recently at the base of Dillon Dam, sponsored by the Coors Beer Company and AMAX Corporation. Large boulders were positioned in the riverbed and gates hung over the water. A popular race takes place here each June, water permitting.

The next four miles pass the town of Silverthorne, sewage ponds, and gravel quarries. Two newly constructed culverts, a short distance below Dillon Dam, present hazards. The Blue River Campground eight miles downriver from the dam makes a good access point. One-half mile below the campground, at the mouth of Boulder Creek, sits the biggest rapid in this stretch—Boulder Creek Rapid. As Captain Adams found to his dismay in 1869 and many people have discovered since, it appears unexpectedly around a sharp corner after miles of placid water. Below Boulder Creek Rapid the Blue tumbles for two miles through a series of exhilarating class II and III drops in a shallow canyon. Then it sweeps into a luxuriant valley of green fields separated from the river by a fringe of pines.

This valley follows a long, narrow basin of sedimentary rock between two granitic uplifts on either side. It passes steep bluffs of black, crumbling Mancos shale, the former bed of the great Cretaceous Sea.

Good take-outs are found at several campgrounds off State Highway 9 near the head of Green Mountain Reservoir.

Blue River: Green Mountain Reservoir to Spring Creek Road Bridge

Physical Data: 4 mi; 180 ft drop; 45 ft/mi average gradient; 220,000 acre-ft average yearly discharge (below reservoir).
Maps: Mt. Powell USGS Quad.
Land Ownership: Mostly public; private last half mile.
Flow Information: BLM, Loveland, CO.

This most endearing run on the Blue lies in Green Mountain Canyon just below the Green Mountain Reservoir. Although only four miles long, it follows one of the few wilderness canyons in the upper Colorado Basin. The river is full of eddies and play areas to stretch out a kayaking run. It is a place for intermediate and advanced paddlers to sharpen their skills while enjoying the solitude of an unspoiled canyon.

Water releases from the dam tend to be erratic. Highest water usually comes late in the season. Any amount greater than 350 c.f.s. would be excellent.

The put-in is found west of the dam down a dirt road that leads to the bottom of the gorge. The Spring Creek Road Bridge (County Road 201) take-out lies on private land. It is best to exercise courtesy to landowners and park a distance from the bridge.

Below Green Mountain Canyon the Blue meanders lazily through private pastureland for a distance of nine miles to the Colorado River.

Piney River

The little Piney River originates in the Gore Range on the opposite side of the divide from the Blue River drainage. It would be better characterized as a large creek than as a river. Despite its puny size, deep canyons and unspoiled wilderness adorn the Piney from its headwaters to its terminus in the Colorado River just above State Bridge.

Piney River: Above Box Canyon to State Bridge

Physical Data: 6 mi; 400-ft drop; 66 ft/mi average gradient; 53,700 acre-ft average yearly discharge (near mouth).

Eagle River Valley looking toward Avon and Edwards.

Maps: State Bridge USGS Quad (incomplete map).
Land Ownership: Put-in on private land, alternating private and BLM land to State Bridge.

Because of its remote location, access can be difficult, especially during high water season when snow often blocks the rough roads leading to the river. Much of the land alongside is leased by a large sportsmen's club, which may try to restrict access. There are two possible routes to the river. The first is over Muddy Creek pass on County Road 405. The second involves driving up the south rim of the canyon on a dirt road meeting State Highway 131 two miles south of State Bridge.

This short run is beset with obstacles. There were five log jams requiring carries in 1979. The water flows swiftly, rating a continuous class II to III, but there are no steep drops. The Box Canyon just below the put-in, though only a mile long, is deeply forested with steep walls of gnarled volcanic rock—a spectacular gorge.

The Piney is too small for any boats except kayaks. It has sufficient flow, ranging from 250 to 500 c.f.s. only from late May through mid-June in average years.

Eagle River

Almost as big as the Colorado at their confluence, the Eagle is a Rocky Mountain river of the primary class. It was given its name by the Ute Indians, who said it has as many tributaries as there are feathers on an eagle's tail.

Though no large dam blocks the Eagle, it has not been forgotten by man. Due to its wide valley and lack of obstructing gorges, the Eagle was chosen as part of the major east-west commerce route across the Southern Rocky Mountains. Along the 40-mile stretch from the Colorado River confluence to Dowds Junction at Gore Creek, the Eagle Valley holds two major highways—Interstate 70 and old U.S. 24, and one railroad—the Denver and Rio Grande Western. In addition, four fair-sized towns straddle the river. A new ski resort complex, Beaver Creek, with accompanying condos, hotels and golf courses, is being built in the valley. With all this activity around the beleaguered Eagle River, one might think it a good place to avoid. But the Eagle steals through the maze of roads and buildings unhindered, encased in a shallow canyon clothed with a fringe of evergreens. On the river, one hardly notices the bustle of activity in the wide valley 50 to 100 feet above. The river corridor is like a linear oasis where hawks still cry and mountain gooseberries and blueberries ripen on vines beneath the forest canopy.

Departed glaciers left an outwash plain filled with large boulders across the Eagle Valley. Many of these boulders still choke the riverbed, providing good sport for kayakers and rafters who come to court the Eagle. Its complex channel is suitable for intermediate and advanced paddlers. The free-flowing river seethes during the high-water months of May, June, and sometimes early July. At such times the swift water and lack of eddies spell danger. As the level drops during July and August, the Eagle becomes practical for a wider range of boaters.

Our investigation of the Eagle begins with the tumultuous upper gorge, rated class V and VI. Below this slot the walls flare out. The river picks up

Gore Creek and continues past the towns of Avon, Edwards, and Wolcott. This second stretch is the most popular one for river running. The final run begins at the town of Eagle and ends at the Colorado River. Here the difficulty eases a bit.

Eagle River: Upper Eagle Gorge (Gilman Run)

Physical Data: 4 mi; 440-ft drop; 110 ft/mi average gradient; 58,000 acre-ft average yearly discharge (below Homestake Creek confluence).
Maps: Minturn USGS Quad.
Land Ownership: Alternating private and National Forest.

The Upper Eagle Gorge is a hidden chasm of the sort common in the Southern Rocky Mountains. The sun's rays rarely reach its constricted belly, and the river appears shrouded in perpetual night.

Wisconsin Age glaciers, which sculpted the canyons above, did not reach down the Eagle far enough to widen this gash, although the valley of Cross Creek, which meets the Eagle at the mouth of the gorge, was broadly scoured by a large glacier that plowed to the river before receding.

In slicing the gorge, the river cuts through ancient Paleozoic limestones and finally into basement granites and metamorphic rocks. The Great Unconformity between the basement complex and the sedimentary rock above is beautifully exposed in the walls of the gorge. Revealed by erosion of the Eagle River, this basement rock has been exploited for its wealth of zinc, copper, and other metals. The huge Eagle mine has an array of shaft entrances and buildings, clattering with machinery, along the river in the middle of the gorge. The mine's support town of Gilman perches precariously on the east rim.

The Upper Eagle Gorge is a spectacle available only to kayakers of expert ability. Because its major tributary, Homestake Creek, is diverted to the East Slope, the Eagle's volume in the gorge is not great enough for paddling except during high water periods, usually June and early July. The gorge holds one 12-foot fall around a blind corner and many smaller falls rated class IV to VI. Jim Gonski summed up the difficulty of several of these in July 1978 when, after careful inspection, he exclaimed, "They're runnable—but I'm walking!"

A good put-in is found at the Red Cliff sewage pond, next to the confluence of the Eagle and Homestake Creek, below the high bridge. A dirt road off U.S. Highway 24 leads down close to the river.

Railroad tracks hug the water on both sides for the first two miles. Rock walls supporting the tracks are located at the edge of the water in many places. The channel is very narrow and steep (over 100 feet per mile) with difficult but navigable rapids. Dilapidated wooden headframes, miners' shacks, and tailings piles dot the steep canyon walls giving evidence of Eagle Gorge's long mining history. About two miles below the put-in, on a curve to the left, the boater reaches the buildings associated with Eagle Mine. It is remarkable to see two railroads, several buildings, and a river in an area hardly large enough for a basketball court. A railroad bridge and Fall Creek entering from the west are on a right turn beyond the buildings. Just past these landmarks lies the biggest hazard in the Eagle Gorge, the 12-foot falls. Portage along the tracks, river left. In the last two miles are some of the most difficult and exhilarating rapids found anywhere.

Slow water above the take-out marks the approach of a deadly cascade. It would be very unwise not to stop here. A take-out lies above a bridge where a dirt road on the east side ends at a gate. This road meets Highway 24 a quarter mile up from the nearby highway bridge that crosses the Eagle.

Eagle River: Minturn to Eagle

Physical Data: 29 mi; 1,370-ft drop; 47.3 ft/mi average gradient; 60 ft/mi maximum gradient (from above Minturn to Avon Bridge); 400,000 acre-ft average yearly discharge (near Eagle).
Maps: Minturn, Edwards, Wolcott, and Eagle USGS Quads.
Land Ownership: Alternating BLM and private; mostly private.

The territory between the towns of Minturn and Eagle is the heart of the Eagle River corridor. Nearly all the best boating runs lie in this stretch.

Put-ins are found above and below Minturn. The run through Minturn has several class IV drops. Watch for man-made obstacles such as broken-down footbridges and low-hanging cables. There is a good put-in below Minturn just upriver from the Interstate 70 Bridge at old Dowds Junction on a grassy flat next to Vail Mountain School. If you put in here, be sure to warm up vigorously. Just below the bridge and the Gore Creek confluence lies Minturn Chutes, a quarter-mile gusher with no good eddies and at least five boat-swallowing holes. Three people have drowned in this rapid in the last few years, all at high water. Scout from the left bank and carefully evaluate it before running. If there is any doubt, put in at the bottom. There is no calm pool in which to rest at the base of the chutes. The river keeps on ripping—around a right turn and under a railroad bridge with a hazardous mid-river piling. The lack of a stopping place is one of the chute's significant hazards. For experienced paddlers, however, a ride down the wild horse current of the Minturn Chutes offers a sporting wallop to end all of life's ennui. For novices—"to hell you ride."

The river keeps up a steady 50- to 80-feet-per-mile gradient for the next nine miles in its tiny canyon. Big water and a maze of holes hold the paddler's constant attention. The main hazards are bridge abutments, sweepers, and possible low-hanging cables. Watch out for flying balls as you pass through the new golf course. A good access point lies at the Avon Bridge, a beautiful, wooden, arched span leading to the Beaver Creek Ski Resort. The Eagle doesn't let up below Avon. It keeps up its continuous, rip-roaring pace.

Suddenly the rapids end six miles beyond the Avon Bridge, pouring the boater as if from a spout into the one mile of dead water that leads past the trailer town of Edwards. Then, just as suddenly, the rapids begin anew with two exciting drops. After these the current moderates, offering time to contemplate the wonders of Eagle Valley. Evergreens beside the water here are gradually giving way to cottonwoods and box elders. A hawk, eagle, or possibly even an osprey might be seen soaring above.

Below Edwards the river passes the exposed vertical strata of a major fault. It then begins a gradual descent through the black Mancos shales, the plateau capping the Dakota sandstone, the dinosaur graveyard of the Morrison mudstones, and the pink cliffs of the Entrada and Wingate sandstones. At the Gates of the Eagle, above the town of Eagle, the towering cliffs are composed of the ubiquitous Red Beds.

A railroad bridge below Wolcott signals another drop, Bridge Rapid, rated class III. It is 100 yards long, with big waves at high water. Scout this one from the bridge. Just below Bridge Rapid, at the Alkali Creek confluence, sits Hidden Rapid. Below Hidden Rapid, the Eagle sweeps around a broad left curve with several good access places off old U.S. Highway 24. Passing under the next I-70 Bridge paddlers reach Texas Chute, class II to III.

In the seven remaining miles to the town of Eagle, the river runs beneath the Red Beds through several easy rapids and finally into cottonwood-lined ranch land. Here old Highway 24 occasionally skirts the river, providing several access points.

Eagle River: Eagle to Dotsero

Physical Data: 15 mi; 470-ft drop; 31 ft/mi average gradient; 408,000 acre-ft average yearly discharge (at Gypsum).
Maps: Eagle, Gypsum, and Dotsero USGS Quads.
Land Ownership: Private between Eagle and Gypsum; mostly BLM between Gypsum and Dotsero.

In its final 15 miles, the Eagle's mood quiets a bit, offering open canoeing and novice kayak runs. If you put in above the town of Eagle, beware of two dangerous, man-made drops beyond the U.S. Highway 24 Bridge. It is probably best to put in at the lower end of town. Between Eagle and Gypsum, the river is sandwiched between Interstate 70 and U.S. Highway 24, winding back and forth through cottonwood flats. Most of this section crosses private land.

Beyond Gypsum the current slows further. The Eagle has established a convoluted meander pattern in its approach to the Colorado River. Two miles above the confluence, a basalt lava flow from a volcanic blowout to the north has pushed the river against the south canyon slope. This is Colorado's youngest lava flow, estimated to be less than 4,000 years old. Upriver and downriver from the flow, contorted beds of Pennsylvanian-age gypsum, squeezed into swirls and folds, color the lower slopes. Several well-developed alluvial fans spread from the mouths of gulches on the left.

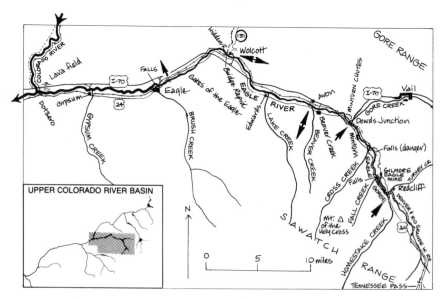

Eagle River.

Roaring Fork River

With easy access, pleasurable rapids, and a scenic course, the Roaring Fork is one of the Southern Rockies' most popular kayaking rivers. Its gradient moderates gradually and steadily from the technical Slaughterhouse Run below Aspen to the gentle lower valley above Glenwood Springs and the Colorado River confluence. Below its chief tributary, Crystal River, the Roaring Fork attracts many rubber rafters.

The valley of the Roaring Fork was fashioned by a number of interesting geological events. One event happened just 20,000 years ago. During the Wisconsin Ice Age, a deep glacier crept down the upper Roaring Fork River Valley pushing ahead of it, bulldozer fashion, a moraine of rock debris. Upon reaching a point immediately east of present downtown Aspen, climatic changes set in, and the glacier began to retreat. The moraine it left behind dammed the Roaring Fork and formed a lake. As the glacier gradually shrank back into the highest cirque valleys, rock flour—a very fine powder formed when rocks imbedded in a glacier abrade underlying rocks—and silt were sent down the river to be deposited in the lake.

Today the lake is filled. A grassy meadow remains on the valley floor. The Roaring Fork, true to its name, comes roaring out of the high Sawatch Range. When it reaches the meadow five miles upriver from Aspen, it suddenly decelerates, meandering slowly to the outskirts of town. Today this glacially created stillwater section provides a place for beginners and novice kayakers to get the feel of moving water before putting themselves in the jeopardy of much swifter water downstream.

Though the Roaring Fork flows free, a transmountain diversion through the Twin Lakes Tunnel has reduced its volume 30 per cent at Aspen. This diversion, with its network of canals and catch dams, becomes especially evident when the snowpack begins to wane. The river drops too low for practical paddling earlier than it formerly did.

Roaring Fork: Slaughterhouse Bridge to Upper Woody Creek Bridge

Physical Data: 5 mi; 360-ft drop; 72 ft/mi average gradient; 175,000 acre-ft average yearly discharge (below Maroon Creek confluence).
Maps: Aspen, Highland Peak, and Woody Creek USGS Quads.
Land Ownership: Mostly private.

The Slaughterhouse run is a wild ride—for advanced and expert kayakers only. The river, filled with big boulders and tumbling down a steep gradient, contains many traps for the unwary. Rafts cannot maintain any semblance of control in the switchback currents. The higher the water, the more treacherous Slaughterhouse becomes. For those who have mastered complex currents, this is a run never to be forgotten.

A put-in is available next to the parking lot across the Slaughterhouse Bridge west of Aspen. If this is your first run, scout the river from the abandoned railroad grade on the north bank. The first rapids, immediately below the parking lot, are extremely technical. John Denver Falls (so named because one of the singer's album covers has a photograph of him standing next to the falls), half a mile downstream, is sometimes run at lower levels on the left side. Because of a strong backwash, however, the falls are dangerous at any time and have claimed several lives. Below the falls the Roaring Fork meets Maroon Creek. This big creek from the Maroon Bells Mountains enhances the flow. The next mile is class III to IV through a wide boulder field and under an abandoned bridge—the start of the annual Aspen Slalom Race—to some flat water next to the sewage plant, a short reprieve. Beyond the sewage plant the steep, complex boulder fields continue. Smoothly rounded, automobile-sized boulders choke the channel. At high water, all the paddler sees ahead is leaping whiteness. Each bend brings new puzzles into view. The run ends—too soon—at the upper Woody Creek Bridge.

Slaughterhouse renews every paddler's appreciation of how the delicate art of kayaking can cleanse the mind of life's mundane problems and fill the spirit with the exhilaration of nature's most wonderful force.

Roaring Fork: Upper Woody Creek Bridge to Basalt

Physical Data: 12 mi; 730-ft drop; 60 ft/mi average gradient; 210,000 acre-ft average yearly discharge (below Woody Creek confluence).
Maps: Woody Creek and Basalt USGS Quads.
Land Ownership: Mostly private.

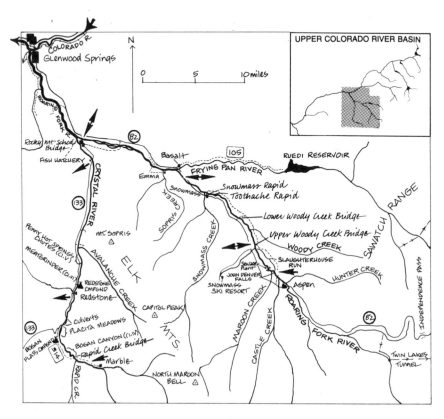

Roaring Fork, Fryingpan, and Crystal rivers.

Below Slaughterhouse the Roaring Fork eases up. Many paddlers feel a personal liaison with the swirling currents and pleasant, rural backcountry along this run. The water is swift and brawling, with many class II and III rapids. With an average gradient of 60 feet per mile, the run from Upper Woody Creek Bridge to Basalt is no place for beginners or novice boaters, especially at high water. One should watch out for the usual hazards—snags, sweepers, and bridge abutments.

The Upper Woody Creek Bridge put-in is reached down the road off State Highway 82 half a mile north of the Snowmass Resort exit. The next access is found at the Lower Woody Creek Bridge, 8.5 miles downriver. A parking area for boaters and fishermen next to the Lower Woody Creek Bridge has been provided by friendly landowners.

Beyond the Lower Woody Creek Bridge the Roaring Fork maintains its fast pace. A steep but straightforward drop lies one mile downriver under a low-hanging footbridge. The next big rapids come in the last mile above the Snowmass Bridge. This bridge crosses the Roaring Fork next to the tiny old town of Snowmass. Toothache is the first of these rapids. Here the river narrows, straightens, and lunges down a steep grade 200 yards long, with Highway 82 skirting the left bank. The rapid's name was conceived after an unfortunate kayaker lost a tooth in the midst of the fracas.

Around the corner from Toothache sits Snowmass Rapid, a difficult one at low water. Stay left around a sharp left turn through some big holes. If you swim, the Snowmass Bridge take-out is just below. A mile and one-half below the Snowmass Bridge, the Roaring Fork passes under Highway 82. At higher water levels, a tricky rapid develops on the approach to and under this bridge. From here to Basalt, the river darts through a series of easy drops. A good take-out is found a few hundred yards above the Fryingpan River confluence next to a 7-11 store.

Roaring Fork: Basalt to Carbondale

Physical Data: 12 mi; 520-ft drop; 43 ft/mi average gradient; 420,000 acre-ft average yearly discharge (below Basalt).
Maps: Basalt, Leon, and Carbondale USGS Quads.
Land Ownership: Mostly private.

Below Basalt, the Roaring Fork's declivity drops off sharply. Though not as popular, this stretch is better suited to those who are hesitant to try the upper runs. The river skirts State Highway 82 for two miles, then wanders away from the highway. It passes under two bridges, each a possible access point. The biggest rapid in the stretch, class II, lies below the second bridge. A number of snags and tricky drops at headgates are scattered along this run, especially in the last three miles. Here gravel islands, some 200 yards long, divide the river and produce sloughs. A good take-out is found at the abandoned Carbondale Bridge next to the State Highway 133 bridge north of town.

Roaring Fork: Carbondale to Glenwood Springs

Physical Data: 13.5 mi; 360-ft drop; 27 ft/mi average gradient; 811,000 acre-ft average yearly discharge (at Glenwood Springs).
Maps: Carbondale, Cattle Creek, and Glenwood Springs USGS Quads.
Land Ownership: Private.

Crystal River near Roaring Fork confluence. Mt. Sopris in background. (Colorado Historical Society photo.)

The Roaring Fork is substantially enhanced by its biggest tributary, the Crystal River. The gradient drops to a more gradual 27 feet per mile. This is a run for novice and intermediate kayakers, rubber rafts, and experienced open canoeists. Rapids are class I and II. No stops should be planned, since the adjoining land is private.

A staircase of floodplains, each step a green pasture, marches up the valley sides from the river. The iron bridge six miles downriver from Carbondale provides access. It is visible below State Highway 82. Three miles beyond this bridge the river begins sweeping around a broad left curve. Here sits the Roaring Fork's final fling, Cemetery Rapid, a quarter-mile-long roller coaster with the biggest waves on this run. Cemetery is usually rated class II. Below it, one passes Fourmile Creek Road Bridge and Rosebud Cemetery on the right bank. The next two miles run through the backstreets of Glenwood Springs to Kiwanas Park, half a mile shy of the Colorado River. This excellent take-out is reached by crossing the Fourmile Road Bridge or the Roaring Fork Bridge at the north end of town.

Fryingpan River

Legend has it two mountain men were attacked by Utes while trapping beaver on this river. One was seriously wounded. His partner left him in a cave by the river and went for help, placing a frying pan in the fork of a nearby tree to mark the cave. When he returned with soldiers, the frying pan helped him locate his friend, who unfortunately was dead. The incident gave this little river its name.

Today the water manipulators have taken the Fryingpan into their relentless grasp. A complicated network of tunnels, catch dams, and canals at the headwaters of the Fryingpan lap up its tributaries. The water is funneled into the Boustead and Carlton tunnels beneath the Continental Divide to be delivered to the Arkansas River as part of the Fryingpan-Arkansas Project. What is left of the Fryingpan is collected by the Reudi Reservoir and released downstream to meet Roaring Fork at Basalt.

The 13 miles between Reudi and Basalt still harbor one of the most scenic little valleys in Colorado. It might be called Red Valley, for its entire length is cut into the Red Beds. When the reservoir releases more than 250 c.f.s., the Fryingpan becomes marginally navigable in kayaks. Most of the run can be scouted from County Road 105. The declivity varies from flat water to steep, technical rapids.

Crystal River

Plunging from the Elk Mountains, this beautiful river flows westward, then due north past that monarch of mountains, Mt. Sopris, to meet the Roaring Fork at Carbondale. Viewed on a map, the Crystal has the shape of a large fishhook. Its valley holds a rich mining history. Three boom-and-bust towns nestle in its lap.

Near the uppermost put-in on the Crystal, a "Mountain of Marble" was discovered. A town, whose name derived from that architecturally valuable rock, grew up below the mountain on the banks of the river. The town of Marble furnished building stone for the Lincoln Memorial, the Tomb of the Unknown Soldier, and many other public and private buildings throughout the United States. It is said to be the purest white marble in the country. In 1941 the city nearly died. A disastrous flood swept down from Snowmass Mountain, wiping out most of the buildings. In addition, the popularity of marble as a building stone declined. The major companies closed their mines. Today, Marble, set among spectacular peaks, remains a popular tourist town.

Eight miles below Marble, where the fishhook straightens, is the ghost town Placita. The willow flats here provide the only break in the constricted valley of the upper Crystal. It was a perfect place for a railroad hub. At the turn of the century, when the Crystal River Valley was booming, two railroads ran on either side of the river. One stopped at Marble. The other, the Elk Mountain Railroad, continued over the mountains to Gunnison. Only a few cabins remain at Placita, but its willow flats provide relief for rapid-weary paddlers.

Redstone, the resort city of mining tycoon J.G. Osgood, sits beside the Crystal four miles below Placita. Osgood entertained the likes of J.P. Morgan, John D. Rockefeller, and Jay Gould in his 42-room Tudor castle built beside the river. Redstone became known as the "Ruby of the Rockies."

Today the aesthetic grandeur of the area makes it a popular haven for artists. The works of such famous painters as Frank Mechau and Ben Turner came out of the Crystal River Valley.

Crystal River: Marble to Roaring Fork Confluence

Physical Data: 31 mi; 1,870-ft drop; 60 ft/mi average gradient; 200 ft/mi maximum gradient (through Meatgrinder Rapid below Redstone Campground);

205,000 acre-ft average yearly discharge (above Avalanche Creek).

Maps: Marble, Chair Mountain, Placita, Redstone, Mount Sopris, and Carbondale USGS Quads.

Land Ownership: Alternating private and National Forest to below Avalanche Creek, then mostly private to the Roaring Fork.

One of the few unfettered rivers in the upper Colorado Basin, the Crystal pulses with natural seasonal rhythms. Highest water levels usually come around the end of June.

The river boasts several classic kayak runs ranging from expert to intermediate in difficulty. The Crystal should not be undertaken lightly. In the heart of the boating corridor lies the Meatgrinder, a class VI cascade, and several other rapids that straddle the thin line of boatability. Most of the Crystal can be scouted from the roads parallel to the river, although several big rapids lurk in hidden canyons.

During high water periods, the Crystal is big enough for kayaks as far upriver as Marble. To avoid dangerous rapids, it is best to put in about two miles below the town where County Road 314 gets close to the water. Just below the Rapid Creek Bridge, the river enters Bogan Canyon, which is hidden from the road by a thick forest. In Bogan Canyon the Crystal tumbles proudly through a mile of continuous class IV whitewater. It dashes around blind corners and doesn't let up until its sudden emergence from the canyon.

Bogan Flats Campground, half a mile beyond the canyon, provides good river access. Beyond the campground the Crystal keeps up its fast pace to

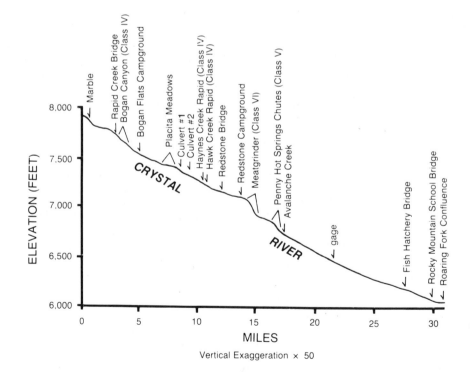

Gradient profile of Crystal River from Marble to Roaring Fork confluence.

Pair of Canada geese with newly hatched gosslings. (Don Grall photo)

Placita Meadows. After a short reprieve in the willow flats, it once again begins its rapid descent. The first of two culverts which carry the river under State Highway 133, one mile apart from each other, lies half a mile below Placita Meadows. These culverts should be portaged for safety. Between the second culvert and the Redstone Bridge are three boulder-choked, class IV rapids. Thereafter the gradient eases to the Redstone Campground Bridge. This last bridge above the Meatgrinder is a mandatory take-out. There are reports of daring kayakers running the Meatgrinder, but a cursory inspection of the cascade will convince most boaters to put discretion before valor.

One mile past the Meatgrinder, Highway 133 skirts the Crystal and reveals another harrowing run, Penny Hot Springs Chutes. The half-mile chutes rate a solid class V at high water. Below the chutes the Crystal meets Avalanche Creek. The gradient eases to 60 feet per mile, with clear sailing the rest of the way downriver. Six miles past Avalanche Creek, the Crystal emerges from her narrow canyon. The gradient moderates further, providing good boating down to the Roaring Fork for less advanced paddlers.

Access is available at the Fish Hatchery Bridge and at the bridge at Rocky Mountain School west of Carbondale. The school sponsors the popular Crystal River kayak races each May. It is also the headquarters of Roger Paris's famous kayak school.

Lower Colorado River Basin

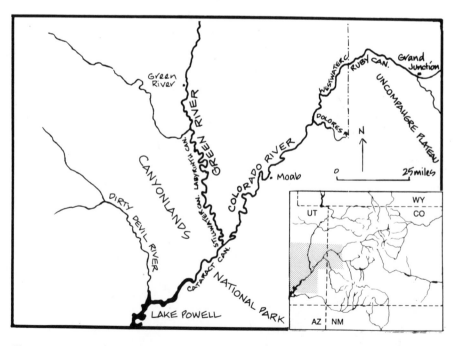

Life sure is easy on a raft, ain't it Huck?
—Tom Sawyer

Metamorphosis of a River

The Colorado's mood changes as it emerges from the mountains, picks up the Gunnison—its largest tributary but for the Green, and becomes the biggest river in the Southwest. The treble music of mountain cataracts gives way to the low rumble of desert rapids. The river's movement becomes more deliberate, less fluttery. Whirlpools appear on the surface, then disappear. Silt and sand in the water beat a steady drum roll on the raft's underside. Kayakers keep their mouths shut during eskimo rolls to avoid the prospect of false teeth. Here the Colorado will lull boaters to sleep, then toss them through a roller coaster of standing waves only to put them to sleep again.

In this book, the lower Colorado is defined as that portion of the river between Grand Junction, Colorado, and Lake Powell in southern Utah.

Close inspection reveals a river that has chosen not the easiest but rather the most tortuous path to the sea. Many unsolved puzzles surround its formation and development in the western deserts. It gives up its secrets grudgingly. All geologists are certain of is that the body of the Colorado contains the great digestive tract of the Southern Rocky Mountains as it courses from granite peaks to beds of sediment on the Pacific Ocean floor.

In contrast to the Colorado's bustling upper valleys, there is little commerce along the banks of the Lower Basin. The river has been deserted by man. The accompaniment of trucks and trains are gone. Only the canyon cliffs, binding the river tightly, hear its song.

Prior to the dam-building era, the river roared with wild fury during the spring melt. It still roars, but more softly. The cement plugs in its narrowest canyons break the ancient rhythms. But it is stronger than man-made obstructions and will ultimately blow them away as the wind blows autumn leaves.

Early Explorers

Fathers Dominguez and Escalante in 1776 were the first Europeans to explore the tributaries of the river their predecessors had named the Rio Colorado—Red River. After traveling north from New Mexico they forded the Green, the Colorado's final and grandest tributary, near the site of Vernal,

Utah, calling it the Rio Buenaventura. Soon after, the Fathers abandoned their plan to reach the California missions and turned back toward Mexico, crossing the great Red River of the West a last time at the "Crossing of the Fathers." This historic site is now beneath the waters of Lake Powell Reservoir. Escalante spoke of a wild and turbulent river on which man could never sail.

Chiseled on rocks in two canyons of the Green—Desolation and Labyrinth —and also in Cataract Canyon of the Colorado is the same inscription: "D. Julien 1836." Sometimes the month is given. The figure of a boat is carved next to the name at several sites. Little is known of Mr. Julien, but he appears to have proven Escalante wrong. The Colorado *would* be sailed. Julien, the mysterious trapper, seems to have been its first navigator.

The first man to set out deliberately to explore the Colorado and to record his findings was John Wesley Powell in 1869. After Powell blazed the trail, many men followed: Brown and Stanton, George Flavell, Nathaniel Galloway, Ellsworth and Emery Kolb. Each of these expeditions began on the Green River at either Green River, Wyoming, or Green River, Utah.

While many explorers ventured down the Colorado by way of the Green, few attempted to run any significant sections of the main trunk. The first to explore the Colorado below Grand Junction was Frank C. Kendrick, a 36-year-old mining engineer from Denver. He was sent down the river by Frank Brown, promoter of the Denver, Colorado Canyon and Pacific Railway. Brown fancied that his tracks could follow the river from Colorado to California. With a touch of bravado, the two men hammered in the first spike of the projected railroad line on March 26, 1889, at Grand Junction. Brown then went East to prepare the main expedition while Kendrick organized a survey team to float the river below Grand Junction. Kendrick planned to proceed to the confluence of the Green, then up the Green to the crossing of the Rio Grande Railway at Blake (present day Green River, Utah), a distance of 277 miles. There he hoped to meet the main expedition returning from the East.

Kendrick purchased from a ferryman a second-hand, open dory made of pine with oak ribs, named the Brown Betty. His assistant engineer and three local men from Grand Junction made up his crew.

The five explorers set off from Grand Junction the first of April. The little skiff did well through Horsethief and Ruby canyons. Upon reaching Westwater Canyon, Kendrick made camp in a cottonwood grove and climbed to the rim for a look at the rapids. After reconnoitering the black-walled gorge, Kendrick was inspired to call the place Hades Canyon. His diary reports: "River narrow and very dangerous." Showing the kind of prudence not exhibited by his boss, Brown (who later drowned on the Colorado), Kendrick eschewed the vicious rapids of Westwater Canyon and began planning a 12-mile portage. After passing the mouth of the Dolores, the party floated into Richardson Amphitheater. "There is the finest scenery here that we have yet seen. Castles and towers of every imaginable kind," Kendrick exclaimed.

The party camped for two days at Moab, then followed the Colorado's winding path to the mouth of the Green. Kendrick's mood varied widely during the voyage. One day he observed: "We have had the grandest scenery yet." The following day he called the place a "barren and godforsaken looking country...." Passing through The Loop, he referred to the canyon as "a grand and gloomy place."

The voyagers enjoyed ideal weather—for the most part. Near the mouth of the Green, however, Kendrick expressed the frustration many later river runners have known in the lower canyons of the Colorado and the Green. "Have not struck a rapid below Moab but today the wind was so strong that it was as bad as the rapids. The water would wash over the sides of the boat and we had all five of us in."

At the mouth of the Green they marked a large sandstone boulder: "Sta. 8489 + 50 DCC & PRR May 4th, 1889." This inscription was noted by Emery Kolb in 1911, but no one has reported seeing it since.

During the long pull up the Green, Kendrick noted that the river was "like an immense snake taking a sun bath and has not room enough to stretch out straight. It must be three times as long as in a direct line."

With their food gone, the men finally reached some signs of life at the mouth of the San Rafael River. A small cabin on the bank belonged to the Wheeler Ranch. Old man Wheeler told Kendrick that, upon spotting his tattered and half-starved band of explorers, he almost ran from them. Instead, he hosted a feast. On May 14 they reached their destination at Blake.

The first boat trip down the Colorado below Grand Junction (with the exception of Westwater Canyon) had been successfully completed.

The following day the men were paid. They received between $45.00 and $61.60 for the job.

Having arrived from the East with five new boats, Frank Brown started back down the Green on May 25 with 15 men. He hoped to survey the river to the Gulf of California, but one disaster after another struck the party. The Brown Betty was destroyed in Cataract Canyon. Brown was drowned in Soap Creek Rapid in Marble Canyon. Several days and two more fatalities later, the expedition ended. Brown's chief engineer, Robert Brewster Stanton, organized a successful survey of the Green and Colorado the following year, but the plan for the Denver, Colorado Canyon and Pacific Railroad had fizzled.

Gates of Lodore Canyon on the Green River. (see The Birth of Rivers, Upper Green River Basin)

Kendrick's reports of Westwater Canyon's impassability kept river runners from attempting the Colorado below Grand Junction for years. Finally, in September, 1916, Ellsworth Kolb and Bert Loper tried Westwater in a cedar canoe. Both men were Colorado River veterans, having successfully run Cataract and Grand Canyon. Westwater, they reasoned, couldn't be worse. It was. Only the skills that made them possibly the two best boatmen in the West brought them through successfully. They traded off at the oars, carefully scouted Skull and the other hazardous rapids, and emerged with their boat intact.

Possibly the most remarkable Colorado River voyage of all was that of Harold Leich in 1933. Leich started high in the mountains at Grand Lake in a wooden kayak. He followed the paddle strokes of Samuel Adams who, 63 years before, had struggled through notorious Gore Canyon. Leich, however, successfully lowered his boat through the falls of Gore with ropes and went on past the point where Adams had called it quits. Portaging the worst drops, he took his kayak through Glenwood Canyon past Glenwood Springs to Grand Junction. At this point he abandoned the kayak, built a punt, and successfully traversed Westwater Canyon. In Cataract Canyon he lost his boat. With the indomitable spirit that had gotten him through the Colorado's most treacherous falls and rapids, Leich walked and swam the 50 remaining miles to Hite, Utah.

The River Takes a New Course

Two million years ago, the Colorado's route was directly westward from the Grand Junction area through Unaweep Canyon. The rapidly rising Uncompahgre Plateau, however, forced the river away from its ancient canyon. It took a new course around the north snout of the Uncompahgre Plateau, carving Horsethief, Ruby, and Westwater canyons (see the "Birth of Rivers" chapter). Below Westwater the Colorado joins the Dolores, which skirts the west flank of the Uncompahgre. The river then crosses several down-faulted anticlines at the north end of the Paradox Basin—Cache Valley, Castle Valley, and finally Spanish Valley, site of the town of Moab.

Brick red walls of the Wingate Sandstone and its neighbors border the Colorado along most of this 88-mile reach. In only two places has the black Precambrian basement rock that supports the Uncompahgre Plateau risen from its hidden depths to river level. In Ruby Canyon (at Black Rocks), it breaks the laminar flow into whirlpools and waves, a warning of things to come.

Nine miles below Black Rocks, the river again meets the basement complex in Westwater Canyon. This time an upthrust plug of hard, black slate and gneiss beneath the Wingate forced the river to forge this constricted gorge. Westwater is famous for its fierce rapids and solemn beauty. The contrast between the gloomy subterranean hole of basement rock and the vital, crimson sandstone above makes the gorge look like the abyss of hell. It is no wonder early explorers called it Hades Canyon. Because of its geological resemblance to Granite Gorge in the Grand Canyon, Westwater is sometimes referred to as Granite Canyon.

Beyond Westwater the basement rock sinks below river level as colorful sedimentary beds again clothe the Colorado's canyons down to Moab.

Colorado River—Horsethief, Ruby, and Westwater Canyons Section

The Colorado below Grand Junction steals through a series of canyons, each with unique beauty and difficulty. In Ruby and Horsethief canyons the river's mood is generally calm, but downstream it growls though the wildwater of Westwater Canyon. Then it glides smoothly past the Dolores confluence into Richardson Amphitheater. Beyond Fisher Towers the current quickens again through a series of modest rapids to Moab.

The canyons above Westwater make an ideal two-day open canoe run. Westwater itself is strictly an advanced kayak and rubber raft stretch. The moderate rapids above Moab are ideal for all types of river boats.

The beauty of this stretch of the Colorado lies in its remoteness. Above Cisco Pumphouse the canyons remain in a wild state. Only a short riverside visit by the Rio Grande Railroad tracks and an occasional backcountry ranch break the solitude. Below Cisco Pumphouse, the Dewey Road borders the river within narrow canyons but departs in the wider valleys.

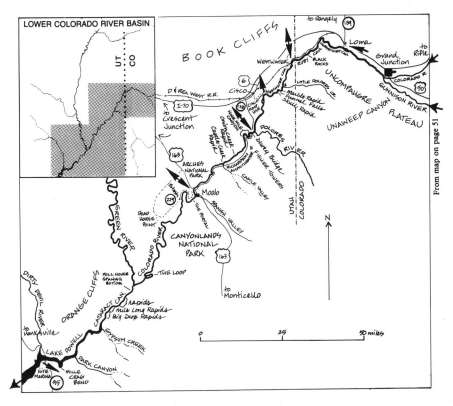

Colorado River from Grand Junction to Lake Powell.

Benches and bottoms are clothed with cottonwood groves, favorite haunts of the great blue heron. Vultures and hawks glide across the unsettled countryside. Bank swallows gather in their bulbous mud nests on the cliff faces. In the spring, mallards, mergansers, Canada geese, and green-winged teal stop here on their migratory flights.

Colorado River: Loma to Moab

Physical Data: 88 mi; 480-ft drop; 5.5 ft/mi average gradient; 20 ft/mi maximum gradient (for four miles through Westwater Canyon); 4,156,000 acre-ft average yearly discharge (near Colo.-Utah state line.)
Maps: Mack, Ruby Canyon, Westwater SE, Westwater SW, Coates Creek, Cisco, Castle Valley, and Moab USGS Quads.
Land Ownership: Alternating private and public land.
Information: Horsethief and Ruby Canyons—BLM Grand Junction, CO; Westwater Canyon to Moab—BLM, Moab, Utah.

A convenient put-in lies a stone's throw south of the Loma-Rangely Exit on Interstate 70 west of Grand Junction. Placid water drifts for nine miles past scenic sandstone cliffs and quiet bottomlands in Horsethief Canyon.

Ruby Canyon begins where the Rio Grande tracks meet the riverbank from the north. Four miles into Ruby Canyon, at Black Rocks, the sandstone walls are broken by a dome of slate basement rock. Good campsites and swirling currents characterize this anomalous site. For four miles below Black Rocks, sluggish current continues past the Colorado-Utah border. At the border, Anasazi footholds can be seen in the sandstone cliff north of the river.

The ranger station at Westwater Ranch is on the right bank eight miles past Black Rocks. A permit from the BLM in Moab is required for passage through Westwater Canyon. Contact the agency for the latest rules and regulations. The ranger station is reached by taking the dirt road south from the Westwater Exit on I-70.

Rapids begin just below Westwater's entrance, where the black slate and gneiss appear at river level. Four miles into the canyon, the Little Dolores enters from the left. This is a popular campsite. A quarter mile past Little Dolores Rapid, around a left-hand bend, sits a sandy beach, Hades, the last campsite before the big rapids.

One mile beyond Hades, the Colorado turns south into Marble Canyon Rapid. The next two miles sport continuous, thundering whitewater. A big drop, Funnel Falls, pours through a chute between two huge boulders half a mile below Marble. Ahead the red Wingate Sandstone is seen above the black inner-canyon slate. One-half mile past Funnel Falls lies Skull, Westwater's worst—or best, depending on your point of view—rapid. The river plunges along a wall on the right. Then, just past the big hole at the bottom, it slams into the cliff face, with half the river's volume gushing into a round whirlpool on the right and the other half proceeding downriver. At high water levels, boats caught in the whirlpool have been unable to escape. Skull should be run left of center at high water. At lower levels, scout the rapid from the rockpile at the base of the left wall.

Three more rapids greet boaters below Skull. Then the whitewater suddenly ends. In the eight miles of flat water to the Cisco Pumphouse take-out, the inner canyon walls gradually drop to river level, giving way to sandstone bluffs again. The take-out is reached by driving four miles south on the dirt road from the nearly abandoned town of Cisco.

Westwater exhibits profound differences at high and low water. At low water, the channel is a maze of boulders and steep drops. At high water it becomes a flusher, pouring through a series of tall haystacks between the narrow walls. Rafts less than 16 feet in length often flip in the two miles of heavy rapids during high water. Only experienced river runners should enter the gorge at these times.

The next good access point below Cisco Pumphouse lies across the Dewey Bridge, a precarious one-lane suspension span 15 miles downriver. The bridge is reached by driving south on the Dewey Road (Utah State Highway 128) from old U.S. Highway 6, two miles west of Cisco. Red Wingate walls rise up again through four-mile-long Nine Mile Canyon below the Dewey Bridge. The mouth of Nine Mile Canyon frames one of the most scenic vistas in Utah. The Fisher Towers—spires of eroded Chinle Shale—stand in the Richardson Amphitheater ahead. Beyond the towers, the granitic peaks of the La Sal Mountains crown the awesome panorama.

Below the mouth of Nine Mile Canyon, in the wide Richardson Amphitheater, a series of moderate rapids punctuate the flat water—Onion Creek, Professor Creek, and Ida Gulch. Eight miles of glorious scenery in the Richardson Amphitheater end at Castle Creek. The creek pushes the Colorado to the north, forming a fairly large rapid. Then the river slices into a final Wingate-walled canyon before Moab. Arches National Park borders this canyon on the north. Groves of scrub oak separated by sandy beaches—good access points—flank the river, which clips through easy rapids between flat water stretches. Most parties take out just above the U.S. Highway 163 Bridge near Moab or, alternately, six miles upriver at the Big Bend Beach Recreation Area.

Colorado River—Moab Through Cataract Canyon Section

The run from Moab to Hite involves 69 miles of flat water in the Canyonlands section, 12 miles of rough rapids through Cataract Canyon, and 33 miles across the upper reaches of Lake Powell to the Hite Marina. The long stretch of dead water on the lake, often afflicted with stubborn headwinds, requires an outboard motor, except for the hardiest paddlers. Passage through Cataract Canyon requires a permit from Canyonlands National Park. Regulations vary from year to year. By hiring a Moab outfitter with a jet boat (Tex's or Tag-Along-Tours) to get you back upriver, a picturesque open canoe trip can be made down to Spanish Bottom at the head of Cataract Canyon.

An alternate launching point is found 17 miles downriver from Moab by following the north bank road through Potash.

Between Moab and Cataract the river cuts down through beds of Mesozoic and Paleozoic strata, taking river runners gradually back through geologic time. In Cataract Canyon, the river follows the axis of the Meander Anticline through a heavily faulted part of the Hermosa Formation. The steep gradient in Cataract might be due to the fact that the river is flowing down the west flank of the huge Monument Upwarp, through which the San Juan River carved its lower canyons 60 miles to the south.

Colorado River: Moab to Hite Marina

Physical Data: 113.5 mi; 250-ft drop; 3 ft/mi average gradient; 25 ft/mi maximum gradient (through Cataract Canyon); 5,463,000 acre-ft average yearly discharge (above Moab).

Maps and Guides: Moab, Hatch Point, Canyonlands National Park, and Glen Canyon National Recreation Area USGS Quads; Canyonlands River Guide, Westwater Books, Boulder City, Nevada.

Land Ownership: Private and public first 18 miles below Moab; Canyonlands National Park to Lake Powell; Glen Canyon National Recreation Area to Hite.

Information and Permit: Canyonlands National Park, Moab, Utah.

Two miles below the Moab Bridge is the Portal. This marks the edge of the downthrown Spanish Valley crustal block and the sudden entrance into canyon country. Petroglyphs are found on the south canyon walls for the next three miles. Powerlines cross the river in several places. The road to Potash hugs the north bank. The Texas Gulf Potash Plant lies 14 miles into the canyon. Here, water from the Colorado is injected into the Hermosa Formation 3,500 feet below river level. Brine is then pumped to the surface where the potash can be recovered in large evaporation ponds.

Beyond the plant the river enters wilderness. Bushy tamarisk lines the bank. Isolated box elders provide shade. Poison ivy is occasionally encountered. Canyon wrens flit among the rocks. Access to the river is found only on steep, rough trails. The colorful walls of the Wingate, Chinle, Cutler, and Rico formations embellish the canyon. Petrified logs, brachiopods, clams, and horn corals—fossils that intrigued Frank Kendrick on his first reconnaisance of the river—are found in the Rico Formation and at the top of the Hermosa from 10 miles below Potash to the Green River. A few Anasazi or Fremont structures can be seen on bluffs along the route.

Ten miles above its great confluence with the Green, the Colorado sweeps through two entrenched meanders called The Loop, bending six miles to cover a distance of one mile as the crow flies. At low water a small rapid is found at The Slide, formed by a landslide on the north wall two miles above the confluence. The first rapids of Cataract Canyon lie four miles below the confluence. Spanish Bottom, river-right just above the rapids, can be reached on a rough trail from The Doll House on the rim above. A hike up to The Doll House offers a spectacular maze of eroded towers and steeples in the Cedar Mesa Sandstone.

The Park Service has placed a sign marking Cataract Canyon's dangerous rapids at the lower end of Spanish Bottom.

At low water, Cataract holds 23 distinct rapids ranging from class I to class IV in difficulty. At high water (from 40,000 to 80,000 c.f.s.) many rapids blend together; and the waves, up to 15 feet tall, are the highest on the Colorado. Rafts smaller than 20 feet can easily flip on these enormous waves even if the river's thunderous holes are avoided. Cataract requires a combination of experience and dexterous boat handling for safe passage.

Cliff Jumping at Black Rocks in Ruby Canyon. (Gene Levin photo)

The first four miles contain 10 rapids. These give boaters a taste of the canyon's power. A two-mile break in the heavy rapids ends at Mile Long Rapids. At high water, the next 1.5 miles are a continuous series of huge waves and holes. At low water the nine rapids, closely spaced, range in difficulty from class II to IV. Inscriptions from early Colorado River expeditions with the words "wrecked," "capsized," "lost," can be found on boulders throughout this area. At the end of Mile Long Rapids, the river makes a sharp right turn around a boulder bar with another difficult drop at the end of the bar. One mile past this point, the "Big Drop" sequence begins. The Big Drop is comprised of three rapids: Upper Big Drop, Satan's Seat, and Satan's Gut. In Satan's Seat, a cabin-sized boulder river-right produces at high water one of the biggest holes found anywhere on the Colorado River.

A quarter-mile-long pool separates Satan's Seat from Satan's Gut. At highest water levels there are no pools, only swooping waves between the last two drops. Satan's Gut is the most difficult in the Big Drop sequence. At most levels it can be run right of center by snaking through the big holes.

When full, Lake Powell almost reaches the end of Satan's Gut. Three or four more rapids are encountered when the reservoir drops below capacity level.

Most parties crank up an outboard for the trip across the lake. Some hire a speedboat from Hite to take them out.

Gunnison River Basin

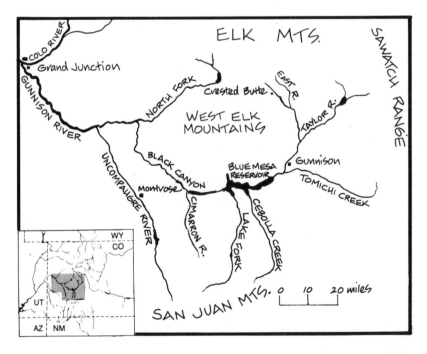

*Through the black canyon's angry foam we hurled to dreamy
bars,
And round in a ring the dog-nosed peaks bayed to the mocking
stars.*
  —Robert Service

Trail of the Gunnison

The Gunnison is the largest river whose entire basin lies within the boundaries of the state of Colorado. It is also the largest instate tributary of the Colorado River. At its junction with the Colorado—"Grand Junction"—it accounts for 40 percent of the Colorado's total volume. Overall, it produces 20 percent of the waters carried by that hub river of the Southwest.

The Gunnison's large tributaries gather among 14,000-foot peaks—the North Fork and East River in the Elk Range to the north; the Taylor and Tomichi in the Sawatch massif to the east; and the Cochetopa, Cebolla, Lake Fork, Cimarron, and Uncompahgre in the high San Juans to the south. These tributary streams are no less inviting than the river itself, providing a wide variety of pleasures to river enthusiasts.

The Gunnison River Basin also has the dubious distinction of housing more large reservoirs than any other river complex in Colorado. Dam builders are currently scrutinizing several of its remaining unbroken canyons.

The staircaselike profile of the river is steep in its upper reaches, after which it levels out only to plunge downward again before its final, gentle approach to the Colorado. (See profile, page 91). It alternately occupies wide valleys and cavernous gorges, the most majestic of which is the famous Black Canyon.

At one time the Gunnison Basin was the heart of Ute Indian territory. The first Europeans were vigorous Spanish explorers. An expedition led by Juan Maria de Rivera in 1765 was the first to reach the Gunnison. Rivera carved the date and his name on a cottonwood at its junction with the Uncompahgre. He was followed by the Dominguez-Escalante expedition in 1776. Father Escalante crossed the Gunnison near the present town of Delta where he found Rivera's inscription. He named the river the San Javier.

In the 1830s came the fur trappers. Such familiar figures as Jim Beckworth, Kit Carson, Jim Baker, and James Pattie trapped beaver up and down the Gunnison and its tributaries. Antoine Roubidoux built a fort on the Uncompahgre near Delta to supply them. These trappers were probably the first to use the river for travel, plying its gentler waters in their bull boats.

Next were the railroad surveyors—Captain John Gunnison in 1853 and John Fremont in 1855. Complete and accurate maps of the region awaited the Hayden Survey of 1875.

The town of Gunnison was founded in 1873, but it amounted to little until the railroad arrived in 1881. The line followed the Gunnison River into the Black Canyon as far as Cimarron, where the tracks left the gorge to reach Montrose, returning to the riverbank between Delta and Grand Junction. The railroad brought miners to the region in the 1880s. Branch lines were built up the tributary rivers to the mines around Crested Butte, Pitkin, Lake City, Ouray, and Paonia.

The first major water project in the basin—forerunner of many trans-basin diversions—was the Gunnison Tunnel from the Black Canyon to the Uncompahgre Valley, completed in 1909. Next to be built were the Taylor Dam and Reservoir, followed by Paonia, Blue Mesa, and Morrow Point Dams in the 1960s. The 1970s brought the Crystal Dam just above Black Canyon National Monument. The latest, Ridgeway Dam on the Uncompahgre, is presently nearing completion. In the planning stages are the Tri County, Cedar Flats, Austin, Smith Fork, Fruitland Mesa, and Dominguez reservoir projects. Coal mining has only begun to make its demands on the river.

Oldest Valley in Colorado

Few river basins illustrate as well as the Gunnison how different geological processes occurring at widely different times can combine to produce a unique river system.

The Gunnison occupies the oldest recognizable valley in the Colorado River Basin above Grand Junction. The river's course follows a broad depression between the surrounding uplifts—the type Powell called a "consequent" drainage. Even its headwater streams—Tomichi Creek, the Upper Taylor above the reservoir, and the East River—meander lazily on marshy floodplains bounded by low hills, with gradients of less than 15 feet per mile. Such signs tell of an ancient valley. In contrast, two steep-walled canyons crack the Gunnison's wide valley, the Canyon of the Taylor and the Black Canyon. Such chasms owe their formation to recent uplifts that raised the floor of the valley and, in these two places, forced the water to commence the erosion process anew. The basement rock at Black Canyon rose over 1,400 feet during the Tertiary Period, resulting in a precipitous gorge which left the ancestral valley high above. The extremely youthful geological characteristics of the Black Canyon—narrow, steep gradient, hanging tributaries—indicate that the area may still be rising.

The Black Canyon's geologic story began 1.75 billion years ago. Magma cooled deep inside the earth's crust, creating the Pitts Meadow granites. About .75 billion years later, the Black Canyon Schist to the west was formed. Subsequently, both were thrust upward within the core of a great mountain range, the Ancestral Rocky Mountains. In late Pennsylvanian time this range washed into the sea, leaving a land of low, rounded hills—the Uncompahgre erosion surface. Still later, great winds blew across a wide, Sahara-like desert. The region was covered with sand dunes, creating the Wingate and Entrada formations atop the roots of the leveled mountain range. After the desert, in late Jurassic time, other terrestrial sediments were laid down—the Wanakah gypsum and the Morrison mudstones. Then the great Cretaceous sea swept over the region. The beach at the sea's leading edge became the Dakota sandstone. As the beach passed, deeper waters accumulated the Mancos shale from eroding highlands to the west.

The Laramide Crustal revolution began 65 million years ago. Tremendous pressures lifted the entire area out of the sea to a height of over 8,000 feet. After the Gunnison River became established on the southwest flank of this upheaval, it eroded its canyon down through the sedimentary strata, past the enormous time gap of the Uncompahgre erosion surface and into the sleeping roots of the Ancestral Rocky Mountains. In this way the Black Canyon and Gunnison Gorge were fixed in the hardest rock to be found anywhere in this part of the Colorado, yet within a few miles of the softest rocks. (See cross sections, pages 95 and 97.)

Other recent events shaping the Gunnison Basin include tremendous Tertiary outpourings of lava and ash from the San Juan and West Elk volcanoes on either side of the river valley. Many of the river's tributaries are incised into these deep volcanic deposits.

Black Canyon of the Gunnison National Monument. (Colorado Historical Society photo.)

Early Conquest of the Black Canyon

Although known from early days of Spanish exploration, the Black Canyon was studiously avoided. Fathers Dominguez and Escalante passed 10 miles east of it in their attempt to reach the California missions in 1776. In 1853 Captain John Gunnison's expedition followed the river, which took his name, from Cochetopa Pass to the Grand River—today's Colorado River—searching for a railroad route through the Southern Rockies. He skirted the Black Canyon as did Fremont's 1855 expedition. In 1873 topographers of the Hayden Survey pronounced it "inaccessible."

The first recorded penetration of the canyon was by Byron H. Brayant's survey in the winter of 1883, commissioned by the Denver and Rio Grande Railroad. His reconnaissance persuaded the railroad to route its tracks south of the Black Canyon over Cerro Summit.

The initial attempt to float the canyon was inspired by an idea for a tunnel from the Gunnison River through the walls of the Black Canyon to supply water for farms in the Uncompahgre River Valley. William W. Torrence led five men from Montrose and Delta on a survey expedition down the river in two wooden boats in the late summer of 1900. After a month in the canyon, they gave up about 15 miles below Cimarron.

Torrence, however, was thirsty for adventure. He returned the following summer with A.L. Fellows, a Bureau of Reclamation engineer. The two made the first successful passage of the Black Canyon—25 miles from Cimarron to Red Rock Canyon—on foot without boats. Describing this feat with bravado if not veracity, they reported at one point jumping into the river and letting it wash them beneath one of the huge boulder piles clogging the canyon bottom. Miraculously emerging on the opposite side of the pile, they leapt onto a flat rock and danced a jig! The Gunnison Tunnel was begun four years later.

Ellsworth Kolb, anxious to make "the most perilous water trip in the West," organized an attempt to float the Black Canyon's twisting corridor in 1916. Kolb was an experienced whitewater adventurer, having traveled the Green and Colorado rivers from Green River, Wyoming, to California with his brother Emery from 1911 to 1913. With a bank president, a stockbroker, and a Grand Canyon guide, he set off from Lake City down the Lake Fork to the Gunnison and on into the Black Canyon. The group carried the best equipment available at the time: a cedar and canvas boat, "air tight swim suits," and an unsinkable trunk containing photographic equipment. The end came about three miles past the East Portal of the Gunnison Tunnel. "After fighting death in the angry whirlpools," reported Kolb, "the trip was abandoned."

Kolb returned in 1917 with the famous river explorer Bert Loper. The two men started at Cimarron and made several trips in and out of the gorge for food and repair supplies. Their boat was eventually wrecked in the tumultuous waters.

In October 1918, the indefatigable Kolb returned to the Black Canyon with renewed determination and a partner named W.A. "Billie" Wright. They abandoned one boat before reaching the East Portal and the second below the Narrows, where Kolb suffered a broken kneecap. He was forced to remain on a ledge by the river for two weeks until his knee had healed sufficiently for him to climb out of the canyon. Undaunted, Kolb built another boat and returned to the canyon four miles below the point of his earlier accident. He and Albert Moore of Montrose completed the last leg to the North Fork in four days.

Torrence Expedition into the Black Canyon in 1900. (Denver Public Library Western History Dept. photo.)

President Hoover established Black Canyon of the Gunnison National Monument in March 1933. During the following summer several trips were made through the monument section, some for survey purposes and some purely for adventure. Robert Davis, topographer for the United States Geological Survey, was sent to make a detailed survey for a topographic map. He and photographer Dexter Walker, Mark Warner, and several others achieved successful foot passage through the monument. Warner wrote a delightful and useful account of the trip, illustrated with Walker's photographs and published by Black Canyon of the Gunnison National Monument.

However, no one had yet taken a boat from Cimarron to the North Fork intact.

On July 9, 1934, Harvey Barsch of Pueblo and Jack Gorsuch of Crawford started on the river at Cimarron. They emerged below the North Fork confluence a remarkably short four days later. Their account disputes the claim of L.E. Orr of Denver, Russell Johnson of Minnesota, and Melvin Griffiths of Montrose that their 1938 trip was the first boat run down the canyon. Is it possible that a boat trip could have been made between the 9th and 13th of July, 1934, well before the usual low water season on the Gunnison? Perhaps. An examination of available water records reveals that 1934 was the Gunnison's worst drought year on record.

One of the most colorful Black Canyon adventures was the first successful solo trip, made in 1949 by Daniel (Ed) Nelson, president of the Montrose Chamber of Commerce. With Jerry Reynolds and Cecil Mash, he put in at Cimarron in five-pound inflatables using ping pong paddles as "oars." Mash and Reynolds pulled out at East Portal. They had had enough!

Nelson went on alone in his mighty craft. "The Narrows weren't bad," he related "I just floated through in the boat, but that stretch from Pulpit Rock to Painted Wall was tough. I mean tough...I had trouble in getting over and around boulders—some 50 feet high. They would have torn my boat to shreds if my luck hadn't held."

He left the canyon at Red Rocks. "There just wasn't enough water in the river for me and the boat. I figured on the boat carrying me from Red Rocks on," he said. "After all, I carried it a couple of hundred miles in that stretch below the Narrows."

Ellsworth Kolb Expedition into the Black Canyon in 1916. (Colorado Historical Society photo.)

Ed Nelson arrived back at Montrose to an unexpected hero's welcome and celebrity status. The city heralded their chamber president's feat and awarded him the nickname "Solo." "I was just on vacation," he quipped.

An ardent champion of the Gunnison, Ed has over 250 raft trips down the now-flooded upper portions of the river to his credit today. He has also led many trips through the Gunnison Gorge.

The most notable recent effort to master the Black Canyon was the first successful kayak descent in August 1975. The attempt was organized by Ron Mason—one of Colorado's well-known native boaters, with over 15 years of experience—against the advice of the National Park Service. "You will be taken by the scruff of your neck and the seat of your pants if you try it," warned park authorities. Mason's team of experts included Bill Clark, one of the country's most experienced kayakers, national wildwater champion Tom Ruwitch, and Filip Sokol. They decided to give it a go.

Starting at East Portal, they portaged four times before reaching the Narrows. The second day was their most difficult, "because we were forced to carry our boats a mile to the bottom of S.O.B. Gully.... This section is almost completely unnavigable because of rock 'filters' and high falls." On the third day Mason described the Gunnison Gorge as "a spectacular narrow canyon of its own with narrow passages and walls which rise vertically from the water. This canyon is unspoiled country which shows even fewer traces of man than the Main Canyon.... It should be emphasized that the Black Canyon is not an easy trip—in fact, it is one of the most difficult I have done. However, it is an entirely feasible trip for the expert paddler who is in good physical condition and prepared for some hard work. The reward, in my opinion, is the ultimate canyon experience."

Taylor River

Taylor River: Lottis Creek to Almont

Physical Data: 16.5 mi; 1,020-ft drop; 62 ft/mi average gradient; 120 ft/mi maximum gradient (Lottis Creek to Lodgepole Campground); 249,000 acre-ft average yearly discharge (at Almont).

Maps: Matchless Mountain, Crystal Creek, and Almont 7.5 minute USGS Quads.

Land Ownership: Mostly Gunnison National Forest. Several private ranches, including the first 3 miles below the Taylor Park Reservoir, miles 6-8, and miles 13-15.

The Taylor is a delectable, high-mountain kayaking stream. It tumbles clear and cold through a rugged granitic canyon paralleled by State Highway 306 and bordered by numerous developed campgrounds and access points.

Taylor Park Dam controls the river's flow, releasing a steady 100 to 400 c.f.s. at the Almont gage (see hydrograph, page 89). This dam both moderates high spring flows and enhances the volume in late summer and fall. As a consequence, kayakers can enjoy the Taylor at times when other rivers are too high or too low for enjoyable boating.

Clear water, a boulder-studded bed, and easy access make the Taylor a popular trout fishery. Bushy alders line the streambank. Behind them, tall stands of timber cling to the canyon walls.

The Taylor's difficulty varies from class II to class V. Its most popular runs lie between Taylor Park Dam and the East River confluence at Almont and include the following:

• *Staircase*—Lottis Creek to Lodgepole Campground (2.5 mi). Rated class IV or harder with an average gradient of over 120 ft/mi. The water is often too shallow here.

• *The Slot*—Lodgepole Campground to below Whitewater Resort (3.5 mi) is the most popular expert run on the Taylor. The first 1.5 miles pass through a private ranch. Small weirs and barbed wire cross the stream in several places. Below the ranch lie several very technical rapids, including The Slot at mile 8.5.

• *Rosy Lane*—Below Whitewater Resort to One Mile Campground (2.5 mi). Gradient decreases offering less demanding class III boating.

• *Harmel's*—One Mile Campground to the Highway 742 bridge (3.5 mi). Increased volume due to Spring Creek and Beaver Creek tributaries, easier class II to III water.

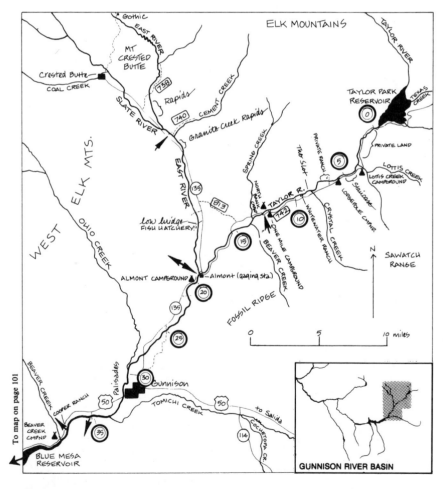

Taylor, East River, and Upper Gunnison River.

• *Almont*—Highway 742 Bridge to Almont (5 mi). This is the gentlest run on the Taylor, class II. There are several access points along the way.

Enjoyed mostly by local kayakers from Gunnison and Crested Butte, the tiny, tumbling Taylor is a recommended side trip on any Colorado paddling expedition. Joining the Taylor at Almont is its physiographic antithesis, the East River.

East River

Both the East River and the Taylor drain the south flank of the Elk Range. Each carries approximately the same volume of water, and each has convenient road access. The confluence of the two streams marks the beginning of the Gunnison River.

Despite its close proximity to the Taylor, the East River differs markedly in appearance and character. Unlike the clear Taylor, which maintains a relatively steady flow from its upstream reservoir, the East River, free of impoundments, roils muddy and full during the spring thaw. Then, in late summer, its volume drops too low for boating.

The structural characteristics and geological histories of the two rivers also present striking contrasts. While the Taylor has cut a narrow, rugged canyon through crystalline granitic rocks, the East River glides across a wide, flat valley of alluvium and glacial drift, dotted with farms and ranches. The East River could easily have cut a deeper canyon into the soft Cretaceous strata in which its valley is set. It was prevented from doing so because its base level (lowest level to which it can erode) is the elevation of the Taylor at their confluence. The Taylor, in contrast to the East River, was forced to erode much more resistant granite, which restrained its downcutting action. Thus, the East River's energy was directed sideward rather than downward, widening its valley and depositing a broad floodplain.

Below the town of Gothic, the East River suddenly plunges through a short, impassable gorge. It abruptly calms two miles downstream from Gothic, meandering tranquilly beneath the shadow of Mt. Crested Butte. Its gentle valley of oxbow lakes, natural levees, and backswamps—typical of such lowland valleys as that of the lower Mississippi—seem incongruous at 9,000 feet. It may be one of the highest rivers in the world displaying these geologic features.

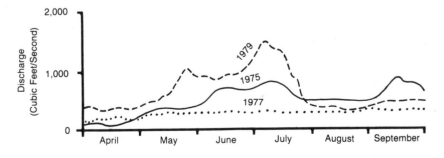

Hydrograph of Taylor River at Almont.

The gradient suddenly steepens to 90 feet per mile two miles above its junction with the more rapidly downcutting Slate River. Even at high water the Slate is barely large enough to sustain a kayak, although it might be possible to run it from the State Highway 135 Bridge.

East River: County Road 740 Bridge to Almont

Physical Data: 11 mi; 560-ft drop; 51 ft/mi average gradient; 251,000 acre-ft average yearly discharge (at Almont).

Maps: Crested Butte, Cement Mt., and Almont 7.5 minute USGS Quads; Gunnison National Forest Map.

Land Ownership: Upper East River below Gothic—alternating private ranches and Gunnison National Forest land; East River below Slate confluence to Almont—mostly private land, state land around fish hatchery.

The most popular section of the East River is the 11-mile stretch from its confluence with the Slate River to the Taylor River. Put-ins are found at the County Road 740 Cement Creek Bridge or the State Highway 135 Bridge.

The East River's channel is sandy, with an even 50 feet per mile gradient and few eddies. The lack of boulders and eddies makes it less desirable than the Taylor for kayaking. At high water it is a "flusher," racing steadily along. Cottonwood sweepers, fences and small weirs present significant hazards at this level due to the speed of the current and the lack of stopping places. Open canoes are suited to the East River at moderate water levels.

Gunnison River—
Upper Gunnison Section

Formed by the union of the Taylor and East rivers at the town of Almont, the Gunnison wanders large and leisurely through rural pasturelands. Its wide, level valley was filled with glacial sediments when the ancient, silt-laden river dropped its load in slacker water behind the natural "dam" of crystalline granites and metamorphic gneiss at the Black Canyon 20 miles downstream.

The river above and below the town of Gunnison has attracted fluvial enthusiasts for many years. The first river runners were John McCloskey, Charles McClaren, and C.W. Chinery from Telluride. On July 14, 1901, they drifted 12 miles in their crude craft from Gunnison to Iola. By 1940 the "Gunnison Navy" was officially established. This slightly off-beat organization consisted of about 30 "Gunnison Kayaks," wooden boats which combined the best features of an Eskimo kayak and a one-man, flat-bottom duck-hunting skiff. The "Navy" was a hodgepodge collection of fishermen and river rats. Annual naval maneuvers were held on the second Sunday in September, when the flotilla would show its colors. Rank was dependent upon the degree of dunking—Full Admiral: dunked all over; Vice Admiral: only the nose and three eyelashes dry; Rear Admiral: a wet rear end. The leader of the Navy was the Grand High Admiral. The group claims its maneuvers were witnessed by such an illustrious Honorary Admiral as Herbert Hoover.

Today all types of rafts, kayaks, and open canoes ply the relatively gentle waters above Gunnison and below the town for five miles to the margin of

Blue Mesa Reservoir. Commerical raft companies take advantage of summer tourists while canoeists sharpen their moving water skills.

Deer are often seen drinking here. Tall cottonwoods adorn the wide floodplain and willows crowd the bank. The rural setting includes many riverside houses.

Twenty-five miles below Gunnison, the narrow opening into the Black Canyon Gorge, with its solid, impermeable rock walls, provided a windfall for dam engineers. In the early 1960s Colorado's largest mountain reservoir, Blue Mesa, was built here. The river was ponded for 20 miles. The Bureau of Reclamation has since taken full advantage of the gorge below Blue Mesa. The result: 45 miles of the Gunnison, including the upper Black Canyon, drowned under a string of three reservoirs comprising the Curecanti Unit of the Colorado River Storage Project.

Gunnison River: Almont to Blue Mesa Reservoir

Physical Data: 18 mi (river miles 20-38); 395-ft drop; 22 ft/mi average gradient; 576,000 acre-ft average yearly discharge (at Gunnison).

Maps: Almont, Signal Peak, Gunnison, and McIntosh Mt. 7.5 minute USGS

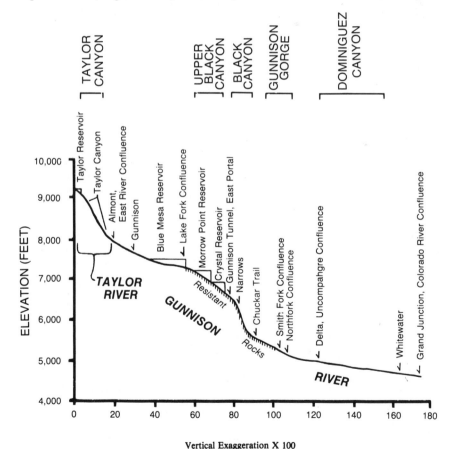

Vertical Exaggeration X 100

Gradient profile of Gunnison River from Taylor Reservoir to Grand Junction.

Quads.
Land Ownership: Private, except first and last miles.

The first mile below Almont has some class II whitewater. The only significant rapids below this first mile lie nine miles downriver along the flank of the Palisades, a volcanic ridge west of Gunnison. Rated class II, these rapids roll up high haystacks when the river runs full during the spring thaw.

Put-in spots are located at the Taylor-East River confluence and at Almont Campground one mile downstream from the confluence. Good access is found on the northwest side of the State Highway 135 Bridge three miles north of Gunnison. Take-outs lie at the bridge at mile 35, the Cooper Ranch riverside recreation area, or on the upper reaches of the Blue Mesa Reservoir.

Gunnison River—
Black Canyon Section

The Gunnison's mid-section, the 50 miles below its confluence with the Lake Fork, is known as the Black Canyon Complex.

Because the narrow, steep walls of the Black Canyon Complex make ideal dam sites, the first half of the canyon has been harnessed for kilowatts. The recently constructed chain of reservoirs—Blue Mesa, Morrow Point, and Crystal—have stolen the river's thunder and calmed its mighty rapids.

Below the three reservoirs, the Bureau of Reclamation drilled the West's first large-scale diversion from one river valley to another, the Gunnison Tunnel. A six-mile bore annually carries about 300,000 acre-feet of water from the Black Canyon to the irrigation ditches of the Uncompahgre Valley. Completed in 1909, the tunnel cost—not surprisingly—three times the Bureau's estimate. The access road to the tunnel's East Portal remains the only rim-to-river road in Black Canyon.

The second part of the Black Canyon Complex lies within the boundaries of Black Canyon of the Gunnison National Monument. This is a paragon of river-sculpted chasms. In this 12-mile stretch the gorge reaches its grandest proportions, with a depth of up to 2,800 feet and the highest cliffs in Colorado. From rim to rim the width of the gorge narrows to 1,250 feet. At the Narrows the river is constricted between vertical walls only 40 feet apart. For several miles it plunges down a 240-foot-per-mile grade, by far the steepest for a large river in the Southern Rocky Mountains. It races over falls, under piles of house-sized boulders, and through menacing cataracts. This section is traversed only at very low water by intrepid kayakers with mountaineering skills in addition to river running skills. Portages between the Narrows and the Painted Wall are long and arudous. Blockading monoliths are difficult enough to climb through without having to drag 50 pounds of loaded kayak. Rafts and open canoes are dangerous and impractical. The journey should be attempted only by kayakers in good physical condition with technical paddling skill and confidence, for a missed eddy carries the risk of entrapment in one of the many rock strainers. Should there be an injury, a rescue operation would prove difficult and costly.

A flow of *less than 500 c.f.s.* is required for safety. Most kayakers prefer 300 to 400 c.f.s., which maximizes navigability and minimizes hazards. Accurate volumetric data has been difficult to obtain in past years. However, with completion of the Crystal Dam in 1977, the Bureau of Reclamation in Montrose or the National Park Service at the monument should be able to provide current and projected volume levels.

The Morrow Point Dam upstream supplies peaking power to cities in the Southwest. At one time this resulted in sharp volume fluctuations in the Black Canyon. Before construction of the Crystal Dam, vigilance and caution were required to avoid surging water while portaging through the boulder fields. One was reminded of John Wayne's immortal line: "God willin' and the river don't rise."

Three or four days is the usual length for a trip through Black Canyon and the Gunnison Gorge. At least one full day is required to travel the two miles from the Narrows to the Painted Wall. Here a 50-foot length of rope will prove a valuable asset in portaging.

Except for the rope, extraneous gear should be held to a minimum. A light sleeping bag or blanket will suffice in the summer months, because the canyon walls absorb the sun's heat during the day and radiate warmth back at night. One luxury worth considering is a foam pad or air mattress. A big flat rock might be the only available level spot for a campsite.

Permission is required for boating trips through the canyon. Ron Mason's trip in 1975 paved the way for good relations between kayakers and monument officials, who have since been extremely helpful.

Gunnison River: East Portal to Red Rock Canyon

Physical Data: 11 mi; 1,080-ft drop; 98 ft/mi average gradient; 240 ft/mi maximum gradient (between the Narrows and S.O.B. Draw); 992,600 acre-ft average yearly discharge.
Maps: Grizzly Ridge and Red Rock Canyon USGS Quads.
Land Ownership: National Park Service.
Information: Black Canyon of the Gunnison National Monument.

This is the National Monument section. The East Portal put-in can be reached from the paved river road branching from the main road just inside the monument boundary. Here much of the river is channeled into the Gunnison Tunnel.

The first mile allows a warm-up on class I to II water. Thereafter, maneuvering becomes much tougher. The first carry, two miles down, skirts a 17-foot drop. This is followed by two miles of classic technical boating with plenty of navigable falls and class IV and V rapids.

One should take time to contemplate this place of stark beauty. Tall pinnacles and towers of Black Canyon Schist are poised high above. The river twists and churns through their remnant boulders, which look like huge lumps of coal.

Douglas fir and ponderosa pines cling to patches of soil on the canyon walls. Box elders sink their roots into the water table. Between the river and canyon walls grow patches of oregon grape, current bushes, poison ivy, and mountain shrub. In the first four miles, cold-water springs emerge from the walls amid gardens of fern. Rainbow and brown trout fishing is excellent. The rim above, bustling with tourists, is quickly forgotten as one enters this "inaccessable" place where the outside world feels a thousand miles distant.

A few hundred yards above the Narrows, the laborious portaging begins in earnest. From here to the Painted Wall it is possible to boat only short

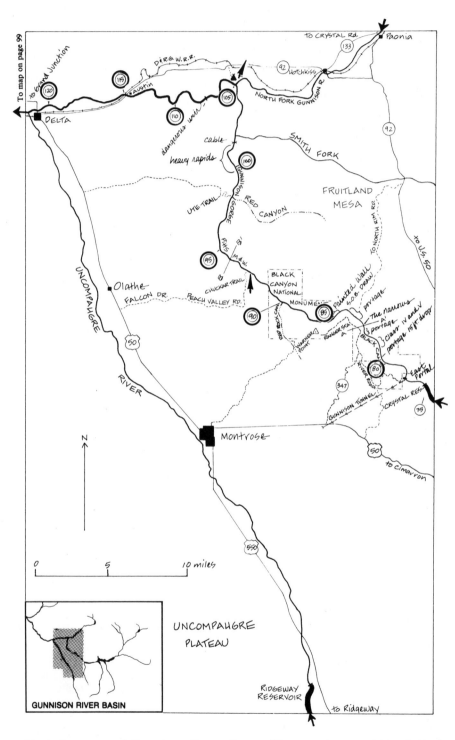

Black Canyon and Gunnison Gorge; Lower Uncompahgre and North Fork.

segments. Fortunately the 40-foot-wide Narrows can be run, or the Black-Canyon would not be traversable. Kayakers must scout every inch of this stretch, evaluating dangers, planning moves, finding eddies and places to put in and take out.

The pinnacled canyon upriver gives way below the Narrows to broad walls with pegmatite vein murals. One becomes mystified by this etheral place and oblivious to the crowds gathering behind the safety rails on the rim, intently watching the slow progress of the antlike specks 2,000 feet below. "What are those idiots doing down there?" is the question reported to be most frequently asked by those above.

Portaging is necessary at least 85 percent of the way down the three-quarter-mile section from what the Torrence expedition called the "place where the river goes underground" to the 45-foot falls above S.O.B. Draw. This long portage includes every obstacle short of a pack of starving wolves. Ropes are essential to drop boats over ledges and down chimneys. A good carry route just below the falls hugs the left wall through dense thickets of poison oak. While usually a matter of some concern, the shrub seems trivial compared to the difficulties offered by any other route.

After passing S.O.B. Draw, we encounter a half-mile navigable section and several unexpected beaches that make inviting campsites. Sandbars appear as the river slows behind the huge talus cone dam at the base of the Painted Wall, Colorado's highest vertical cliff. Beyond the talus pile, the Gunnison makes its final 60-foot plunge. Here boaters carry their boats for the last time and are rewarded for their labors with 20 miles of marvelous wilderness canyon ahead: the Gunnison Gorge of the Black Canyon.

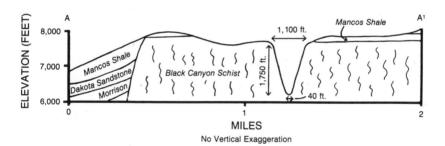

Cross Section of the Black Canyon at the Narrows.

Gunnison River— Gunnison Gorge Section

The dizzying abruptness characterizing the Black Canyon within the national monument moderates in the Gunnison Gorge. This is the Black Canyon Complex's final event. Here the river turns northward. The nearly vertical walls give way to a more jagged, but wider canyon. A narrow inner gorge carved in the Pitts Meadow granites winds through the bosom of the colorful, stratified outer canyon.

The steep, semi-arid country in and around the gorge has never been considered good for any development. Hence it remains one of the few remaining

The Narrows of the Black Canyon. Note kayaker lower left.

wilderness canyons in Colorado and a sanctuary for wildlife. The river plays host and parent to a wide variety of fish including cutthroat, german brown, and rainbow trout. Northern pike and the endangered roundtail chub inhabit its lower reaches. Beaver and muskrat burrow in its banks. River otters have been reintroduced.

The most commonly witnessed raptors are golden eagles and red-tailed hawks. The rugged cliffs are prime nesting and hunting habitat for prairie falcons and great horned owls. The gorge is an historic nesting area of the peregrine falcon, although the last official sighting occurred in 1973. An estimated 10,000 ducks visit the canyon during their winter migration, as do stately sandhill cranes and snowy egrets. Hordes of cliff swallows, endlessly in pursuit of insects, dash about overhead. Next to the river, in squeaking colonies of mud nests, the swallows' voracious young devour mouthful after mouthful of insects supplied by their busy parents.

On slopes adjacent to the river, mule deer and bighorn sheep graze amid sagebrush, oakbrush, saltbrush, mountain shrub, and greasewood. A sparse pinon-juniper forest covers the hillsides. Leafy box elders inhabit the floodplain, and tall ponderosa pines cling to jagged, northfacing inner canyon slopes.

Several trails—Chukar, Duncan, and Ute—enter the inner gorge from the west rim. These were first used for trans-canyon travel by the Utes. Later they served cattlemen and settlers—the Duncans and Howells—who tried to eke out a living in the 1930s through mining. Several stone and wood cabins built by these early families still stand along the river.

Presently, various large power projects are planned for the Gunnison Gorge that would flood all or parts of it. Unless National Wild and Scenic River protection is achieved, this magnificent, last free-flowing portion of the Black Canyon Complex will be flooded for electrical power.

An intense battle is being waged over use of the Gunnison Gorge. If a fourth dam should be constructed, the entire 50-mile Black Canyon Complex would be stilled except for the 12 protected miles within the national monument.

Lack of road access to the inner gorge necessitates carrying boats. Mules have been used for this purpose. Inaccessibility has limited floating in the Gunnison Gorge. Use is increasing, however, as more people seek the wildness of this place and the pleasure of its water. Newer, lightweight rafts and kayaks make the portage more feasible.

The rate of flow varies from place to place, through pools and eddies in which motion is scarcely measurable, past narrows and over rapids where it becomes strong and swift.

Most boating parties float the 13 miles from Chuckar Gulch to the North Fork in one day. If supplies can be carried in, a two-day trip is an excellent

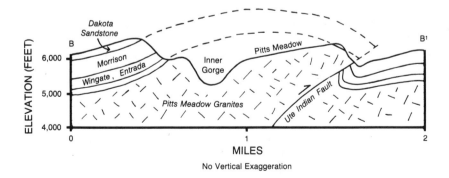

Cross section of Gunnison Gorge at mile 94 (adapted from Black Ridge quadrangle; Hansen, 1968).

choice; it provides the opportunity to camp at one of the many primitive sites along the river.

The Gunnison Gorge can be run at any level in excess of 300 c.f.s. The higher the water, the more difficult the boating. As in the monument portion of the Black Canyon above, discharge is regulated entirely by releases from Crystal Dam and Reservoir and by diversions through the Gunnison Tunnel. The tunnel reduces the total volume of discharge. The dam tends to decrease high flows, increase low flows, and maintain a minimum flow of 200 c.f.s. from March to September. Below the tunnel, the Bureau of Reclamation expects to maintain a 400 c.f.s. minimum when the Blue Mesa Reservoir is full. (Before the reservoirs, discharge reached a record 19,000 c.f.s. in June 1926 and dropped to zero in dry years.) Discharge information can be obtained from the Curecanti Unit of the Bureau of Reclamation in Montrose.

Gunnison Gorge: Red Rock Canyon to North Fork of the Gunnison

Physical Data: 16 mi; 381-ft drop; 24 ft/mi average gradient; 40 ft/mi maximum gradient (between Red Canyon and Smith Fork); 992,600 acre-ft average yearly discharge (below Gunnison Tunnel).
Maps: Red Rock Canyon and Smith Fork USGS Quads.
Land Ownership: Public land, BLM administered.
Information: BLM District Office, Montrose, CO 81401.

There are five access points. The most strenuous involves driving to Warner Point at the west end of the Black Canyon National Monument road. From here a mile-long cross-country climb down the steep draw reaches a point at the bottom of the canyon only half a mile below the Painted Wall. The entire Gunnison Gorge lies ahead, including several gnarly rapids in the first two miles. Due to its difficulty, however, this access is not recommended.

Three miles downriver from Warner Point, there is a trail to the river down Red Rock Canyon (not to be confused with Red Canyon farther down). This trail can be reached by the main dirt road out of Montrose leading northeast in the direction of the canyon. It is not recommended either, because it crosses a patch of private land to reach the river.

The most popular put-in trail follows Chukar Gulch, three miles downstream from Red Rock Canyon. It may be reached by jeep (or car with high clearance) by turning east on Falcon Drive off U.S. Highway 50. Falcon Drive becomes Peach Valley Road and leads to a BLM picnic site at the Chukar trailhead. From here, a good one-mile trail leads to the river.

Duncan and Ute, the remaining downstream access trails, are rarely used today because they are longer than Chukar and offer the boater fewer river miles.

The river roughly follows the Ute Indian fault zone, which is well exposed at Chukar Canyon, at a point just south of Ute Trail, and at several other locations where it crosses the canyon (see cross section, page 97).

Caution should be exercised in the last narrow inner gorge below the Ute Trail and Red Canyon. Numerous delightful rapids punctuate this stretch, the most difficult being those encountered just above the Smith Fork confluence. Holes and haystacks in these rapids have flipped several rafts at high water.

The take-out is located at the campground beside State Highway 92 at the North Fork-Gunnison confluence. Here the river emerges from the deep recesses of the Gunnison Gorge, flowing out upon the broad, fertile plain of the Grand Valley.

Gunnison River— Dominquez Canyon Section

Emerging from the Black Canyon Complex and picking up the North Fork and the Uncompahgre, the Gunnison becomes the state's second largest river. Only the Colorado is larger. The river could have taken its course across any part of the 12-mile-wide Grand Valley but chose to snuggle up against the eastern flank of the Uncompahgre Plateau, where it has cut a shallow canyon —Dominguez Canyon. This is one of the few places in the Southern Rockies which offers a lengthy, gentle, out-of-the-way canoe trip. Sloping beds of grey, maroon, black, and purple Morrison strata at its upper end give way to red walls of Wingate and Entrada sandstones downstream. Bones of the largest land-dwelling animals ever known, the giant sauropods, were recently discovered in the Morrison mudstones above Dominquez Canyon. Small ranches and apple orchards dot the river banks as the Gunnison murmurs through this pastoral canyon. The tracks of the Denver and Rio Grande Railroad parallel the widened stream. Several large petroglyph panels near the

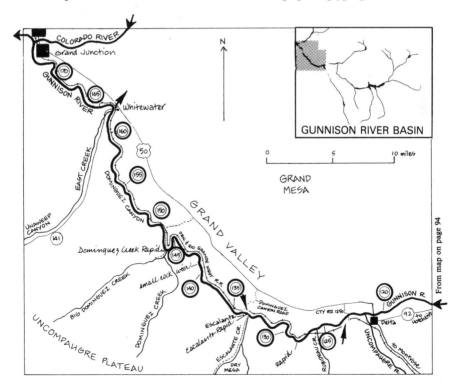

Dominguez Canyon of the Gunnison.

river attest to the former presence of the Anasazi Indians. The area is an April breeding ground for Canada geese, while two tall cottonwood stands hold great blue heron rookeries.

Gunnison River: Delta to Whitewater

Physical Data: 39 mi; 260-ft drop; 6.7 ft/mi average gradient; 1,800,000 acre-ft average yearly discharge (below Uncompahgre confluence).
Maps: Delta, Roubideau, Point Creek, Dominiguez, Triangle Mesa, and Whitewater USGS Quads; Glade Park Area Map from Colorado Fish and Game or BLM shows private and public lands along the river.
Land Ownership: Half private, half public land administered by BLM.

There are two good put-in spots. The upper one, above the entrance to the canyon, is next to the County Road 1250 Bridge just west of Delta. The other lies 10 miles downstream where the Dominguez Canyon Road, leading from U.S. Highway 50, crosses the river within the canyon. An excellent take-out is found river-left at the State Highway 141 Bridge in the town of Whitewater. There are many good campsites along the river, but care should be taken to avoid private land. Likely spots beside Escalante Creek (with dirt road access) or on the public land between miles 151 and 157 are recommended campsites.
Flat water predominates in Dominquez Canyon, but there are several riffles and four class I to II rapids. Three of these rapids cross boulder fans at the mouths of side creeks originating on the Uncompahgre Plateau. One is formed by a rock diversion weir.
The Dominguez Dam is planned for construction in the mid-1980s in a narrow part of the canyon just upriver from Whitewater. It will back a 26-mile-long reservoir through Dominguez Canyon. A local dam opponent has stated, "Taxpayers everywhere should begin questioning the merit of this project before spending $400 million to inundate a beautiful slickrock canyon, destroy wilderness potential for adjacent areas, eliminate productive farms and ranches of 15-20 families, and flood numerous petroglyph panels and other prehistoric and historic sites."

Cebolla Creek

Cebolla Creek and its larger neighbor, the Lake Fork, spill from the Alp-like San Juan Mountains northward into Blue Mesa Reservoir. Tiny Cebolla Creek cuts a hidden canyon through the ash flows from the San Juan volcanoes into the underlying basement complex of foliated gneiss and schist. The sparsely settled canyon reaches a depth of 1,000 feet and is penetrated only by small dirt roads periodically meeting the stream at ranches and homesites. Wild onions, from which the name Cebolla comes, still grow in the lower reaches of the canyon.
The put-in lies at the State Highway 149 Bridge on the Wilson Ranch. Despite an average gradient of 45 feet per mile, the drop is continuous rather than concentrated in steep drops. Though the flow is fast in many places, the run is highlighted by only one well-defined rapid, Wolf Creek, near the end of the run.
Cebolla Creek has a single, critical disadvantage for floaters: it's too small. It can only be run at peak high water (May and early June), in years of above

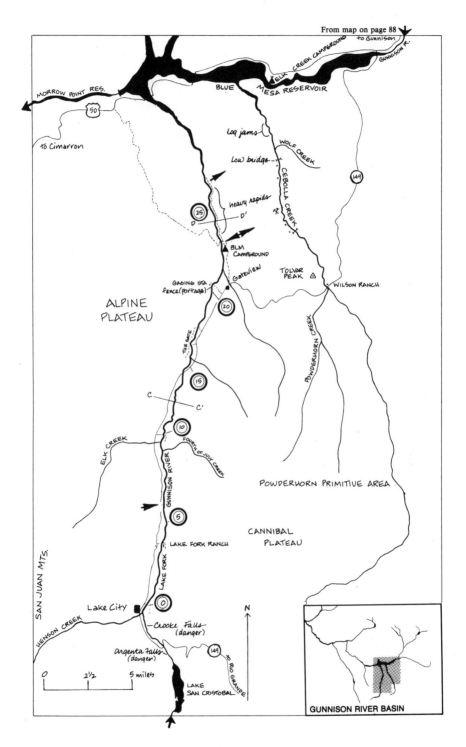

Cebolla Creek and Lake Fork of the Gunnison.

average runoff when the discharge may reach 250 to 350 c.f.s. Any river of this size is typically infested with obstacles. Rafts are not recommended because of the small volume, the portages, and the long paddle to the Elk Creek Campground take-out on Blue Mesa Reservoir.

Portaging in the Black Canyon. (Bill Tuthill photo.)

Lake Fork of the Gunnison

Cebolla's parallel neighbor to the west, the Lake Fork of the Gunnison, crosses terrain of volcanic origin deposited by relatively recent massive eruptions from those mountains. What a display of steaming fury must have occurred 30 million years ago when molten lava and searing ash clashed with this young stream! The river eventually leaves the lava pile, knifing through a narrow canyon of metamorphic basement rock as it approaches the Blue Mesa Reservoir (see cross section, page 104).

The Lake Fork, though a small river, is roughly three times the size of Cebolla Creek. It is naturally free-flowing, with adequate boating volume from mid-May through mid-July in most years (see hydrograph, page 105). Easy access and unique scenery contribute to delightful day boating on this little-known river.

A sudden change in the character of the canyon, combined with a sudden increase in gradient below the town of Gateview, divides the Lake Fork into two parts. The upper canyon, a 35-feet-per-mile stretch for advanced open canoeists or novice to intermediate kayakers, is a good run—provided one does not mind portaging a possible snag or low bridge. State Highway 149 occasionally meets the river. In the last six river miles before Blue Mesa Reservoir, the lower canyon of the Lake Fork narrows, and a dirt access road hugs the river bank. The boating challenge suddenly intensifies as the river flows over a series of steep drops.

Lake Fork of the Gunnison: Lake City to BLM Campground (Upper Lake Fork Canyon)

Physical Data: 24 mi; 840-ft drop; 35 ft/mi average gradient; 179,000 acre-ft average yearly discharge (at Gateview).
Maps: Lake City, Alpine, Plateau, and Gateview 7.5 minute USGS Quads; Gunnison National Forest Map.
Land Ownership: Alternating private and BLM land.

The first five miles of bulldozed and fenced floodplain below Lake City are undesirable for boating. Good put-in places are found between miles five and six where State Highway 149 skirts the river.

From below this put-in to mile 21, the Lake Fork is deeply incised into its floodplain, forming a canyon within a canyon (see cross section, page 104). The highway, built on the old floodplain, is not visible from the bottom of the 100-foot-deep inner canyon. Occasionally, varicolored greens of the distant Alpine Plateau can be seen framed by bare, light brown inner canyon walls of contoured ash, breccia, and tuff. At "The Gate" (mile 17), the river slices through a hard lava flow exposing tightly packed, vertical colonnades of columnar basalt. A difficult carry is required at the gaging station near Gateview.

The BLM campground at mile 23.5 is an excellent take-out.

Lake Fork of the Gunnison: BLM Campground to Blue Mesa Reservoir (Lower Lake Fork Canyon)

Physical Data: 5 mi; 260-ft drop; 52 ft/mi average gradient; 80 ft/mi maximum gradient; 179,000 acre-ft average yearly discharge (at Gateview).
Maps: Gateview and Carpenter Ridge 7.5 minute USGS Quads.
Land Ownership: BLM land.

Below Gateview the Lake Fork departs from the lava-bed country of its upper reaches and knifes into the region's basement rock, the Black Canyon Schist. The character of the valley shifts abruptly to a precipitous gorge, and the river responds with a steeper, less consistent gradient. A series of class IV to V drops can be scouted from the parallel dirt road. Blue Mesa Reservoir backwaters reach up the canyon, ending the Lake Fork only five miles into the gorge.

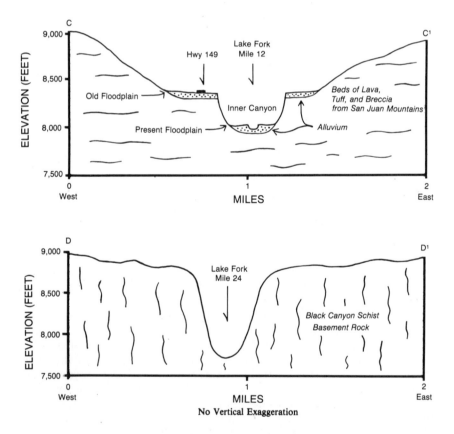

Cross sections of Lake Fork of the Gunnison showing contrasting structures of the upper and lower canyons (adapted from Gateview Geologic map; Olson Hedlund, 1973).

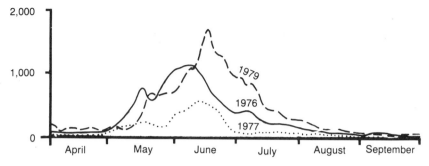

Hydrograph of Lake Fork at Gateview.

North Fork of the Gunnison

Coursing down a wide valley of quiet ranches, the North Fork is not an outstanding river for boating. But some canoeists enjoy the gentle, out-of-the-way canyon from the town of Lazear past the Gunnison confluence to Austin. The canyon's foundation sandstone (the Entrada) is overlain by the Wanakah and Morrison formations. Dakota sandstone caps the surrounding mesas

Paddling through "huge lumps of coal" in Black Canyon.

as it often does in the stratified western flank of the Southern Rocky Mountains. An irrigation diversion weir 1.5 miles below the Gunnison confluence can be very dangerous.

The 10-mile stretch below Paonia Reservoir contains fast-moving water. Here State Highway 133 hugs the river bank, providing convenient scouting points.

Unnavigable Box Canyon of the Uncompahgre just upriver from Ouray.

Uncompahgre River

The Uncompahgre River Valley was the center of Ute territory before settlers arrived in the 1880s. Its name comes from the Ute words *unca-pah-gre,* or hot-water-spring. Several such springs issue from its mineralized headwaters high in the San Juan Mountains.

The river descends a black gorge below the Million Dollar Highway (U.S. Highway 550). Above Ouray it plunges through the narrowest box canyon in Colorado. Although this chasm is more than 150 feet deep, it is so constricted that some claim to have jumped across it from rim to rim with the aid of a good running start!

Below Ouray the Uncompahgre escapes from its confines, pouring as from a cave into the sun onto a boulder-strewn floodplain at the edge of the mountain mass. The descent from below Ouray to near Ridgeway should be carefully evaluated in advance from the highway. It is rated class IV to V and looks rather unpleasant.

Beyond Ridgeway, the river crosses a glacial moraine and enters a scenic, rural canyon of pinon-juniper woodland rooted on strata from the floor of the great Cretaceous Sea. Here it separates the east snout of the Uncompahgre Plateau. The water is generally class I to II, with some big waves at high water. Ridgeway Dam is under construction in the middle of this canyon. It is scheduled to flood the upper reaches.

Beyond the canyon, the Uncompahgre emerges into the broad upper Grand Valley, one of the richest agricultural areas of Colorado. The riparian environs of the upper Grand Valley are typical of the state's irrigated flatlands, with tall cottonwoods bordering a heavily utilized river bed which has been bulldozed, fenced, and diverted into ditches.

The Uncompahgre meets the Gunnison just downriver from the Black Canyon Complex at the town of Delta.

Dolores River Basin

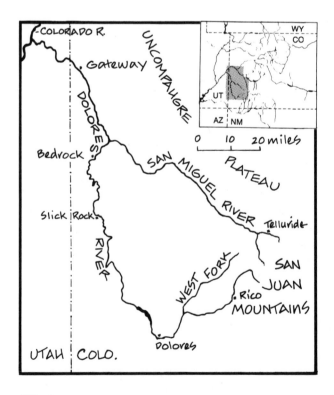

The map shows the Dolores River Basin region. Labels include: COLORADO R., Gateway, UNCOMPAHGRE, DOLORES, Bedrock, SAN MIGUEL RIVER, PLATEAU, Slick Rock, RIVER, Telluride, WEST FORK, SAN JUAN, Rico, MOUNTAINS, Dolores, UTAH, COLO. Inset map shows WY, CO, UT, AZ, NM state locations. Scale: 0 10 20 miles.

Yet, fair as thou art, thou shunnest to glide,
Beautiful stream! by the village side;
But windest away from haunts of men,
To quiet valley and shaded glen.
    —William Cullen Bryant

Men, Mines, and the River

Man arrived on the banks of the Dolores River early. Projectile points found near the river may date to 7,000 B.C.

Near the town of Dolores—a point where the river, having just emerged from the San Juan Mountains, makes an acute turn to the north—there is much evidence of Anasazi culture, which reached its climax at Mesa Verde only 16 miles to the south. The "ancient ones" settled the area perhaps 3,000 years ago and ultimately established a full-scale, corn-based horticultural society of about 5,000 people. Archeological sites become scarcer downriver beyond the entrance to Dolores Canyon, but evidence of the Anasazi can be found all the way to Paradox Canyon and the town of Bedrock. By the middle of the 10th century, for unexplained reasons, the Anasazi abandoned the Dolores Valley.

Today an extensive dig, the Dolores Archeological Project, is being undertaken in the area around the town of Dolores by Colorado University Professor David Breternitz and others. Little is known about the Dolores Anasazi. Although archeologists are uncovering important clues, they are working against the clock. In 1984 or 1985 the backwaters behind the McPhee Dam, under construction downstream, will fill the valley and bring the study to a gurgling halt.

On August 13, 1776, Fathers Dominguez and Escalante, on their journey to find a route from New Mexico to the California missions, reached the Dolores near its Big Bend (later to become the town of Dolores). Here they rested a day before pushing downriver. At this time the Dolores region was the domain of the gentle Ute tribe, whose relationship with the Spanish friars was a congenial one.

The expedition explored the Dolores River for 120 miles. Upon reaching Slick Rock Canyon, however, the fathers found the terrain too rough for efficient travel, forsook their intended northwesterly route, and turned eastward away from the river up Big Gypsum Canyon toward the Gunnison.

Author David Lavender, who spent many years in the region, believes Father Escalante first named the river El Rio de Nuestra Senora de las Dolores—The River of our Lady of Sorrows—after one of his men drowned during their layover at the Big Bend. A century later, on early mining maps of the Southwest, the name of the river was shortened to Dolores.

The Dolores Utes enjoyed a century of obscurity following the Dominguez-Escalante expedition. But the lust for precious ore led to a rapid decline of their quiet culture. Prospectors discovered the region in the late 1860s, finding placer gold on both the upper Dolores and the San Miguel. By 1875 numerous mines—Liberty Bell, Tomboy Smuggler, Union, Pandora, and others—poured out precious ore from the mountains surrounding the newly established town of Telluride. Nestled on the banks of the San Miguel and enclosed on three sides by evergreen and aspen forests, 14,000-foot peaks, and majestic waterfalls from surrounding hanging valleys, Telluride's residents call it the most beautiful spot on earth.

Telluride was the site of several historical events. William Jennings Bryan delivered his famous "Cross of Gold" speech from the downtown Sheridan Hotel. Jack Dempsey's career began as a bouncer at a local bordello. Alternating current was discovered here and used for the first time on Telluride's street lights.

Over Lizard Head Pass on the banks of the Upper Dolores, another rich silver lode was found in the spring of 1879. The boomtown of Rico (Spanish for rich) was born. The rich discovery drained hundreds of miners from Telluride.

While Telluride has continued to prosper as a tourist and ski resort, Rico is nearly a ghost town today. But there is much evidence of past glory. Stagnant lavender and chartreuse tailings ponds amongst dilapidated hotels and abandoned mining structures provide rich diggings for history buffs who visit the scenic mountain valley of the Dolores.

The region's last major ore discovery was made north of Rico at the headwaters of the West Dolores River. It gave rise to the town of Dunton. When

Remains of flume above Dolores River (Colorado Historical Society, Doc Marston photo)

Butch Cassidy and his "wild bunch" robbed the San Miguel National Bank of Telluride on June 24, 1889, they made their getaway over Lizard Head Pass and down the West Dolores, stopping in Dunton for a rest. The outlaws enjoyed a meal, a dip in the hot springs, and several rounds at the saloon before riding downriver out of the mountains and disappearing into the recesses of the Lower Dolores beyond Big Bend.

Dunton hasn't changed much since. One can still enjoy the hot springs and sit at the same bar where Butch and his gang took their respite.

Poor transportation on whiplash roads from Big Bend and Montrose stalled economic development on the upper Dolores and San Miguel until Otto Mears, "pathfinder of the San Juans," built his Rio Grande Southern Railroad between Ridgeway and Durango in 1890 and 1891. The tracks, which connected the southwest corner of Colorado to the rest of the state, extended over Dallas Divide to Placerville on the San Miguel, then up the San Miguel with a spur into Telluride. The main line followed a tortuous route over Lizard Head Pass through the Ophir Loop and down the banks of the Upper Dolores past Rico to Big Bend, where it left the river and extended east to Durango. The economic boost brought by the Rio Grande Southern increased Telluride's population to over 5,000. "To-hell-you-ride!" bellowed the conductor as the little train pulled into town.

The 1893 silver crash threatened to ruin the railroad and the towns it served. Telluride and Dunton were saved when gold ore replaced silver. Coking coal from nearby veins rescued Rico. The Rio Grande Southern, acquired by the larger Denver and Rio Grande, continued to roll until 1951.

Today the abandoned rail bed can be seen along the banks of the Dolores, and picturesque wooden trestles still stand precariously above the South Fork of the San Miguel.

Mining was less lucrative beyond the mountain valleys of the Dolores and San Miguel. Nevertheless, several gold placer operations strove for profitability. Auriferous deposits below the San Miguel-Dolores confluence were located on "high bars," ancient remnant floodplains above the river. Those who laid claim to one such deposit, the Lone Tree Placer on arid Mesa Creek Flats, fully expected it to hold a fortune. However, the source of that fortune was located 400 feet above the Dolores River. Hand operations were impossible since pumps couldn't raise water from the river to such a height. "How will we get water to the Lone Tree?" asked the overseers of the claim. A ditch carrying water from upriver was the only solution. The ditch began the diversion eight miles up the San Miguel. When it reached the edge of the sandstone cliffs at the Dolores confluence, construction began on a four-by-six-foot flume box. The flume was supported by cantilevered brackets anchored to the vertical face. Workers suspended from a shelf road 400 feet above the river set thousands of brackets. At least one worker lost his grip and was saved by falling into the river. Since riverbank cottonwoods and stunted pinon trees on nearby slopes were inadequate for constructing the long flume, it became necessary to haul over 1,800,000 board feet of pine lumber by wagon from the forests of the high Uncompahgre Plateau. The planks were floated down the completed portion of the flume where the flume box was constructed on the brackets. The project—a mammoth and daring engineering feat—was largely completed in 1891. The flume worked, but it failed to produce due to a miscalculation: The Lone Tree Placer gold was too fine to be profitably recoverable. The engineer blew his brains out.

Sections of the useless, crumbling flume still cling to the cliffs above the

Dolores. They offer river runners a chance to recall a dramatic though nearly forgotten episode in Colorado's mining history.

In 1881, across the river from the Lone Tree Placer, near the banks of Rock Creek, the Talbert brothers' gold mine shaft entered a vein of soft, canary yellow material—carnotite. A rich uranium ore, carnotite was to have as much of an impact on the lower reaches of the Dolores and San Miguel as the gold and silver at their headwaters. A sample of the stuff was sent to a French chemist in Denver who, discovering its radioactivity, relayed it to Marie and Pierre Curie. Thus Dolores carnotite was used in pioneering radioactivity work and in the discovery of radium. Radium had limited usefulness in those days. Nevertheless, mines appeared up and down both rivers from their confluence, which was the heart of the carnotite-rich region. The tiny cattle towns of Nucla and Naturita on the San Miguel River and Bedrock on the Dolores were transformed with hundreds of miners, mills, and reduction plants. In the early 1900s the region produced half the world's carnotite.

Discovery of cheaper Belgian Congo pitchblende in 1923 brought the mines and mills to a halt. Quiet descended once again on the Dolores country, but only until World War II. Vanadium, which is used to harden steel, can be extracted from carnotite, and uranium was needed for the atomic bomb. In 1942 a Paradox Valley cattle rancher described the change: "Desperate men raced back to the ruins. New monsters belch fire and smoke. . . . Now the valley mills are thundering again on a scale never dreamed by the old radium miners. Towns stand on once-desolate flats. Scores of crisp, efficient ore buyers swarm where formerly a chance cattle speculator might wander in and drive a long-winded bargain. Trucks snort about where we had only trails." Effluent from the mills at Vanadium, Naturita, and Urvan on the San Miguel and Bedrock on

Lunch on the river. (Tim Haske photo.)

the Dolores turned the two rivers, born so beautifully in the high San Juans, into grey, miserable, flowing cesspools.

Although the uranium mining activity in the region has died down, crumbling momentos of the boom days are in evidence on the canyon walls and in the valleys of the two rivers.

In 1889 a gigantic engineering feat upriver near Big Bend brought an end to the Dolores as a naturally free-flowing river. Several million years ago, when the river left its southerly channel to the San Juan and turned north, it left a broad, flat, and fertile plain; but the Montezuma Valley was without sufficient water. Why, reasoned early homesteaders in the valley, let the Dolores flow uselessly through untillable gorges in the desert when it is so close to us? In November, 1885, James W. Hanna and others founded the Montezuma Valley Ditch Company. They intended to connect two great river basins—the Dolores and San Juan—with an irrigation canal across the low divide between them and bring the Montezuma Valley into bloom. Completed in 1889, the "Great Cut" and mile-long tunnel through the divide supplied Dolores River water to 35,000 acres of farmland. A second canal and the Narraguinnep Reservoir were completed in 1907, giving the system enough capacity to entirely eliminate the Dolores from its natural bed except during periods of high water. By early July the great canyons either are dry or hold barely a trickle. The Montezuma Ditch Company, however, brought beans to the desert. The tiny farmtown of Dove Creek in the center of the Montezuma Valley proudly displays a sign declaring itself the "Pinto Bean Capital of the World." The American armies of World Wars I and II can thank Dove Creek (perhaps with some ambivalence) for a good portion of their rations.

Mining and irrigation were not man's only uses of the Dolores and San

An open canoeist solos the Dolores. (John Berg photo.)

Miguel and their picturesque valleys. The San Miguel was the home of one of the West's first experiments in communal living, and the Dolores became a gold mine for timber barons and the empire of cattlemen.

In 1896 the Colorado Cooperative Company, a utopian enterprise where "equality and service rather than greed and competition were the basis of conduct," established the town of Pinon on the San Miguel at Cottonwood Creek. Near Pinon a 15-mile irrigation canal, parts of which are still in use, was built by the communalists. It extended from the river to croplands around their main townsite at Nucla. The canal's route required an enormous flume 108 feet high and 840 feet long across Cottonwood Creek. The Cottonwood Trestle, finished in 1903, was at the time the longest and highest irrigation flume in the world.

Today, when floating by the all-but-deserted Pinon townsite, one is reminded that communal living was not solely a phenomenon of the 1960s.

In 1915 the New Mexico Timber Company, headed by C.D. McPhee and J.J. McGinnity, made good a bid for nearly 100 million board feet of timber along the river mesas of the Dolores. The two men built a railroad spur from Dolores (Big Bend's new name) to a millsite four miles downriver. The millsite logging town of over 500 people was named McPhee in 1924. By 1927 it had become Colorado's biggest sawmill. Unrestricted cutting (125,000 board feet per day at the peak) caused severe damage to this part of the Dolores's watershed. In 1933 the Great Depression brought the operation to a halt. The town is gone now, soon to be replaced by a dam and reservoir named, appropriately, McPhee.

With discoveries and economic changes, mines and mills have appeared and disappeared. One enterprise, however, has consistently embraced the valleys and canyoned mesas across the path of the Dolores: cattle ranching. There was plenty of grass and mild winter weather in Paradox, Gypsum, and the lower San Miguel valleys. Their proximity to lush summer range on the Uncompahgre Plateau and the San Juan Mountains was another advantage. By the turn of the century, the town of Bedrock on the Dolores in Paradox Valley burgeoned into a wild west mecca ringed with reminders of hoofed adventure—Wild Steer Mesa, Bull Canyon, Muleshoe Bend, Maverick Draw, Horse Range Mesa, and Horsethief Canyon.

"Doc" Marston and the First Dolores River Run

On May 13, 1948, an unlikely group of adventurers gathered on the banks of a roiling river that had just emerged from its mountain genesis. They were about to begin the first exploration of the Dolores River.

The leader was Otis "Doc" Marston, World War I submarine commander and pioneer of the Grand Canyon, Salmon, Snake, and Green rivers. He was accompanied by his wife Margaret, Preston and Becky Walker of Grand Junction, and a runty black dog, "Ditty."

Doc was doubtful whether their skills or craft, a small wooden San Juan boat, would be up to the job. The river was swollen by meltwater from a heavy winter snowpack in the San Juan Mountains. The boat had been designed by Norman Nevills for trips on the relatively gentle San Juan. Nevills's San Juan boat was about the shape and size of a duck hunting skiff turned up at both ends, with big freeboard and watertight compartments fore and aft. It was as primitive in comparison to today's craft of neoprene and fiberglass as Doc's World War I submarine had been to modern undersea monsters. If the Dolores were to match their worst fears, they could be courting disaster.

The party entered the river one mile below the town of Dolores. Doc's destination was Moab on the Colorado, 250 miles and at least two weeks away. Pres pulled into the current, and they felt that exciting surge of power and speed as the river took hold. In the first two days the canyon walls grew. A fringe of tall pines on the banks inspired them to name the deep canyon of the second day "Ponderosa Gorge." The pace quickened as the river swept the tiny craft around the turn at Glade Canyon on the third day. Shortly the explorers came to a half-mile of whitewater. "A rapid-happy riverman in a cataract boat and a covered cockpit might run it, but he would need to be very happy," declared Doc. In the difficult task of lining past the rapid, which they named "Old Snaggle Tooth," the boat foundered and nearly capsized.

There were several close calls, but no mishaps in the miles of rapids below Old Snaggle Tooth. That afternoon the water slackened and the walls began to break down as they emerged from Dolores Canyon. They entered Disappointment Valley with its tiny town of Slick Rock marked by "a group of houses and trailers."

The following day, the group ran through a canyon swinging to the right and east. This canyon opened into a valley. (The small canyon has recently taken the name Little Glen Canyon in remembrance of its namesake drowned under Lake Powell Reservoir.) Here, in Big Gypsum Valley, they expected to resupply at the Bedrock Store. Bedrock, however, was in Paradox Valley, 35 miles downstream. Doc remarked optimistically that "we were lost......but not too lost."

In the space of less than 100 yards the river leaves Big Gypsum Valley, piercing its north wall and then "running deep with many close loops." The explorers found themselves on the incised meanders of Slick Rock Canyon. Two days in this beautiful canyon brought the party to Paradox Valley which, like Disappointment and Big Gypsum, "stretches one way, while the river enters, crosses, and passes out the other." After floating past the Bedrock Store, Becky realized from the air maps that the sought-after landmark must be in the vicinity. They stopped and found it one mile back upriver. There they "bought supplies, phoned Walkers and listened to Warner, the cowpuncher, tell stories of the [Paradox] Canyon."

The following day and a half brought them through several difficult rapids in Paradox Canyon, past the San Miguel confluence, through a relatively placid Mesa Canyon, and on to the town of Gateway where they rested two days.

On the afternoon of May 23, five miles below Gateway near the Utah-Colorado border, the group "sighted a gathering of cars and trucks and 75 people on the rocks. This was 'The Narrows' so we landed for a look-see." At high water levels this rapid is second only to Old Snaggle Tooth in difficulty. It is long with very big waves. They would succeed only with a perfect run.

"We decided the ladies would like to see the show from the shore and took off," Doc related. "In the first drive through the narrow gate we took some water and then some more. With the boat water-loaded Pres was unable to pull to the right of the rock below as planned, but did manage to clear the upper end of the island, to the right.

"All the current drove us toward the rock in mid-channel and we missed it just exactly right but with no safety factor. I started bailing as we were taking much water with the boat heavy and we ran another quarter mile before we could land left and bail. The whole run was almost a mile.''

They knew it was mostly luck that had prevented a flip, and they smiled wryly at one another when an old timer said, ''By God! Those men sure knew what they were doing every minute of the time, didn't they?'' The running of The Narrows became the chief talk of the town of Gateway. Remarked one native, ''If I hadn't seen it, I wouldn't believe it. And I still don't believe it.''

The ladies reentered the boat and the party left their ''fan club,'' entering Gateway Canyon, the final canyon on the Dolores. A mile-long series of difficult rapids near the entrance of Beaver Creek was negotiated with care. Finally the river slowed on its approach to the Colorado. Another day on the Colorado brought them to Moab, ''completing the most successful boat trip yet.''

A Geologic Spectacle

The Dolores River and its major tributary, the San Miguel, are the master streams of the west flank of the San Juan Mountains. Their waters gather in the La Plata and Rico ranges to the south, the San Miguel Range between the two rivers, and the Uncompahgre Range to the north. These mountains present a bold escarpment above the deserts of the Southwest. A two-mile-thick blanket of strata, raised high on the uplifted sides of the mountains and dipping toward the southwest, is deeply embayed by the canyons of the upper Dolores and San Miguel. Here erosion has exposed the Permian and Triassic Red Beds, whose colorful slopes support and give life to deep forests of spruce and fir.

After emerging from the mountains, the Dolores turns northward abruptly and unexpectedly, cleaving a series of high desert canyons through gently undulating strata on the roof of the Paradox Basin. The basin sits between the protruding Uncompahgre Plateau on the east and La Sal Mountains to the west. The Dolores took this course through the Paradox Basin only recently. It originally followed a route south from the mountains to merge with the San Juan River in the Four Corners area. Then, about 10 million years ago, subterranean igneous activity began uplifting Ute Mountain and the Mesa Verde highlands across the ancestral Dolores's path, forcing its 180 degree turn to the north.

For centuries the Dolores meandered quietly across a level plain while it fashioned this new route to the Colorado. Afterwards, in late Tertiary time, earth deformation once again disturbed the path of the Dolores. An undulating series of anticlines threatened to turn the river from its established course once more. The deformation was slow, however, and this time the river held fast, incising its meanders into the gradually rising domes of strata and forming what Powell termed ''antecedent'' canyons. Dolores, Little Glen, Slick Rock, Paradox, Mesa, and Gateway Canyons were born.

The first, Dolores Canyon, cracks a nearly level plain. Standing 100 yards from the rim, one would not know he was on the edge of a deep gorge. Dolores Canyon breaks through the axis of a broad, gentle arch in the strata known as the Dolores Anticline.

If the Dolores Anticline had risen long ago, the river would have had time to even out its gradient through the canyon, but it has not accomplished this.

Geologists believe the anticline may still be active and therefore may still be affecting the fluvial characteristics of the river. It performs the function of a huge, gentle, rising dam. In its approach to the axis of the Dolores Anticline, (cutting into older and older layers) the river flows sluggishly. Upon reaching the axis, however, its gradient suddenly steepens dramatically through a steady series of rapids, including Old Snaggle Tooth, as it flows "down" the back side of the huge upwarp.

The anticlines in the central section of the Dolores corridor (and possibly the

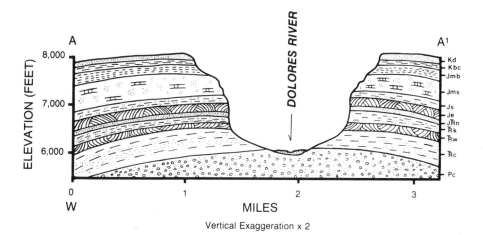

Age	Symbol	Formation	Description	Thickness
Cretaceous	Kd	Dakota	fine grained, hard quartz sandstone, beach deposit	150 ft.
	Kbc	Burrow Can. fm.	intertoungues with Morrison, gray qtz. ss., greenish shale, limestone, cheut	150 ft.
	Jmb	Morrison-upper member	reddish-brown mudstone, sandstone lenses	400 ft.
	Jms	Morrison-lower member	brown quartz sandstone, interbedded lenses of limey mudstone, source of most uranium and vanadium	350 ft.
Jurassic	Js	Summerville	sandy siltsone, reddish-brown	150 ft.
	Je	Entrada	light orange, buff, cross bedded, desert sandstone	150 ft.
	JR̄n	Navajo	light brown to white cross bedded quartz sandstone	100 ft.
	R̄k	Kayenta	purplish gray, purplish red siltstone and sandstone. Interbeds shale and mudstone	180 ft.
Triassic	R̄w	Wingate	red cross-bedded quartz sandstone, forms tall cliffs	200 ft.
	R̄c	Chinle	red to brown shale and siltstone, friable slope former	200 ft.
Permian	Pc	Cutler	arkose, conglomerate, arkosic sandstone	

Cross section of Dolores Canyon near Snaggle Tooth Rapid.

Dolores Anticline, also) were powered by elongate masses of salt from the underlying Paradox Formation. Less dense than surrounding rocks, the salt masses sought the surface, as do chunks of ice held underwater. In doing so they bowed the overlying strata upward. The highly soluble salt masses, however, proved a weak foundation and the anticlines collapsed, leaving steep-walled, dry canyons—Paradox and Gypsum—athwart the Dolores. The river, instead of flowing through these canyons as a normal stream should, enters and leaves them as though crossing great hallways through side doors.

Because the river was already established, the collapse of the anticlines did not affect its course. A notable exception is Glade Graben, a narrow downthrown block in the Dolores Anticline paralleling the upwarp's northwest-trending axis near mile 150. Upon reaching this small trough, the river abruptly turns southwest and follows it for a couple of miles before resuming its original northerly course.

The deep canyons of the lower Dolores River owe their existence in part to an erosion-resistant sandstone formation atop the surrounding high-desert plateaus. The tightly cemented Dakota sandstone, deposited on the leading edge beach of the advancing Cretaceous Sea, today provides a protective roof in many places over the softer underlying strata of the Paradox Basin. The Dakota has been breached only by the downcutting action of the Dolores and its tributaries and by the collapsed salt anticlines. Otherwise, acting as a protective capstone, it sustains the mesas and high plains.

The desert canyons of the Dolores are unusual in the uniformity of the strata layers exposed in their walls. Through other Colorado Plateau canyons, travelers find themselves either descending in time, through successively older strata, or the reverse. Each canyon of the Dolores, however, exposes essentially the same formations.

The bottom formation revealed by the river, the Triassic Chinle shale, appears as Arizona's Painted Desert far to the south. The Chinle is also the home of the famous Petrified Forest. Following deposition of these shales, dunes of

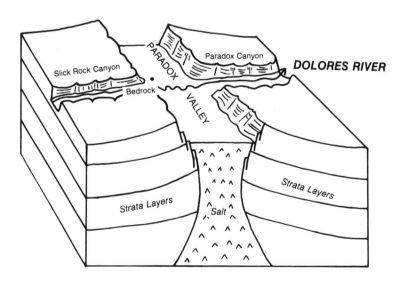

Generalized structure of the collapsed salt anticline at Paradox Valley.

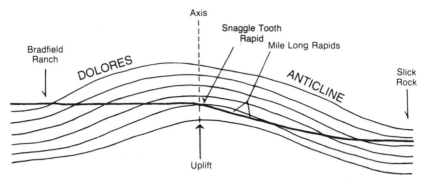

Generalized gradient profile of Dolores River through Dolores Canyon. Note sharp gradient change where the river reaches the axis of the Dolores anticline.

a great desert spread over the region. The desert waned for a time, then returned, bringing into existence the three members of the Glen Canyon Group. The basal member and the dominant rock in each of the desert canyons is the vermillion-colored Wingate Sandstone, a vertical cliff 200 feet high. Above, a ledgy Kayenta Sandstone forms a topographic break from the wall-like Wingate. The Kayenta is topped by another dune formation, the white Navajo Sandstone. This top member of the Glen Canyon Group has a thickness of less than 200 feet in the Dolores canyons, but thickens westward to more than 2,000 feet where it reaches its maximum development in the colossal white cliffs of Zion National Park. Another cross-bedded sandstone, the Entrada, tops the Navajo, followed by the Summerville and Morrison shales. Capping the canyon rim high over the river is the ubiquitous Dakota Sandstone.

Nowhere do the Dolores or its mountain twin, the San Miguel, encounter crystalline basement rock, with whose upthrust masses almost all other Southern Rocky Mountain rivers had to contend.

The land surrounding the Dolores River canyons, called Montelores Country by the locals, is rich both in natural resources and in scenery. Numerous competing interests—agriculture, mining, oil and gas, archeological discovery, wilderness preservation, and tourism—today contend for these riches as never before.

A Doomed Watercourse?

In 1973, the Dolores and 11 other Colorado rivers were proposed for inclusion in the study phase of the federal Wild and Scenic Rivers Act. The Dolores headed the priority list. In 1980, wild and scenic designation for the Dolores finally appeared to be nearing approval, but a heavy price had to be paid: construction of McPhee Dam and Reservoir. Bureaucratic support for protection of the river hinged, ironically, on a dam that would largely destroy it for floating by diverting most of its water out of the Dolores Canyon.

Alas, the Dolores may soon become America's first Wild and Scenic Dry Gulch. The reservoir will not destroy the most scenic canyons, but many conservationists wonder which is worse, to flood beautiful canyons or to take away their life blood.

For perhaps the next two years, however, the river will remain, in the words of a long-time advocate, "one of the most beautiful in the United States and one of the most interesting for rafts, canoes and kayaks."

It is best to plan an early trip on the Dolores. The river peaks earlier than almost any other Southern Rocky Mountain river, often in mid- to late April (see hydrograph, below). Phone the Bedrock Store (Bedrock, Colorado) for flow information. With swifter current and livelier rapids, high water is the best time for a Dolores float trip. Even during high water years, diversions dry up the riverbed by early July. The lower canyons from below the McPhee construction project to the Colorado River can be run in about a week. A single canyon—Dolores, Slick Rock, Mesa, or Gateway—can be run in a weekend. Dolores Canyon is the most difficult.

Dolores River—Mountain Canyons Section

The Upper Dolores and West Fork are tucked into forest-blanketed canyons in the uncrowded southwest corner of Colorado. Roads parallel both rivers. Numerous landslides down colorful canyon walls of Mesozoic strata have helped to shape these rivers. The main fork drops 140 feet in half a mile at the Peterson Slide, one mile upriver from Rico. The river becomes boatable below Rico.

Dolores River: Rico to Dolores

Physical Data: 37 mi; 1,850-ft drop; 50 ft/mi average gradient; 318,000 acre-ft average yearly discharge (at Dolores).
Maps: Rico, Orphan Butte, Wallace Ranch, Stoner, Boggy Draw, and Dolores East USGS Quads; San Juan Natonal Forest Map.

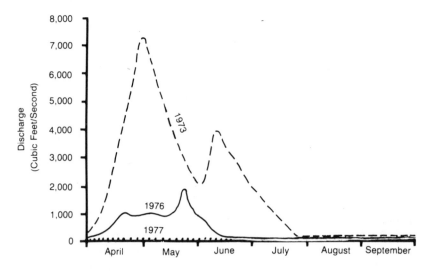

Hydrograph of Dolores River at Bedrock.

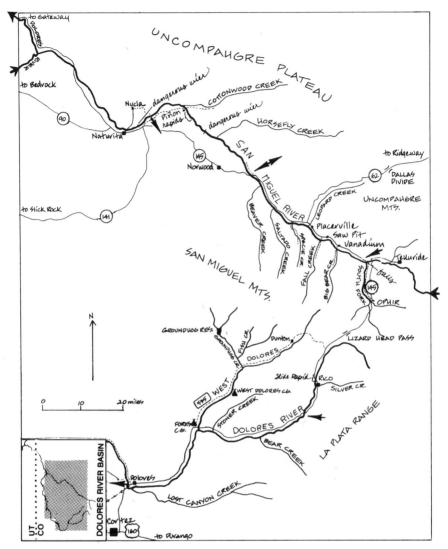

Upper Dolores and San Miguel rivers.

Land Ownership: Alternating private ranches and National Forest land.

Here the Upper Dolores flows through a tranquil valley of shady, forested stretches alternating with open ranchland. U.S. Highway 145 parallels the river, providing scouting and access.

A steep average gradient of 50 feet per mile between Rico and Dolores suggests difficult running. The river has graded itself, however, resulting in an evenly sloping bed without steep, sudden drops or falls, and relatively few big boulders. These fluvial characteristics apply to many mountain rivers which, like the Upper Dolores, flow across soft sedimentary strata. The only river-level exposure of igneous rock is a short, class III canyon composed of white porphyry two miles below Rico.

The upper Dolores has a steady current usually rated between class I and III. At high water it is a flusher: fast water, big waves, and few eddies. This is a potentially dangerous situation for open canoeists and inexperienced rafters and kayakers. The river is much more pleasant at moderate to low levels when the water is crystal clear. The abandoned Rio Grande Southern Railroad bed follows the river.

With the exception of Groundhog Reservoir on a tributary of the West Fork, the Upper Dolores and its West Fork are entirely free-flowing, responding to natural seasonal rhythms. Paddlers usually find the best boating between mid-June and mid-July. By late July there is usually enough water only below the confluence of the two forks.

West Fork of the Dolores

The West Fork, with historic Dunton near the head of its canyon, is a smaller copy of the Upper Dolores. Its flow characteristics are the same, and its steeply inclined canyon walls are even more heavily forested. There is plenty of National Forest land between small ranches along its course. The small size of the West Fork means boating only during high water—usually late May and early June. Watch out for log jams and barbed wire fences. Above Fish Creek, on the West Fork, log jams prevent boating. The best put-in lies at the Stoner Mesa Road Bridge, just off County Road 535, one mile below Fish Creek. Four National Forest Campgrounds in the 12 miles down to the confluence of the West Fork and Upper Dolores make excellent access points.

Dolores River—Desert Canyons Section

Dolores River: Dolores Canyon Ranch to Slick Rock (Dolores Canyon)

Physical Data: 50 mi;1,000 drop; 20 ft/mi average gradient; 60 ft/mi maximum gradient; 260,000 acre-ft average yearly discharge.
Maps: Doe Canyon, The Glade, Secret Canyon, Joe Davis Hill, and Slick Rock USGS Quads.
Land Ownership: San Juan National Forest, BLM. Public land except in first and last 2 miles.

This is one of the Southern Rockies' most superb river runs. Most boaters plan an early trip during April or May high water periods. At such times much excitement awaits them on the swift, muddy river.

Good put-ins lie just upriver from the Dolores Canyon Ranch, five miles east of Cahone, or upriver on the dirt road. The first 10-mile stretch is gentle, with class I rapids at side canyon boulder fans as the river cuts into the uplifted plateau. Thick forests of 100-foot-high Douglas fir and ponderosa pine cover the river's narrow floodplain, where many excellent campsites can be found. This section of Dolores Canyon is fittingly called the Ponderosa Gorge. It harbors the wildest country along the Dolores outside Slick Rock Canyon. Watch for Old Blockhead on the left.

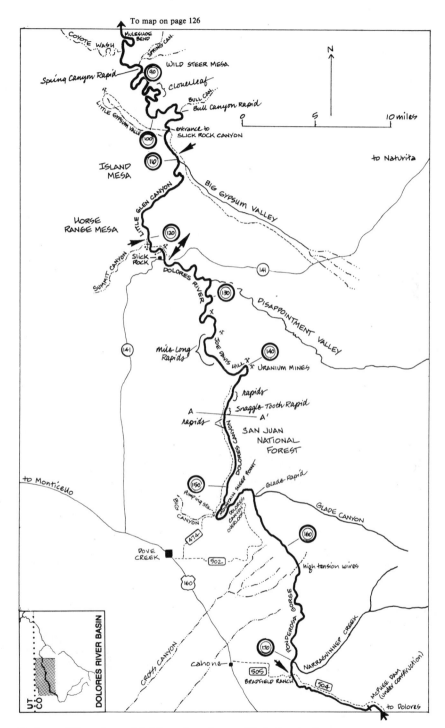

To map on page 126

Dolores River from McPhee damsite to Slick Rock Canyon.

The first moderately heavy rapid is reached at the mouth of Glade Canyon, where the river makes a sharp bend to the west. After two miles it doubles back, reestablishing its northerly course at Mountain Sheep Point.

The Dove Creek town pumping station is located on the left just past Mountain Sheep Point. A rough dirt access road to the town reaches the river here and follows the west bank for 10 miles.

Downriver, the flora changes swiftly and dramatically as the river drops from the mountain to the upper sonoran life zone. The tall evergreens of the canyon bottom give way to scrub oak, saltbrush, sage, and cacti. Cottonwoods and box elders sink their roots into the water table on the low floodplains. The canyon walls bristle with pinon and juniper. Greasewood, russian thistle, cheat grass, and milkweed depend on the sparse rainfall inside the canyon.

On an early spring trip, a tall, intermittent waterfall can be seen plunging off the east wall of the canyon near mile 144. The canyon achieves its grandest proportions, with a depth of 2,500 feet and a width from rim to rim of two miles. The Dakota Sandstone caps the rim high above. The axis of the Dolores Anticline crosses the river here. For the next 10 miles the water picks up its pace, plummeting down the back side of the uplift. Near mile 145, about six miles from the big bend at Mountain Sheep Point, boaters reach the first big rapids. Two class III rapids, Molar and Canine, greet river runners a short distance above Snaggle Tooth.

Snaggle Tooth can't be missed. The river disappears, falling away ahead. Pull over on the left and scout from the dirt road. The gentleman who named Snaggle Tooth, Doc Marston, said he caught a severe case of "rapid fever" (butterflies, sometimes accompanied by nausea) while scouting this one. It is long, steep, and boulder studded—class IV to V. Most rafters portage. Those who run it are put to the test. In the first 200 yards the river drops over a field of crashing holes; then the difficulty eases, but class III water continues for a

Snaggle Tooth Rapid. Art Hutchinson at the oars. (Tim Haske photo)

quarter of a mile around a small island.

Below Snaggle Tooth difficult rapids continue, interspersed with flat stretches. The old Mucho Grande and Uncle Sam uranium mines can be seen near the canyon rim ahead. The river sweeps around a U-shaped curve to the left near mile 140. One-half mile below the curve begins a series of long, continuous class II to III rapids—Mile Long Rapids. At higher water levels, big waves and room-sized sandstone boulders provide an exhilarating run through this section. The rapids finally dissipate near mile 135.

At mile 131 the Wingate Sandstone walls give way to more open country as we pass out of the Dolores Anticline. Flat water continues to Slick Rock. A good take-out lies on the east side of the river 50 yards above the Slick Rock Bridge.

Dolores River: Slick Rock to Bedrock (Little Glen and Slick Rock Canyons)

Physical Data: 45 mi; 440-ft drop; 10 ft/mi average gradient; 260,000 acre-ft average yearly discharge (at Slick Rock).
Maps: Slick Rock, Anderson Mesa, and Paradox USGS Quads.
Land Ownership: Mostly BLM; private land just below Slick Rock, at Big Gypsum Valley, and last two miles above Bedrock.

Slick Rock Canyon is smaller and tighter than Dolores Canyon. The river follows serpentine meanders encased in the surrounding plateau, offering a backdrop of red, orange, and white sandrock formations. It is a canyon of unparalleled beauty, completely unique.

Between the towns of Slick Rock and Bedrock the gradient eases considerably, offering a good run for skilled open canoeists as well as rafters and kayakers. Again high water is best, and the earlier the better. One often finds high water here as early as late March. Phone the Bedrock Store for flow information.

One put-in—on private land—lies at the gravel quarry above the Slick Rock Bridge. Watch out for the second bridge—many rafts have broached on its narrowly spaced pilings. A better put-in lies three miles downriver on a floodplain just beyond Summit Creek and the gas plant on Poverty Flat.

The strata immediately buckle upward as the boater enters Little Glen Canyon, only five miles long but full of wonders. It was named for the drowned canyon under Lake Powell 300 miles downriver which, though much larger, was contained within the same strata of frozen sand dunes of the Mesozoic Era—the Entrada, Navajo, Kayenta, and Wingate.

The country opens up as the Dolores comes out into Big Gypsum Valley. Watch out for barbed wire across the river here. A road leads down the valley from State Highway 141. Many parties put in here for a shorter trip. The river turns west following Big Gypsum Valley for two miles. Then it suddenly bends south, passing beneath a small bridge and crashing unexpectedly into the great wall of Wingate Sandstone that it has been paralleling. Entering Slick Rock Canyon for the first time can be as shocking as coming upon some monstrous edifice in the Mayan jungles.

In Slick Rock Canyon the river picks up its pace, washing up against ancient sandstones as it sweeps around tight curves. The first tricky rapid comes below the point where Bull Canyon enters. Bull Canyon rapid can reach class III difficulty at higher water levels. Several miles below the rapid the river follows

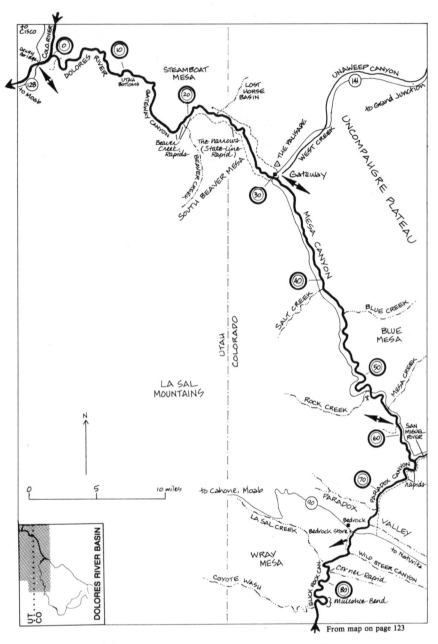

Dolores River from Slick Rock Canyon to Colorado River.

the outline of a three-leaf clover, meandering three miles to go 200 feet.

The river undercuts its sandstone walls in many places. This can be a hazard at high water levels.

Slick Rock Canyon, because it is so narrow, does not have a large number of wide campsites. Pinon and juniper trees cling to tiny patches of soil on the canyon walls. Prickly pear cactus is everywhere. Graeme McGowan, an early Dolores explorer, recalls this favored delicacy of the southwest tribes: "The picture of our second camp in Slick Rock Canyon is vivid in my memory...a great hillside covered with luxuriant growth of fat and succulent prickly pear. To think that we camped in the midst of this field of manna and departed without savoring this gourmet's delight."

A class III rapid, good campsite, and scenic side hike are found at Spring Canyon, mile 89. Three miles below, Coyote Wash from the La Sal Mountains to the west meets the river. Just downriver from Coyote Wash lies Muleshoe Bend, a perfect example of an entrenched meander about to be cut off.

Below Muleshoe the canyon begins to open up. Another class III drop is found at Corner Rapid just before La Sal Creek. A small dirt road from Bedrock follows the river to La Sal Creek. You can take out at the State Highway 90 Bridge on the right, or one mile upriver on the dirt road. The Bedrock Store offers refreshments to weary river runners. In the past the proprietors have allowed boaters to leave a shuttle car at the store.

Lounging in the shade of looming Slick Rock Canyon on the Dolores. (Jerry Mallett photo.)

Dolores River: Bedrock to Gateway (Paradox and Mesa Canyons)

Physical Data: 44 mi; 460-ft drop; 10.5 ft/mi average gradient; 20 ft/mi maximum gradient (end of Paradox Canyon); 679,000 acre-ft average yearly discharge (at Gateway).

Maps: Paradox and Gateway USGS Quads.

Land Ownership: Alternating, approximately 50% private land.

This run has much variety. The first four miles, with no rapids, crosses the Paradox Valley. The river then slices into the north wall of the valley to enter

Paradox Canyon, only five miles long but with several class III to IV rapids. Just below Paradox Canyon the Dolores meets the San Miguel; this confluence often more than doubles the size of the river. The wider canyon between the San Miguel and Gateway, called Mesa Canyon, contains no rapids more difficult than class II. State Highway 141 parallels the river here.

Historic sites abound along this section of the Dolores. The Bedrock Store was built in 1898 near the now-abandoned Cashin Copper Mine. Since then it has supplied ranchers, miners, outlaws, and now river runners with dry goods, food, and liquor. The flat floor of Paradox Valley holds many abandoned homesteads. Below the San Miguel confluence, remains of a 19th century wooden flume are seen hanging from the canyon wall. Mesa Canyon is full of abandoned gold placer mines in the valley floor and uranium mines higher on the canyon walls.

Access locations include Bedrock, the small dirt road in Paradox Canyon, several spots up the San Miguel, or any of a number of places along Highway 141 in Mesa Canyon. The Colorado Highway Department lot just above the Gateway Bridge offers a good take-out.

Dolores River: Gateway to Colorado River (Gateway Canyon)

Physical Data: 32 mi; 420-ft drop; 13 ft/mi average gradient; 50 ft/mi maximum gradient (2 mi above and below Beaver Creek); 679,000 acre-ft average yearly discharge (at Gateway).

Maps: Gateway, Polar Mesa, and Coates Creek USGS Quads.

Land Ownership: Private land at beginning and end of run; public land in the middle.

Gateway Canyon, the Dolores's final fling, is every bit as beautiful and challenging for river runners as the canyons upriver. In addition it has a longer season, because the free-flowing San Miguel contributes to its waters.

The recommended put-in lies at the Highway Department lot on the east side of the river just above the Gateway Bridge. A wide valley with dirt roads on both sides of the river brings boaters to The Narrows or State Line Rapid. This long rapid around a rock island is rated class IV or V at high water, but only class III at low water. It should be scouted. Two miles below, the river swings to the southwest and enters Gateway Canyon, where a heavy, continuous set of rapids begins. These rapids were produced by the Beaver Creek outwash pushing the river against the north wall of the canyon and by big blocks of Wingate Sandstone which have fallen off the cliff above. Below the rapids the river turns northwest again. This is the heart of Gateway Canyon, one of the narrowest and most imposing on the Dolores corridor.

The river leaves Gateway Canyon at about mile 13, slows, and meanders across broad bottomlands to the Colorado.

A good take-out can be found just above the Dewey Suspension Bridge, about a mile down the Colorado.

San Miguel River

The San Miguel is the Upper Dolores's twin. Like the Dolores, it flows westward from the San Juans, cutting its canyons deep into the Permian and Triassic Red Beds.

The massive San Miguel Glacier plowed through the upper valley where Telluride now sits, leaving its tributaries hanging high above. Today this upper valley is like a miniature Yosemite. Surrounding creeks plunge over dramatic waterfalls: Ingram, Bridal Veil, and Cornet. Along the wide valley floor the river wanders sluggishly for about five miles past Telluride before it reaches the terminal moraine left by the great San Miguel Glacier. Here it tumbles 400 feet in half a mile down the back side of the moraine to its junction with the South Fork. Below this confluence, the San Miguel can be run in May and June, and well into July during high water years.

San Miguel River: South Fork Confluence to Norwood Bridge

Physical Data: 25 mi; 1,500-ft drop; 60 ft/mi average gradient; 250,000 acre-ft average yearly discharge (at Naturita).
Maps: Gray Head, Little Cone, Placerville, Gurley Canyon, and Sanborn Park USGS Quads.
Land Ownership: Alternating private and BLM land.

Highway 145, which parallels the river along this stretch, provides scouting and access to this run. Although the gradient is relatively constant, it is steep. At high water the river is a flusher with big waves and cottonwood strainers, so be careful. Low and moderate water levels provide a safer, more interesting run.

The Bureau of Reclamation plans to build a dam in the San Miguel Canyon four miles below Placerville.

San Miguel River: Norwood Bridge to Naturita

Physical Data: 29 mi; 1,100-ft drop; 40 ft/mi average gradient; 250,000 acre-ft average yearly discharge (at Naturita).
Maps: Sanborn Park, Norwood, Redvale, Big Bucktail Creek, and Naturita USGS Quads.
Land Ownership: Alternating private and BLM land.

This is a little-known marvelous run, largely through wilderness. Easy floating for the first six miles leads past white sandstone bluffs and abandoned homesteads to Horsefly Creek. A stop and a hike up Horsefly Creek are recommended—excellent trout fishing.

A small diversion dam two miles below Horsefly Creek requires portage over private land with permission required. There are several class III rapids above and below the bridge.

From here the river enters a shallow, scenic canyon for a distance of five miles. A large powerplant is below the second bridge. This bridge is a good alternate take-out. It can be reached by turning north from State Highway 141 three miles east of Naturita. Just beyond the powerplant another dangerous weir sits in the river. The bridge at Naturita furnishes a second take-out.

San Juan River Basin

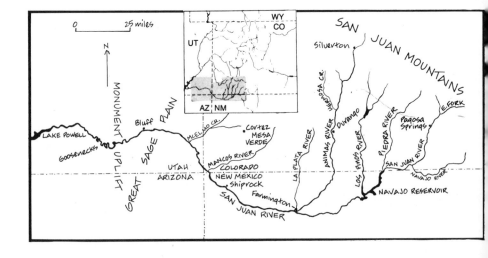

For real companionship and friendship,
there is nothing outside of the animal
kingdom that is comparable to a river.—Henry Van Dyke

The "Mad" River

The San Juan and its four major navigable tributaries—the Animas, Piedra, Los Pinos, and Navajo—drain the southern flank of the massive San Juan Mountain Range in Southwestern Colorado. At first they flow through rugged mountain canyons offering expert level kayak and raft runs. Emerging from their canyons onto the edge of the high plateau country, their decreased gradients make them enjoyable for a wider range of river runners.

The four mountain tributaries of the San Juan join the main branch as it courses westward across northern New Mexico. Near Farmington, the augmented San Juan turns gradually northwestward, entering the Navajo Indian Reservation and the arid, open country of the "four corners." Across this Great Sage Plain, sections of the river divide and rejoin around sandy islands, and steplike terraces build gradually outward from the river banks.

Downstream from Bluff, Utah, the San Juan has carved several canyons through the Monument Uplift, a north-south trending bulge in the predominantly flat strata of the Colorado Plateau in the midst of which is the town of Mexican Hat. Now an aging river, the San Juan follows the twisting, chambered labyrinth of the Great Goosenecks and finally drifts by centuries-old Anasazi ruins to meets its end in the still waters of Lake Powell.

The San Juan is one of the master rivers of the Southwest. With an average annual runoff nearing 900,000 acre-feet, it contributes about 10 percent of the Colorado's volume.

The many moods of the San Juan led the Navajo to call it Powhuska, "the mad river." Roiling dark brown with suspended mud in spring and early summer, it can carry a volume of 10,000 to 15,000 c.f.s. past the town of Bluff. At such times, the swift current with its load of sediment produces tall "sand waves." These appear in rows, creep upstream and down, then vanish only to reappear again. Late in the summer the flow sometimes diminishes to a trickle of less than 100 c.f.s. At any time, however, thunderstorms in the high mountains can raise the river to flood stage in a few hours.

Today, extremes in volume on the lower San Juan are moderated by controlled discharge from the Navajo Reservoir on the Colorado-New Mexico border. Above and below this reservoir, the San Juan, Piedra, Navajo, and Animas rivers are free-flowing. With the exception of the Animas, each is depleted to some degree by trans-basin diversions into the drainage of the Rio Grande. This loss is partially offset by ditches from the nearby Dolores River that carry as much as 700 c.f.s. southward into the San Juan Basin. The stolen Dolores irrigates farms in the Montezuma Valley and supplies municipal water to Cortez, Colorado before reaching the San Juan via McElmo Creek. Completion of the McPhee Dam on the Dolores will probably increase the volume of this diversion.

Animas River

The Animas is the largest tributary of the San Juan. It boasts some of Colorado's most imposing canyon scenery, colorful history, and enticing river running. In its southerly journey from lush mountains to desert, the character of the Animas changes swiftly and dramatically.

Beginning in snowfields on the western bulge of the Continental Divide, the Animas meets Mineral Creek at the historic mining town of Silverton. One mile downriver lie the jaws of a 5,000-foot chasm bisecting the bold and preciptious Needle Mountains. This wild canyon is intruded only by the Durango and Silverton (formerly the Denver and Rio Grande Western) narrow-gauge railroad. Beginning in 1881, steamed-powered locomotives puffed up and down the banks of the Animas hauling precious silver and gold ores from the mines around Silverton to the mills at Durango. Today the railroad carries not ore but tourists, Colorado's current golden treasure.

The 28-mile run from Silverton to Rockwood will delight experts who love the art of wilderness kayaking. Technical water and the strenuous hike out of the canyon at Rockwood serve to eliminate others.

Imposing entrance into Animas River Canyon. Needle Mountains in distance.

For a distance of two miles below Rockwood, the Animas thunders through an impassable gorge as it seeks the far edge of the mountain mass of gneiss and granite in which it has spent its youth. At the end of the gorge it reaches a transition point between resistant, crystalline bedrock and soft sedimentary strata. A dramatic change now occurs in the river. The storm calms. The river turns sluggish and glides to Durango in wide, looping meanders.

The boater is now on a floodplain as much as two miles wide, flanked by ridges of tilted, sedimentary strata which lap up against the igneous mass of the San Juan mountains. Millions of years ago, upthrusting magma burst through these sedimentary strata and erosion consumed the older overlying layers. The boater floats by what remains of the cataclysm.

Below Durango the gradient again steepens to nearly 25 feet per mile. Here, amid pleasant rural scenes, is the most popular run on the Animas for rafters, kayakers, and canoeists. Farther downstream the bluffs gradually fall away and the river flows out upon a sea of strata to meet its master, the San Juan, among the mesas.

The Animas is a free-flowing river, dependent upon the melting winter snowpack for its summer flow. After a snowy winter it will rise from 400 c.f.s. in April to over 6,000 c.f.s. in June. At very high levels the river can be treacherous. Early Spanish explorers gave it the name "El Rio de las Animas Perdidas" or the "River of Lost Souls." The name was prophetic: more than a few ill-prepared rafters have come to grief in its rapids.

Animas River: Silverton to Rockwood (Upper Run)

Physical Data: 28 mi; 2,130-ft drop; 80 ft/mi average gradient; 250,000 acre-ft average yearly discharge (near Silverton).
Maps: Silverton, Snowdon Peak, Mountain View Crest, Electra Lake, and Hermosa 7.5 minute USGS Quads; San Juan National Forest Map (U.S. Forest Service).
Land Ownership: National Forest, private, BLM.

The Animas River Canyon is safe only for expert kayakers—and then only at moderate water levels. Attempts to run the canyon in rafts have sometimes been attended with tragic results; the continuously steep gradient simply makes it too difficult to maintain consistent control of a raft. Moreover, all boats must be carried out of the canyon at the end of the run.

Rafting accidents have unfortunately tended to give the upper Animas a bad name. A Durango outfitter once called it a "killer river." On the other hand, the skilled kayaker who treats the river with knowledge and respect can capture the miracuous energy of its tumbling descent. The kayaker must be capable of quick, accurate appraisal of the river ahead, be decisive in maneuvering and eddy catching, and be willing to carry his or her boat out of the canyon. The result is a true adventure, a virtuoso ballet amid wild peaks and deep forests.

The Silverton put-in, at 9,230 feet, is among the highest in Colorado. Therefore, an early run in April or May means risking bad weather. The water is extremely cold. In years of above average snowpack, the river is considered unsafe during the high runoff between mid-May and mid-June. In late May 1978, a party of very competent kayakers reached a unanimous decision 10 miles below Silverton that the growing river was becoming too dangerous—they

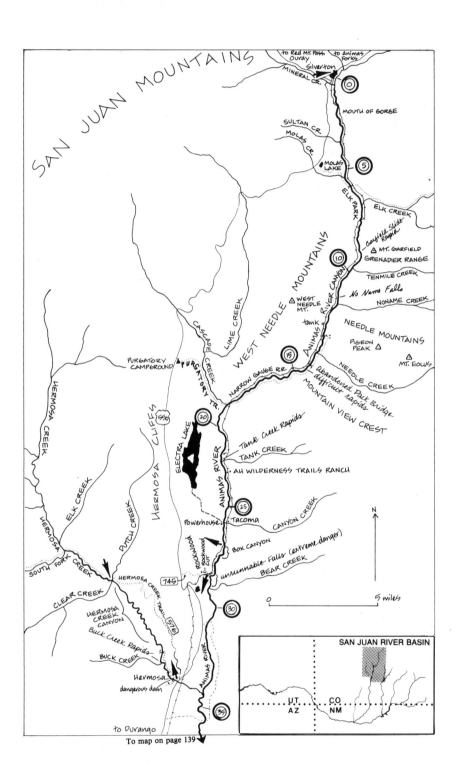

Animas River Canyon, Hermosa Creek.

pulled out even though it meant carrying their loaded boats all the way back to Silverton along the narrow-gauge tracks. In most years, the best time for moderate water and weather conditions ranges from mid-June to early August.

A few have run the river from Silverton to Rockwood in a single day. However, the distance of this run (28 miles), the need for many inspection stops, and the demanding water make a one-day run an exhausting effort. Two days is an ideal length. Forested campsites abound. The river is so enjoyable and the canyon so wildly spectacular that a leisurely three-day trip, averaging about 10 miles per day, is also an excellent choice.

The put-in at Silverton lies just south of the railroad station at a gravel quarry. A quarter of a mile downriver the Animas nearly doubles in volume with the addition of Mineral Creek. Seen from this spot, the black entrance to the Animas River Canyon frames distant peaks of the Grenadier and Needle ranges—a striking view. A low railroad bridge is reached in another half-mile. A steel fence spans the river under the bridge. At high water boaters can get by on the right. At low water it is a portage. Rapids begin shortly after the entrance to the canyon beyond the railroad bridge. From here to Elk Park (four miles) the gradient is a comparatively moderate 60 feet per mile. One difficult, boulder-studded drop in this section requires scouting. Foaming white cascades of tributary creeks, such as Cataract Gulch, Deadwood Creek, Kendall Gulch, and Sultain Creek, tumble down the nearly vertical walls of black metamorphic rock from snow-filled cirques above. As one approaches Elk Park, Mt. Garfield (13,074 feet) towers directly above the east side of the river.

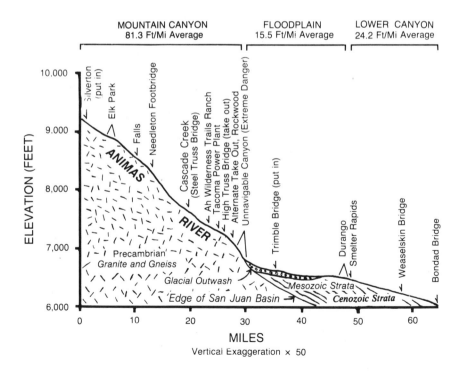

Gradient profile of Animas River from Silverton to Bondad Bridge.

A footbridge crosses the river at the upper end of Elk Park. Here, a trail leads out of the canyon. If the first five miles have proven to be too difficult, a carry-out is possible at this point. The rapids to come are far more demanding.

The next two miles through Elk Park and a short distance below it are relatively easy. A mile below the railroad bridge (mile 8.5), the rapids begin in earnest. The second of these rapids, "Slide Rapid," is reached at the base of the Garfield Slide. This is the first major rapid in the Animas Canyon; it rates class V at high water. It is nearly a quarter mile long with dangerous rails in the water on the right side. Slide Rapid should be scouted carefully.

From here to the Needleton Packbridge (six miles), boaters enjoy continous class III to IV water. In the middle of this section, however, is an eight-foot fall—class IV at lower levels to class V at high water. Difficult water occurs both above and below the fall, making it hard to spot when approaching and causing the recovery to be onerous. Successful runs are usually negotiated by taking the fall to right of center. If needed, a quick roll is advisable as the next drop (class IV) lies only 20 yards below. A take-out at least 75 yards above the fall is suggested for inspection and a possible portage on the tracks.

This part of the run lies in the heart of the canyon. The river is sandwiched between the precipitous peaks of the East and West Needle Mountains. For the next seven miles these jagged summits, several of which are over 14,000 feet, rise 5,000 feet or more above the river, crowning a dense blanket of evergreens and aspen. The Mountain View Crest, almost 13,000 feet high, dominates the skyline to the south. Do not be surprised if that muskrat swimming across the stream climbs the bank in the form of a ponderous black bear.

Two miles below the packbridge at Needleton at the base of Mountain View Crest, the Animas turns westward under an abandoned steel-truss footbridge (mile 15). The next 200 yards holds one of the most difficult rapids on the river. An inspection stop here is recommended.

Jim Gonski approaches falls at Mile 12 in Animas River Canyon.

In the following five miles the boater passes numerous pine-covered benches, several cabins, and a few teetering footbridges. There are many excellent camping spots. Passing under the second active steel-truss railroad bridge, the Animas meets Cascade Creek, a major tributary entering from the west. Below Cascade Creek the river changes character, becoming wider and less boulder-choked. It passes alternating ponderosa-covered benches and short box canyons. Alders along the bank give way to tall cottonwoods. Scrub oak covers the slopes. Here the rapids are better defined, and there are easy stretches between them. They include several rated class IV. At mile 23, Tank Creek Rapid, which is reached half a mile below a guest ranch on the left, is the biggest on this part of the river. It consists of three drops in a shallow inner gorge. The first drop is the most difficult with a huge hole in its mid-section.

After passing several private ranches one reaches the hydroelectric power plant at Tacoma that has generated power for Durango since 1906. Water from Electra Lake drops down the canyon wall through penstocks into generators housed in an old brick building at river level. The turbine-whipped froth gushes into the Animas from a pipe in the red brick facade.

The high steel-truss bridge one mile downriver from Tacoma is the usual take-out, particularly at higher water levels. A two-mile walk down the railroad tracks through a cut leads to the road at Rockwood. It is preferable, however, to run the river for the next two miles to a final take-out where a small side valley leads up to the Rockwood Cut. The first mile of this run below the bridge is in a vertical-walled slot that hides several ferocious class IV rapids. The first rapid in the slot should be run on the far right, up against the wall. Look for a short, boulder-strewn rapid where the river emerges from the slot. At high water this difficult rapid is impossible to scout. Above the rapid, one can observe the railroad turning westward to leave the Animas River gorge. Four more rapids in the next half-mile lead to the take-out. The carry from the final take-out to the Rockwood Cut is steep but short and avoids all but a few hundred yards of track.

Do not attempt the river below Rockwood. The next three miles consists of a tortuous, boxed-in tumult with a 250-foot-per-mile gradient. In the middle is a massive and deadly log jam. This section can't be run at any level.

Most of the riverbed from Silverton to Rockwood is on National Forest and BLM land. There are several private ranches along the last eight miles. Check the railroad schedule to avoid trains, in case you must walk on the tracks.

Animas River: Trimble Bridge to Durango (The Middle Run)

This is a pleasant 10-mile run for open canoes and flat water enthusiasts. The gradient is only five feet per mile. Most people put in at Trimble Bridge to the east of U.S. Highway 550 seven miles north of Durango. The Animas meanders in wide loops across an open floodplain of glacial drift dumped here at the base of the Needleton granite block during the last ice age. Red-tailed hawks soar low over the fields, and spotted sandpipers bob on the banks. Meanders have a nasty habit of growing by erosion of the outer bank. Some ranchers use old auto bodies in an effort to solve this problem. Courtesy toward the owners of these riverside ranches will help insure continued enjoyment of this tranquil run. Most canoeists take out at the 32nd Street Bridge in north Durango.

Animas River: Durango to Bondad Bridge (Lower Run)

Physical Data: 20 mi; 485-ft drop; 24.2 ft/mi average gradient; 635,000 acre-ft average yearly discharge.

Maps: Durango West, Loma Linda, Basin Mountain, and Bondad Hill 7.5 minute USGS Quads.

Land Ownership: Southern Ute Indian Reservation; National Forest.

Information: Southern Ute Indian Tribe, Ignacio, CO 81137; San Juan National Forest, Animas District, Durango, CO 81301.

This is a popular novice- to intermediate-level run. Rafters, kayakers, and open canoeists all find gentle water and quiet beauty in the Animas Valley.

Put-ins are found along the dirt road skirting the west side of the river just north of the U.S. Highway 160 Bridge on the west side of Durango. The biggest rapid on the entire run lies about a half mile downriver from this put-in area on an "S" curve beside the stack of an abandoned smelter. Smelter Rapid is class II to III, with big waves at high water.

A second Highway 160 Bridge is encountered beyond Smelter Rapid, then a K-Mart Shopping Center and a last U.S. 160 Bridge before the Animas leaves town. The biggest rapids on the run lie in these first two miles.

West of the last highway bridge La Posta Road, a dirt road, takes off downriver following the west side of the valley. This road provides several good access points. Railroad tracks follow the east side of the Animas Valley. The tracks and road are visible only occasionally from the river.

A good alternate access point can be found a stone's throw off the La Posta Road one mile downriver from the last Highway 160 Bridge, just past an abandoned cable bridge across the river. The Animas is good for open canoeists below this point.

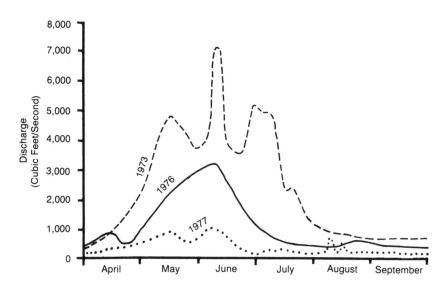

Hydrograph of Animas River at Durango.

Three miles below Durango boaters enter Southern Ute Indian land and are the tribe's guests down to the Bondad area take-out. The Southern Ute tribe requires a permit for travel on their land.

There are plenty of rocks to dodge at low water and waves at higher levels. Several small rock weirs along the way produce minor rapids.

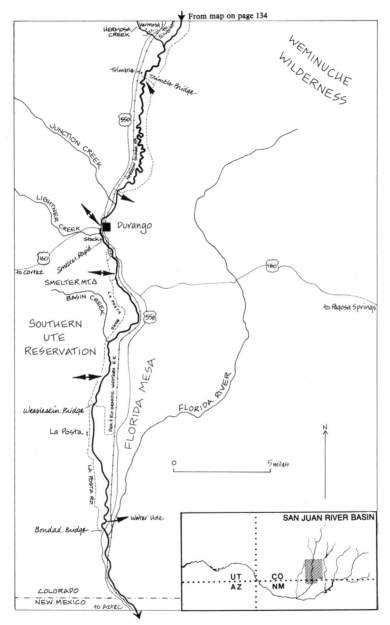

Animas River from Hermosa Creek confluence to Colorado-New Mexico border.

Bottomlands harboring old homesteads and an occasional mining ruin are seen. Benches of glacial outwash from the high San Juans lie in the foreground. There are three levels of terrace gravels. The terrace 20 feet above the river represents the most recent Wisconsin Age glaciation. The terrace at about 50 feet consists of remnants from the older Durango Age glaciation. The highest outwash terraces tower 200 feet above the Animas. They represent the first and oldest glacial stage in the San Juans: the Florida stage. The reddish outwash gravels capping the terraces contrast sharply with the Tertiary Age beige and grey shales underneath.

Along the river corridor we find a large variety of vegetation including alders, mountain mahogany, box elders, and lots of scrub oak. The distant hillsides are dotted with a sparse pinon-juniper forest.

Eleven miles below Durango, about halfway down the run, the Weaselskin Bridge spans the Animas. It can be reached by driving two miles west from U.S. Highway 550 but is not recommended because it lies on private land. A much better access point is found two miles upriver from the Weaselskin Bridge in a cottonwood grove off La Posta Road.

Below the Weaselskin Bridge the character of the valley changes. The river slows and meanders through low floodplains covered with tall cottonwoods. Low bluffs are encountered just above the Bondad Bridge. The Bondad Bridge is not a recommended take-out due to a strenuous climb and private land. A much better access point, though still on private property, is found one mile upriver from the Bondad Bridge at a place called Water Hole. A small fee is charged for use of Water Hole. Another access point is found one mile downriver from the Bondad Bridge opposite a road cut.

Below the Bondad Bridge, the Animas leaves the broad glacial terraces and enters a scenic canyon. Its gradient is about 15 feet per mile here. Highway 550 and the tracks of the Denver and Rio Grande Western Railroad can be used to scout the river.

Soon the Animas leaves its canyons and meets the San Juan near Farmington, New Mexico.

The proposed Animas-La Plata Project is of concern to river runners because it would severely reduce the volume of water in the Animas Valley. The Bureau of Reclamation plans to shift part of the Animas west to the smaller La Plata River Basin. This could mean the end of late summer and fall boating.

Hermosa Creek

Here is another of Colorado's hidden forest gems. Since it requires a four-mile hike to the put-in, Hermosa Creek is rarely kayaked. But if one enjoys small, technical rivers that require constant attention and provide endless entertainment, there is none better. Hermosa Creek is an advanced to expert kayak stream.

Only the last 10 miles of this tiny river are considered navigable. It has carved a narrow, twisting gorge in Pennsylvanian-age strata of the Hermosa Formation. Wildlife abounds along its banks. Dippers play endlessly in the tumbling descent. A deep, mixed spruce-fir forest clothes the canyon. Hiking along the banks is so tortuous that the only practical way to visit this halcyon stream is by kayak. At the end of the run, the dark canyon of Hermosa Creek quickly opens into the light of the wide Animas River Valley north of

Railroad water tanks in Animas Canyon. Mountain View Crest in distance to the south.

Durango.

To reach Hermosa Creek, turn westward from U.S. Highway 550 on County Road 576 at the town of Hermosa, nine miles north of Durango. This road follows the north rim of the inner canyon for about four miles until it deadends at the trail head. The trail upriver from this point is well traveled and relatively smooth. A small, wheeled rig attached to one end of your kayak will help you up the trail. Boats can also be carried two by two or dragged. The four-mile trail gradually descends to the river at the triple confluence of Dutch

Unnavigable gorge on the Animas, downriver from Rockwood.

Creek, Clear Creek, and Hermosa Creek. From here the distance downriver to Highway 550 is about eight miles. For those who wish a longer run, the trail continues up to the north bank of Hermosa Creek three miles to its South Fork.

With its 100-foot-per-mile gradient, Hermosa Creek contains continuous, complex rapids and small falls—a marvelous conundrum. There are no falls that can't be run, but several of these, varying between four and six feet in height, should probably be scouted.

As is typical of small, forest-draped rivers, snags and logs will often be encountered in the water. During two runs in 1979 and 1981, however, there were no log jams necessitating a carry except at the end of the dark canyon where the Hermosa Creek gorge opens out into the Animas Valley. Here at a sharp right turn is Buck Creek Rapid, a double drop. The first drop holds a log jam with no easy passage. The second drop is a long, complex, class IV rapid. From this rapid to Highway 550, watch for irrigation intake structures. The first, half a mile below Buck Creek Rapid, is a crude pile of rocks and cement, about five feet high and runnable. The second, just 300 yards upsteam from the highway, is a dangerous dam with sinister cement teeth at its base—a mandatory carry. The best take-out lies just downriver from this dam at a small bridge 200 yards upstream from Highway 550.

Do not judge Hermosa Creek by viewing it from the Highway 550 Bridge. The big irrigation intake dam 300 yards upstream could be diverting nearly the entire creek. Instead, to make your observations, drive up the north side past the irrigation diversions into the rural village of Hermosa. In an average year, Hermosa Creek is navigable from early May to about mid-June at a recommended volume level of 300 to 800 c.f.s. In a dry year, the run can be made only toward the end of May. Because of steep gradient and abundant snags, very high water levels are considered hazardous. If there has been heavy snowpack, it is advisable to stay off the creek during the high water period from late May through early June. At high water the volume can approach 2,000 c.f.s.

Piedra River

The Piedra is a rare jewel in Colorado's crown. It was originally named "Rio de la Piedra Parada," or "River of the Rock Wall," by explorers Dominguez and Escalante.

Rising on the southwest face of the Continental Divide, this little sister of the Animas carves a fascinating 20-mile canyon through alternating forest-blanketed slopes and narrow box canyons of ancient, crystalline rock. The Piedra is steep, free-flowing, clear, and cold. Its bed is boulder-strewn, its banks lined with twisting alders. Trails follow and cross the river in places. A rough dirt road meets the river halfway down the run at Hunter Campground. The upper section, from the Piedra Road Bridge to the campground at First Fork, is a remote 10-mile run suitable for upper-intermediate paddlers. The lower half, which includes First Box Canyon, is exhilarating and technical. It is for skilled paddlers only. Precipitous First Box Canyon could be the rock wall that inspired the naming of the Piedra.

The upper section has proven too small and the lower section too technical for consistently good rafting. Logs in the water are a common obstacle on this small, forest-sheltered stream. Arduous and exposed portages greet those who come upon rapids beyond their capabilities. A climb out of either of the two box canyons, whether due to loss of confidence or loss of boat, would be a notable mountaineering achievement. As always, special caution is advised at high water levels. At such times, the flow is very swift for a two-mile stretch in First Box Canyon. It plunges over big drops. The nearly vertical walls close in, offering few places for a paddler to get ashore.

The Piedra is currently receiving long-overdue consideration for possible inclusion in the National Wild and Scenic Rivers System. A perfect candidate for wild river status, this wilderness stream possesses the qualifying value: "outstandingly remarkable." Timber companies, for obvious reasons, strongly oppose inclusion.

The Piedra Canyon has been incised into a small plateau on the southern flank of the San Juan Mountains. The Piedra plateau is capped by resistant Cretaceous Dakota Sandstone, which boaters pass in a short, sheer canyon a quarter of a mile downriver from the Piedra Road Bridge. The Dakota Sandstone forms the canyon rim beyond.

Driven by the volcanic energy that raised the San Juan Mountains, plugs of ancient metamorphic rock were thrust upward into the underbelly of the plateau. In its relentless downcutting, the Piedra encountered these resistant, crystalline domes. Having already established its course, the river was forced to cut through them, forming precipitous box canyons along its course.

One of the most interesting geologic windows on the past, the predepositional erosion surface known as the Great Unconformity is splendidly revealed in the box canyons. Here Paleozoic limestones are in angular contact with the continental basement rock in the canyon walls. With their narrow inner gorges of ancient basement rock, planed off by erosion and capped by marine strata, the box canyons of the Piedra are miniatures of Granite Gorge on the Colorado River.

Outside the boxes the river cuts through softer Paleozoic and Mesozoic formations, which are responsible for the more gently sloping valleys. These marine-deposited rocks contain numerous crinoids, brachiopods, and other invertebrate fossils. Above the limestones, red, orange, and white cliffs of Entrada and Wingate sandstone, laid down in the Jurassic Period, rise above the spruce-fir forest.

A sharp, south-dipping monoclinal fold is the principal geologic feature where the Piedra emerges from its canyon close to U.S. Highway 160. Here the river encounters much younger strata before it meets the San Juan River on the roof of the San Juan Basin.

Piedra River: Piedra Road Bridge to U.S. 160

Physical Data: 20 mi; 1,100-ft drop; 55 ft/mi average gradient; 100 ft/mi maximum gradient (first box canyon); 234,600 acre-ft average yearly discharge (near Highway 160).

Maps: Oakbrush Ridge, Bear Mountain, Devil Mountain, and Chimney Rock 7.5 minute USGS Quads.

Land Ownership: National Forest, except private ranches in first mile and last two miles.

This superb 20-mile run is usually paddled in one or two days. Numerous inspection stops and tempting play areas invite a two-day trip. It is possible to cache camping equipment in a car parked at Hunter Campground opposite First Fork, approximately half-way down. Some parties run with loaded kayaks, anticipating the many delicious, solitary, spruce-draped campsites along the river.

Like other rivers flowing out of the southwestern Colorado Mountains, the Piedra peaks early, usually in mid-May. The volume drops quickly through June and July (see hydrograph).

Water Level at the U.S. Highway 160 Crossing	c.f.s.	Comments
Low	350 to 500	Sufficient water only in lower section.
Moderate	500 to 1000	Sufficient water in both sections for kayaks, and expert rafters; upper section rocky.
High	1000 to 2000	Swift; big holes; kayaks only.
Very high	Over 2000	Hazardous.

In an average runoff year, the best time to kayak the Piedra is in May and June. In a heavy runoff year, plan your trip before or after high water.

At the put-in near Piedra Road Bridge ten miles north of Pagosa Springs, the river is no more than a large creek. During the next five miles, three major tributaries enter from the high San Juans to the north, each boosting the river's volume significantly. This pristine valley has not yet been invaded by roads. You will feel a sense of solitude drifting on a clear, quiet stream through deep green forests.

The first difficult rapid is encountered one mile downriver from the Piedra's confluence with Sand Creek near the entrance to Second Box Canyon. (The numerical designations of the two canyons may seem confusing, since this is the first box canyon reached. However, if the names were given to the canyons by explorers pressing upriver, this would have been the second box canyon they encountered.) Second Box Canyon Rapid is a long one (approximately

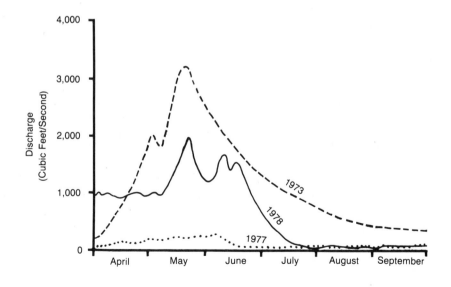

Hydrograph of Piedra River near U.S. 160 Bridge.

100 yards) with many holes, rated class IV at most levels. Two more drops, easier than the first, greet the boater in Second Box, where knifelike edges of Precambrian and Paleozoic metamorphosed strata plunge nearly vertically down the steep walls into the river. Limestone Rapid lies 200 yards past the area where the river begins to emerge from Second Box. This class IV drop features a slot through large limestone blocks followed by a sharp right turn at a wall on the left.

In the remaining four miles to Hunter Campground at First Fork, the Piedra's wilderness canyon offers continuous class II to III boating. Watch for log jams.

If the water level in the upper section is too low, you can put in at Hunter Campground for a run on the lower section of the Piedra. The campground is located halfway between the put-in and Highway 160.

Enlarged by First Fork, the river below Hunter Campground rushes due south into First Box Canyon through glades of pine and fir. Here it flexes its muscles. If one has had any difficulty on the upper section, it would be wise to save the more difficult First Box for another day. A block-filled rapid culminating in a low falls is encountered at the narrow entrance to the canyon. A steep series of drops on a left turn, a short pool, and a walloping 15-foot, boulder-studded drop follow. Inspection of this drop is best accomplished river-left. At low water, the left side is clogged and the right falls can be run. Three more class IV rapids, interspersed by smooth pools, are encountered in First Box. The eerie, sheer canyon walls meet the river for lengthy stretches.

The boater emerges abruptly from First Box. The dark shadowy canyon suddenly gives way to luminous slopes blanketed with evergreens. Rectangular blocks of white limestone lie jumbled in the riverbed. An intricate rapid, through which it is difficult to execute a clean run, sits at the canyon's mouth.

In 1979 a tremendous landslide brought down the right side of the canyon about half a mile past the First Box. The slide shoved the river into a narrow slot against its left wall and created a new rapid—Eye of the Needle. Automobile-sized blocks from the slide remain in the river. At low water the river slips between them through a slit barely wide enough for a kayak. At high water the blocks create a vertical fall seven feet high with a tremendous backwash—a mandatory portage.

Immediately below Eye of the Needle lies the Piedra's final class IV rapid, Climax. Complex maneuvering is required to get through this one. There is no practical portage, due to vertical walls on both sides.

As one approaches Sheep Creek, the Piedra's difficulty eases considerably. Enjoyable class I to II boating as far as the Lower Piedra Campground allows one's attention to be diverted to the abundant wildlife.

The Lower Piedra Campground, one mile north of the Highway 160 Bridge, is the most convenient take-out. Several ranches are crossed in the final two miles above the campground take-out. Barbed wire has been found spanning the river in this area.

Piedra River: Highway 160 Bridge to Navajo Reservoir

Below Highway 160, the gradient eases to about 20 feet per mile. The Piedra meanders southward through groves of cottonwoods across a narrow flood-plain. There are no difficult rapids in the 10-mile stretch to the Navajo Reservoir, but boaters should be alert for sweepers and barbed wire when passing through this ranch country. There are several take-outs along State Highway 151 above the Navajo Reservoir. Many Pueblo Indian ruins are found east of the river in the Chimney Rock Archaeological Area.

Upper San Juan River

The Upper San Juan gathers in the high mountains of the same name, east and west of Wolf Creek Pass. The east and west fork of the river join near U.S. Highway 160 10 miles from Pagosa Springs. The West Fork is not attractive for boating. The East Fork, on the other hand, can be boated for several miles up from the confluence, where its narrow canyon sports some challenging class IV and V whitewater. The most difficult rapids on the entire San Juan River await the boater in this lower section of the East Fork and for several miles downriver from the confluence.

The San Juan loses much of its attractiveness as it approaches Pagosa Springs. Below the town, however, lies Mesa Canyon—a charming, remote stretch of novice to intermediate difficulty. Then the country opens up and an uncrowded dirt road parallels the river in the wide valley from Mesa Canyon to the Navajo Reservoir. Most of the land south of Pagosa Springs is part of the Southern Ute Reservation.

The canyons of both the east and west forks of the Upper San Juan River cut through lavas, breccias, and tuffs of the eruptive Tertiary Period. The edge of the volcanic rock is at their confluence. From here to the Navajo Reservoir, the San Juan crosses first Cretaceous, then Tertiary age strata. Below Pagosa Springs the river splits Eight-Mile Mesa, capped by the resistant Dakota Sandstone. Here in Mesa Canyon, black basaltic dikes jut from the canyon slopes, and several cross the river, forming natural weirs.

Below Mesa Canyon the river reaches younger Tertiary strata, including the coal-bearing Mesa Verde Sandstone, purple conglomerates of the McDermott Formation, and the white Animas Sandstone.

Like the Animas and Piedra, the Upper San Juan leaves the San Juan Mountains through successively younger strata, approaching the apex of the huge structural syncline known as the San Juan Basin. It encounters no granitic basement rock, however, and thus lacks the deep, precipitous canyons found along the Animas and Piedra.

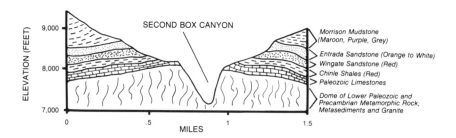

Cross section of Piedra Canyon at Second Box Canyon (generalized geologic stratigraphy).

Upper San Juan River: Sand Creek Confluence to U.S. Highway 160 Bridge

Physical Data: 8 mi; 920-ft drop; 115 ft/mi average gradient; 160 ft/mi maximum gradient (below Sand Creek); 95,000 acre-ft average yearly discharge (East Fork).
Maps: Wolf Creek Pass 15 minute USGS Quad; San Juan National Forest Map.
Land Ownership: East Fork is National Forest. Beyond confluence, alternating private ranches and National Forest.

This is exclusively an expert kayak run. It leads down the final three miles of the San Juan's East Fork, past East Fork Campground to the West Fork confluence, and onward five miles to the U.S. Highway 160 Bridge. Extremely challenging rapids lie on the upper portion of the run.

Immediately below the Sand Creek put-in lies horrendous East Fork Gorge, a half-mile class V torrent. Scout it carefully from just off the road on the south rim. This run can be avoided by putting in at the bridge at the end of the gorge or one mile downriver at the East Fork Campground. A tiny river, the East Fork can be run only during high water periods. Log jams are a hazard in this densely forested canyon.

At the West Fork confluence, the canyon widens as boaters pass Saddleback Ranch. Several steep, boulder-filled rapids catch the paddler's attention as the river's volume more than doubles. The water becomes progressively easier through alternating forests and pastoral ranchlands to the take-out at the Highway 160 Bridge. From here to Pagosa Springs the San Juan's bed, heavily bulldozed for gravel, has been stripped of its beauty and transformed into a grotesque ravine.

Upper San Juan River: Pagosa Springs to Trujillo (Mesa Canyon)

Physical Data: 16 mi; 500-ft drop; 31 ft/mi average gradient; 275,000 acre-ft average yearly discharge.
Maps: Pagosa Springs 7.5 minute and Pagosa Junction 15 minute USGS Quads; San Juan National Forest map.
Land Ownership: San Juan National Forest, Southern Ute Reservation.

The put-in is adjacent to the downtown Pagosa Springs Bridge across the San Juan. A sulfurous smell permeates the air from a nearby hot springs. Before leaving town, boaters must pass sweepers, several unkempt backyards, the sewage disposal pond, and the tiny La Plata powerplant. Ahead lies remote, serene Mesa Canyon.

The rapids in Mesa Canyon reach class III at higher water levels. The run is suitable for intermediate kayakers and advanced open canoeists. Rubber rafts of the six- to ten-person size are excellent choices.

A small portion of the area is included within the San Juan National Forest, but most of the canyon crosses an extension of the Southern Ute Indian Reservation. This may explain why the scenic canyon has not yet been developed. Many local people hope it never will be.

An occasional abandoned homestead; rusted mining implements; and weathered, log-bridge abutments are the sole evidence of human intrusion here. Junipers dot the south-facing slopes while ponderosa pines cover those facing north. Ducks are common, especially during their early May migration. Golden eagles and soaring hawks, including both red-tailed and swainsons, en-

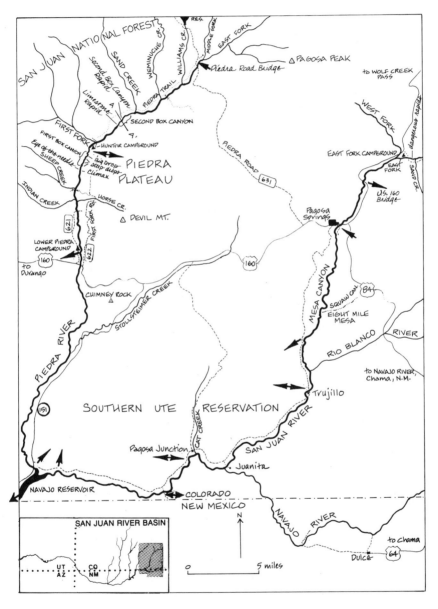

Piedra, Upper San Juan, and Navajo Rivers.

joy the more open habitat. Other birds which frequent Mesa Canyon on migratory stops include western bluebirds, western tanagers, Lewis's woodpeckers, and numerous species of warblers.

Below Squaw Canyon, entering from the east, are several long, fairly complex rapids and a basaltic dike over which the water pours into a recirculating hole. In April 1977, a barbed wire fence spanned the river where it crosses ranchland north of the Rio Blanco. Near the San Juan's confluence with what remains of the tiny Rio Blanco River (which can't be run since most of it has been exported to the Rio Grande River Basin), a local dirt road approaches the river. A take-out is possible here, at the Trujillo Bridge or at any of several spots further downriver.

Upper San Juan River: Trujillo to Navajo Reservoir

Physical Data: 27 mi; 540-ft drop; 20 ft/mi average gradient; 320,000 acre-ft average yearly discharge.
Maps: Pagosa Junction and Carracas 7.5 minute USGS Quads.
Land Ownership: Southern Ute Reservation.

Dominguez and Escalante, after traveling down the Navajo River from near Dulce, reached the San Juan near Pagosa Junction August 7, 1776. They described this country as having "leafy forests of white poplars, low oaks, cherry trees, apple trees, citron (lemon) trees and cacti." Little changed, it remains one of Colorado's enchanting, rural canoeing valleys.

Boaters can scout much of this stretch from the dirt road paralleling the river. Access is found at the Juanita Bridge above the Navajo River, the Carracas Bridge, the Navajo Reservoir, or several other places where river and road converge.

The gradient here is gentler than in Mesa Canyon above. North of Pagosa Junction are several class I to II rapids. Between these and Navajo Reservoir one finds mostly flat water.

Pines cover the 1,000-foot-high slopes along this stretch behind a floodplain embellished with groves of tall cottonwoods and box elders. Small ranches nestle between the cottonwoods.

Navajo River

Rising high in the southeast edge of the San Juan range, the Navajo River glides westward through canyons hidden in the wild country of the Jicarilla Apache and Southern Ute Indian reservations, near the Colorado-New Mexico border. It is the easternmost of the major San Juan tributaries.

The Navajo was a good backcountry canoe trip before 1970. That season the Azotea Trans-basin Tunnel began diverting the river through the Continental Divide eastward into the Rio Grande Basin via the Rio Chama River. The total volume of diversion, including the Rio Blanco river diversion, reaches 110,000 acre-feet per year, the equivalent of a small river. Since 1970 the river has averaged a meager 55,000 acre-feet per year, less than half of its original volume.

Today it is only marginally possible to run the last 25 miles of the Navajo at high water. Boating is class I. Secluded camp spots, abandoned homesteads, and steep walls of Mesa Verde and Animas sandstones embellish the canyon. One finds many annoying fences. The abandoned grade of the Denver and Rio Grande Western Railroad parallels the river, and several small dirt roads enter the canyon. Access is found on roads leading north and west from Dulce, New Mexico. A convenient take-out lies at Pagosa Junction on the San Juan River, just below its confluence with the Navajo.

Lower San Juan River

From Farmington, New Mexico, to Lake Powell, a distance of 182 miles, the San Juan lazily traverses the desolate southwest corner of the Colorado Plateau. The Great Sage Plain from Farmington to Bluff, Utah, is rarely boated. Below Bluff, however, the river has sculpted two wild canyons through resistant strata. The shorter canyon ends at Mexican Hat and the longer, lower canyon winds through the Great Goosenecks to Lake Powell. These canyons, bisecting the north-south trending Monument Uplift, have enchanted river runners for many years.

Free-flowing tributaries of the San Juan—including the Animas, La Plata, and Mancos—contribute about half the river's water in its lower canyons. The remainder of the lower San Juan's volume is controlled by releases from the big Navajo Reservoir east of Farmington. A glance at the hydrograph shows that the river can be run all year after a heavy snowpack season in the San Juan Mountains. The high water months of May and June, when the river's volume can exceed 10,000 c.f.s., remains the most popular season.

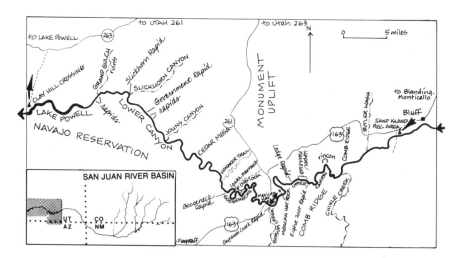

Lower canyons of the San Juan River.

An unusual weather phenomenon occurs frequently in the lower canyons: intense windstorms. These have acquired some notoriety for sandblasting river runners. Such a storm can be so violent it is often best to stop and wait it out, sometimes for a day or more.

Studies have shown that at high water as much as 20 per cent of the lower San Juan's volume consists of silt and sand. Thickened by such suspended sediments, the lower San Juan is referred to as the "river of concrete," or as a "butterscotch milkshake."

Lower San Juan River: Farmington, New Mexico to Bluff, Utah

In this 100-mile stretch, the San Juan sweeps gently through the sage desert of the Navajo and Ute Mountain Indian Reservations. Stream terraces, formed during ancient floods, rise laterally from the river like giant steps. The water divides and reforms in braided patterns among lenticular sandbars and islands.

At low water the river is both shallow and sluggish. A trip during high water offers livelier passage. Few people use the San Juan in this barren region, and quiet solitude can be found here. Canoe and raft trips of beginner level are worth consideration. Rough dirt roads, some leading to oil and gas fields, skirt the river in places.

Good access is available at the town of Shiprock, the U.S. Highway 164 Bridge, the town of Aneth, and near Bluff. The gradient diminishes from 15 feet per mile below Farmington to less than six feet per mile above Bluff. Tamarisk on sandy bottomlands give way to cottonwood groves downriver. Jurassic sandstones support the low bluffs and mesas that dot the horizon.

Lower San Juan River: Bluff to Clay Hills Crossing

Physical Data: 84 mi; 670-ft drop; 8 ft/mi average gradient; 1,895,000 acre-ft average yearly discharge (at Mexican Hat).

Maps: Bluff, Mexican Hat, Goulding, and Grand Gulch 15 minute USGS Quads; Scroll Map, available from Les Jones of Heber, Utah.

Land Ownership: Navajo Indian Reservation south of river; Glen Canyon National Recreation Area from Goosenecks to Lake Powell; remainder BLM.

Information: San Juan Area Office, BLM, Monticello, Utah 84535.

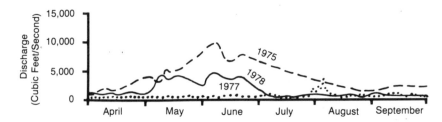

Hydrograph of San Juan River near Mexican Hat.

San Juan River between Goosenecks and Lake Powell.

The lower San Juan has been described in detail in other publications and will not be considered at length here. Probably the best source of information is *Geology of the Canyons of the San Juan River* by D.L. Baars. This small book is available from the Four Corners Geological Society in Durango. It contains an excellent mile-by-mile description of the run in addition to historical and geological information. For those interested in the wildlife and natural history of the region, Ann Zwinger's *Wind in the Rock* is recommended.

The two lower canyons of the San Juan offer a superb wilderness expedition. No rapids greater than class III will be found. The most popular crafts are the five-to-ten-person rubber rafts. Light rapids and warm water also help make this an ideal training ground for the novice kayaker. At lower water levels, advanced open canoeists can negotiate the rapids with ease.

The 84-mile stretch from Bluff to Clay Hills Crossing on Lake Powell is usually run in four to six days. Anasazi ruins, good camping, and numerous side canyons to explore encourage a leisurely expedition. The arid climate allows little vegetation except cactus, sage, and rabbitbrush. Tamarisk lines the river in many places.

Permits (issued by the Bureau of Land Management, San Juan Office, at Monticello, Utah 84523) are required for the run from Bluff to Mexican Hat. The Glen Canyon National Recreation Area authorities (Page, Arizona 86040) issue permits for the stretch from Mexican Hat to Lake Powell.

The 27 miles from Bluff to Mexican Hat can be run in one day at high water, although a longer trip is preferable. Sand waves provide excitement along this stretch when water is high. They appear as a series of parallel waves perpendicular to the channel and up to six feet in height. They move slowly upstream, building, then breaking. Such waves can look ferocious to individuals unfamiliar with them. They provide rare surfing thrills.

Just below Butler Wash (five miles downstream from Bluff) there is a large panel of well-preserved petroglyphs chipped into the Navajo Sandstone wall on the right. Ruins are abundant along the river and up the side canyons in this area.

The river enters the upper canyon suddenly, slicing into Comb Ridge on the

Kayakers run big drop in first box canyon of the Piedra.

east flank of the Monument Upwarp. The average gradient increases to 10 feet per mile through the upper canyon with several class II to III drops, including Eight Foot and Ledge rapids.

Two and a half miles into the upper canyon, a perched, abandoned meander (or rincon) is visible on the right providing an interesting side hike.

The appearance of Mexican Hat Rock after the upper canyon signals the approaching access point. There is a boatramp off U.S. Highway 163 east of town and another at the base of a steep dirt road just upriver from the highway bridge. The valley of Mexican Hat is formed by the Mexican Hat Syncline, a small downwarp in the huge Monument Uplift.

Below Mexican Hat the river drifts again into a deep, narrow canyon which reaches a depth of 1,300 feet through the famous Goosenecks. Here the looping river incised itself into the west side of the Monument Uplift. Through the Goosenecks the dominant riverine vegetation is bothersome tamarisk. Several class I rapids break the flatwater as the canyon deepens. Make sure your taxes are paid before entering Government Rapids, rated class II to III. Below Government Rapids, the gradient again increases slightly, with some lively running past Slickhorn Canyon and Grand Gulch to Lake Powell. When the reservoir is filled, its waters come up almost to Grand Gulch.

A 10-mile dirt road reaches the take-out at Clay Hills Crossing from Utah Highway 263 east of Clay Hills Divide.

The colorful canyon wilderness through which the San Juan once ran to its juncture with the Colorado is drowned today. Old timers like Bert Loper, Norman Nevills, and Georgie White introduced many people to this beautiful canyon. Great rapids like Paiute, Syncline, and Thirteen Foot are now lost forever beneath the still waters behind Glen Canyon Dam.

Upper Green River Basin

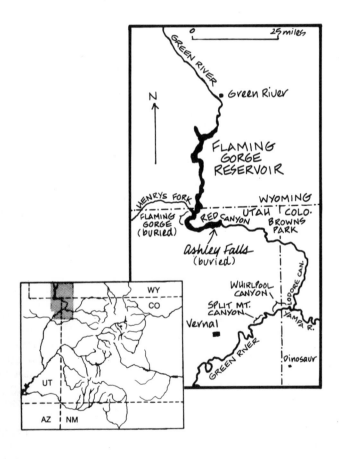

As we passed along between these massy walls, which in a great degree excluded from us the rays of heaven and presented a surface as impassable as their body was impregnable, I was forcibly struck with the gloom which spread over the countenances of my men; they seemed to anticipate (and not far distant, too) a dreadful termination of our voyage, and I must confess that I partook in some degree of what I supposed to be their feelings, for things around us had truly an awful appearance.

—William Ashley

Pioneers on the Green

Long before the well-planned expeditions of John Wesley Powell, the Kolb brothers, and the Geological Survey, two hastily organized voyages were launched down the Green from southern Wyoming. The first was headed by William H. Ashley.

The impulse to go West took young Ashley from Virginia to Missouri early in the 19th century. Here he displayed military and political talent as a general in the Missouri militia and as the state's Lieutenant Governor. Having failed in a bid for the governorship, however, he was left heavily in debt.

With an experienced partner, Andrew Henry, he again headed westward in 1822 to recoup his fortunes in the blossoming fur trade.

The two partners recruited "enterprising young men" to accompany them into the wilderness. Their plan was to venture up the Missouri, fan out to trap beaver, and then assemble at a designated rendezvous point rather than at a traditional trading post. Many of the men Ashley and Henry selected would later become legendary. Among them were Kit Carson, scout for Fremont's exploring expeditions, emigrant guide, and Indian expert; Jim Bridger, discoverer of the Great Salt Lake at the end of a bull boat run down the Bear River; John Colter, discoverer of the Yellowstone region; Jedediah Smith, explorer of a central route to the Pacific and first to cross the Sierra Nevada and the Great Basin from west to east; William Sublette, discoverer of Sublette's Cutoff on the Oregon Trail; Thomas "Broken Hand" Fitzpatrick, chief of mountain men; Jim Beckworth, a mulatto, teller of tall tales, and honorary Crow Indian war chief; Bill Williams, after whom mountains and rivers are named; Jim Baker, greatest explorer of the Southern Rocky Mountain territory. In short, Ashley's recruits were the most important group of territorial explorers ever brought together in America. In succeeding years these men would open up the entire western half of the country.

The company's first two years in the far northern headwaters of the Missouri were difficult ones. Increasing Indian hostility and competition from other fur trading companies led Ashley and Henry to look southward toward the Southern Rockies, as yet untrapped and little known. In November 1824,

Ashley's party started westward up the Platte from its confluence with the Missouri.

The Platte has been described as "a thousand miles long and six inches deep." For this reason, horses rather than boats were used on the initial leg of the journey. Ashley and his men followed the South Platte, reaching the Rocky Mountains near the mouth of the Cache la Poudre in the dead of winter (see South Platte River Basin). After crossing the Continental Divide near the present Wyoming-Colorado border, they ran afoul of a war party of Crow Indians, who stole 17 of their best horses. They struggled on, the men burdened with packs that the horses had carried. On April 18, Ashley recounted, "We traveled west about fifteen miles to a beautiful river running south. This stream is about one hundred yards wide, of bold current, and generally so deep that it presents but few places suitable for fording." (Ashley's account of the Green River trip is continued in a letter printed in *The Ashley-Smith Explorations and Discovery of a Central Route to the Pacific* by Professor Harrison Clifford Dale, 1918.)

The river was the Buenaventura to Father Escalante. Trappers knew it by its Crow name, Seedskedee or Seedskedee Agie (Prairie Hen River). To the Utes farther downstream it was the Bitterroot. One of its names was Colorado but, in the end, there could only be one Colorado. Fremont later named it Rio Verde, and this was the name that stuck—Green River.

The river permitted Ashley to relieve his men of some of their heavy burdens and at the same time accomplish an efficient reconnaisance. He divided the party into four groups, three to explore by land in different directions and the fourth, which he led, to descend the river.

He told his men that somewhere down the river he would mark a place for a rendezvous to be assembled "on or before the 10th of July following." A large bull boat was hastily constructed. Forty miles downriver, another boat was built to divide the load. On April 25 they reached a "beautiful bold running stream" entering from the west. Ashley marked this valley, at the mouth of the Henry's Fork, for the rendezvous. The spot was just above the Flaming Gorge. The party spent several days here scouting their first rapid in the gorge, which Jim Beckworth memorialized with the name "The Suck." Beckworth claimed to have saved Ashley from The Suck's savage rapids. He claimed that later the party went six days without food and was ready to select one man to eat.

Ashley's authentic record is an entirely different story. Although he describes the river as difficult and dangerous through Flaming Gorge, he says the journey was without incident until the boats reached what today is called Red Canyon. Here was a major obstacle, a drop that John Wesley Powell later named Ashley Falls. After lowering his boats over the falls, Ashley painted "Ashley, 1824" on a rock above the drop. This inscription was seen and puzzled over by Powell, who had scarcely heard of the enterprising explorer who preceded him on the river by almost 50 years. Remarkably, Ashley's inscription was still visible 86 years later when the Kolb brothers navigated the river. In the 1960s, Flaming Gorge Dam, built just downstream from Ashley Falls, buried the historic rapid and flooded the canyons northward for 60 miles.

Two days past Ashley Falls, the adventurers paddled into the quiet valley of Browns Park and camped two miles above the Gates of Lodore on a beautiful, cottonwood-covered bottom where, Ashley wrote, "several thousand Indians had wintered during the past season." In the following years, until 1840, this was the scene of some of the greatest rendezvous ever staged by the fur companies. Fort Davy Crockett was built on this bottom.

Ashley and his men entered Lodore Canyon on May 8. He wrote: "We proceeded down the river about two miles, where it again enters between two mountains and affording a channel even more constricted than before.

"As we passed along between these massy walls, which in a great degree excluded from us the rays of heaven and presented a surface as impassable as their body was impregnable, I was forcibly struck with the gloom which spread over the countenances of my men; they seemed to anticipate (and not far distant, too) a dreadful termination of our voyage, and I must confess that I partook in some degree of what I supposed to be their feelings, for things around us had truly an awful appearance.

"We soon came to a dangerous rapid which we passed over with a slight injury to our boats. A mile lower down, the channel became so obstructed by the intervention of large rocks over and between which the water dashed with such violence as to render our passage in safety impracticable.

"The cargoes of our boats were therefore a second time taken out and carried about two hundred yards, to which place, after much labor, our boats were descended by means of cords."

The 200-yard portage was probably made at Disaster Falls. Why Ashley didn't describe other heavy rapids, such as Triplet Falls or Hells Half Mile, is not known. He identified the mouth of the Yampa (which he called the Mary's River), Echo Park, Whirlpool Canyon, and Island Park. At the mouth of the Uinta the voyage was terminated. Ashley continued downriver 50 miles on foot, well into Desolation Canyon, which he aptly described as being "as barren as can be imagined." After buying horses from the Utes, he started back to the designated rendezvous at Henry's Fork above Flaming Gorge by way of the Uinta River.

Ashley pioneered the Green without careful planning and with only two days of preparation. He had no boats built especially for the rigors of the river. Using only axes, his men constructed their bull boats out of the materials at hand. The bull boat, made by pulling sewn-together skins over a willow frame, is light and of shallow draft, but difficult to maneuver. Ashley's river sense must have been superb. With only 16 portages through a series of very rough canyons, he must have run numerous tricky rapids in these less-than-ideal craft.

Ashley's exploits were not well known until long afterward. For years it was commonly thought that Powell had been the first to master the Canyon of Lodore and its neighbors. Upon finding cooking utensils and a piece of a boat at Disaster Falls, Powell assumed Ashley had been wrecked here. Powell's decision in naming Disaster Falls was influenced not only by his own difficulties (he lost a boat there) but by what he thought was Ashley's misfortune. His erroneous judgement about Ashley's fate was to be cleared up by a second young adventurer, who also preceded him through the canyons of the upper Green: William Manly.

Manly yearned to venture from his family's farm in Michigan into the romantic West. In 1849, when news came of the discovery of gold in California, he could resist no longer.

The beginning of his journey westward was a foretaste of things to come. With a friend, Orrin Henry, he built a boat, packed it with provisions, and set off with seven dollars in his pocket on a river called the Grand, just eight miles from the family farm in Michigan. "The stream ran west," he wrote, "that we knew, and it was west we thought we wanted to go, so all things suited us...."
(Manly's adventures are chronicled in his autobiography, *Death Valley in '49.)*

The two young men floated easily on the quiet current, a mild preview of the river that waited for them a thousand miles to the west. The only portage was made at Grand Rapids. Thirty more miles brought them to the river's mouth on the eastern shore of Lake Michigan. For a dollar and fifty cents they caught a schooner to the western side of the lake. Their first rough water experience was on the lake where the passengers all became seasick, "pretty hard usage for a landlubber like myself," Manly recounted.

In St. Joseph, Missouri, Manly hitched up with one of the many wagon trains headed for the gold fields. The party marched up the Platte River, reaching South Pass and the banks of the Green in the late summer.

Manly recalled the auspicious beginning of his journey on Michigan's Grand River. By now, he was convinced of the advantages of water over land travel. He hated the thought of spending the winter penniless in Salt Lake City, waiting for the snows of the Sierra Nevada to melt, and so proposed a "new scheme" to his bullwhacking friends:

"We put a great many 'ifs' together and they amounted to about this:—If this stream were large enough; if we had a boat; if we knew the way; if there were no falls or bad places; if we had plenty of provisions; if we were bold enough to set out on such a trip, etc., we might come out at some point or other on the Pacific Ocean. And now when we came to the first of the 'ifs', a stream large enough to float a small boat; we began to think more strongly about the other 'ifs'."

Enough "ifs" were satisfied. Manly was elected captain of the six who volunteered. A 12 foot ferry boat was loaded with provisions. The party started down the Green "with ease and comfort, feeling much happier than we would had we been going toward Salt Lake with the prospect of wintering there."

The first few days were a picnic. Each man had a setting pole with which he fended the boat off the rocks. At one point Manly's pole became lodged, yanking him into the current. "I struck pretty squarely on my back," he re-

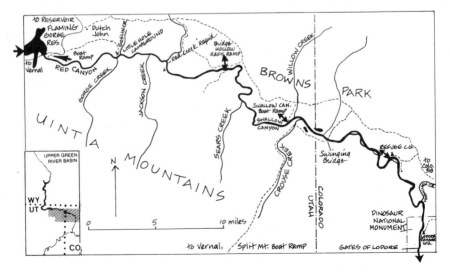

Green River from Flaming Gorge Reservoir to Gates of Lodore.

PIONEERS ON THE GREEN

counted, "and so got thoroughly wet, but swam for shore amid the shouts of the boys, who waved their hats and hurrahed for the captain when they saw he was not hurt."

The captain estimated they made 30 miles a day for the first four days, "which beat the pace of tired oxen considerably." There was plenty of game to shoot. On the fifth day they reached Flaming Gorge. Manly's thoughts at that moment will be familiar to river runners who have suddenly come upon the abrupt entrance to many of the Colorado's antecedent canyons:

"While I was sleeping the boat came around a small angle in the stream, and all at once there seemed to be a higher, steeper range of mountains right across the valley. The boys thought the river was coming to a rather sudden end and hastily awoke me, and for the life of me I could not say they were not right, for there was no way in sight for it to go. I remembered while looking over a map the military men had [given us] a place named Browns Hole, and I told the boys I guessed we were elected to go on foot to California after all, for I did not propose to follow the river down any sort of a hole in any mountain."

But a crack appeared. Through it they went, carefully lining and portaging the bad spots, still in high spirits. Upon reaching Ashley Falls they made the fatal mistake made by many a greenhorn river runner—they broached. The plan was to float down to the upstream side of the large boulder that blocked the river, climb onto it, and let the boat down through the boiling water below. However, Manly reported, "the current was so strong that when the boat struck the rock we could not stop it, and the gunwale next to us rose, and the other end went down, so that in a second the boat stood edgewise in the water and the bottom tight against the big rock, and the strong current pinned it there so tight that we could no more move it than we could move the rock itself." Their provisions had been unloaded before this calamity, but with the boat destroyed it seemed a very sudden ending to their voyage. Rather than continuing on foot, however, Manly decided to hack a couple of dugout canoes from nearby pine trees. "We never let the axes rest, night or day till we had them completed." The two dugouts were lashed together, Georgie White style, for extra stability. Finding they were too small to carry the load, a third, 25 or 30 feet long, was built. At this point Manly noticed the "Ashley, 1824" inscription. The question as to whether they were the first into these canyons was answered.

At Disaster Falls, Manly found a deserted camp, a skiff, and some heavy cooking utensils, along with a notice posted on an alder tree. The note said the party was abandoning the river and starting overland to reach Salt Lake. Heavy articles that could not be carried on foot were left behind. This was the abandoned camp that John Wesley Powell assumed to be that of William Ashley. We will probably never know the identity of this party or how many river miles they had covered.

Hells Half Mile was true to its name with "great, rolling waves in the center," of a kind Manly had never seen anywhere else. The waves flipped the double canoe and rolled it "over and over, bottom side up and every way." Alfred Walton, who could not swim, held onto the canoe with a deathgrip. In the midst of this disaster, Manly didn't lose his sense of humor, commenting that the black-haired Walton looked like "a crow on the end of a log." The canoe and a half-dead Walton were pulled ashore just above the next rapid. This event deeply discouraged the boys. Everything in the double canoe that would sink, including several guns, was lost. Rodgers pulled $3.50 out of his pocket and said sadly, "Boys, this is all I am worth in the world." To this, their captain quipped that they would have been no richer had they possessed a thousand in gold. After all, in this remote canyon, "there was no one to buy from and nothing to buy." They went on.

Near Steamboat Rock in Echo Park they shot three mountain sheep. Manly commented, "We were having better luck with one gun than with six, so we had a merry time after all." Manly accurately identified Whirlpool Canyon, as well as Island Park and Split Mountain.

Downriver, Utes beckoned the party to shore at a village near the mouth of the Uinta. While showing Manly's party his newly acquired guns, blankets, and knives, the Ute Chief uttered the word "Mormonee." Manly thought fast: "I had seen enough to convince me that these Indians were perfectly friendly with the Mormons, also. So we put our right hand to our breast and said 'Mormonee,' with a cheerful countenance, and that act conveyed to them the belief that we were chosen disciples of the great and only Brigham and we became friends at once, as all acknowledged.

"The fierce-looking Indian who sat as king in the lodge now, by motions and a word or two, made himself known as Chief Walker, and when I knew this I took great pains to cultivate his acquaintance."

Manly was now convinced they had "got through the troublesome navigation and could now sail on, quietly and safely to the great Pacific Ocean and land of gold." When he told Chief Walker, through sign language, of their plans, the chief seemed very much astonished. He kept shaking his head, then led them to a sandbar and sketched a map in the sand that showed his remarkable knowledge of the territory. After seeing an accurate sketch of the portion of the river they had just been through, Manly decided Chief Walker knew what he was talking about. Continuing the map downstream, the chief piled stones high on the edges of the sketched river, indicating a deep gorge.

"Then," wrote Manly, "he stood with one foot on each side of his river and put his hands on the stones and then raised them high as he could, making a continued e-e-e-e-e-e as long as his breath would last, pointed to the canoe and made signs with his hands how it would roll and pitch in the rapids and finally capsize and throw us all out. Then he made signs of death to show us it was a fatal place."

After completing this gruesome picture—it is not clear whether he was describing Cataract Canyon or the Grand Canyon—Walker got his bow and arrow, drew it back, and put it into Manly's chest, indicating the presence of hostile Indians downriver. Convinced of Walker's reliability, Manly held a council with his boys. He decided he would "as soon be killed by Mormons as by savage Indians," and that he was ready to travel overland from this point on.

If Manly had not met Chief Walker, he surely would have led the first exploring party into the Colorado's lower canyons. It is possible he would have been the first through the Grand Canyon.

Manly's adventure, however, was not over. In Salt Lake City he joined another wagon train which, after coming to grief in the unknown deserts of California, gave Death Valley its name.

Manly's voyage was remarkably similar to Ashley's. Both of them started at the Big Sandy and ended at the mouth of the Uinta. Ashley did not record the reason for halting there; perhaps he too was dissuaded by the Utes. both men accurately described the canyons, although Manly's account was in a much lighter vein. Both of them made the decision to run the river on the spur of the moment, and neither knew whether anyone had gone before.

The warmth of Manly's account makes it one of the most delightful stories of Colorado River exploration. His high spirits carried his party along. It is good to know that even these earliest of river runners laughed as they tackled the dangerous canyons.

It was not until 1869 that the organized, funded, and well-publicized journey of Major John Wesley Powell brought the upper canyons of the Green out of the darkness of myth and mystery into the light of scientific examination. Powell gave the river its names. Every canyon and almost every rapid bears a Powell name. A popular poem of the day, "The Cataract of Lodore" by Robert Southey, provided Powell with a name for one of the most spectacular of all canyons. Many of his names are vividly descriptive—Flaming Gorge, Red Canyon, Split Mountain Canyon, Desolation Canyon, Triplet Falls, Hell's Half Mile, Whirlpool Canyon. Much has been written about Powell's journey and it will not be dealt with at length here.

In the years after Powell, the solitary trapper, Nathan Galloway, made the river his own. Using his newly perfected, stern-first rowing technique and nimble cataract boat, he was able to run without hazard the rapids that Ashley, Manly, and Powell were forced to portage. By 1906, Galloway had tallied five trips through the upper canyons.

In 1911 the Kolb brothers made a photographic expedition down the river. They were able to accomplish William Manly's dream, going all the way to California.

Bus Hatch opened the first commercial guide service on the river. In 1936, Hatch began carrying "dudes" on ten-day voyages from Green River, Wyoming to Jensen, Utah. By the 1950s he was making regular commerical runs through Dinosaur National Monument in his big World War II surplus inflatables. Bus's sons today operate the largest guide service in Dinosaur Monument.

Battle Over Dinosaur

Dinosaur National Monument is the site of one of the few reservoir battles won by conservationists. In the 1950s the Bureau of Reclamation proposed a big dam at the narrow entrance to Whirlpool Canyon below Echo Park, in the heart of the monument. It would stand 525 feet high, backing up the Green through Lodore Canyon and flattening the Yampa for 44 miles.

Ulysses S. Grant III, former official of the Corps of Engineers who led the fight against the dam, called the project a Trojan Horse. He said the Bureau was trying to infiltrate the National Park System with dams under the guise of a benefactor. "It's easy to fool lay people with idyllic dreams of beautiful reservoir lakes," he said. Grant exposed many erroneous figures in the Bureau's proposal. But support for the dam was strong. Every member of Congress from the Upper Basin states approved of the proposal. The debate dragged on through the first five years of the 1950s.

When Congress authorized the project in 1955, the Sierra Club under David Brower aroused tremendous public support for protection of the river. Finally, on June 25, 1955, Echo Park Dam was excluded from the Colorado River Storage Project. The greatest conservation battle in half a century had been won by conservationists.

Flaming Gorge and Red Canyon, upstream, were sacrificed instead.

Today hundreds of thousands take on the mighty rapids of what dam supporters had called a "menacing and wastrel river" and call it the experience of their lives.

Green River—Red Canyon Section

Green River: Flaming Gorge Dam to Swallow Canyon Boat Ramp (Red Canyon)

Physical Data: 27 mi; 230-ft drop; 8.5 ft/mi average gradient; 1,500,000 acre-ft average yearly discharge (below dam).

Maps: Dutch John, Goslin Mt., Clay Basin, Warren Draw, and Swallow Canyon USGS Quads.

Guide: Dinosaur River Guide, Westwater Books, Boulder City, Nevada.

Land Ownership: Ashley National Forest and BLM.

Flow Information: Bureau of Reclamation at Dutch John, UT.

The upper canyons of the Green require only brief treatment since excellent guidebooks are already available.

What is left of Red Canyon has recently become a popular rafting area. The water issuing from the dam is very cold, about 40 degrees. The flow varies each day with distant power demands. The river is usually highest in the afternoon. Numerous small rapids accent the stretch.

The spillway boat ramp put-in is located a quarter-mile below the dam in the midst of Red Canyon. Intermediate take-outs can be found at Little Hole and Bridge Hollow Raft Ramp, seven and 16 miles downriver respectively. The largest rapid in Red Canyon, Red Creek Rapid (usually class III in difficulty) is at the mouth of tributary Red Creek, almost two miles before the river leaves Red Canyon. The river thereafter glides into an open area, full of waterfowl, for nine miles before entering the steep walls of two-mile-long Swallow Canyon.

Green River—Lodore, Whirlpool, and Split Mountain Canyons Section

Green River: Gates Of Lodore To Split Mountain Boat Ramp (Lodore, Whirlpool and Split Mountain Canyons)

Physical Data: 45 mi; 570-ft drop; 12.7 ft/mi average gradient; 27 ft/mi maximum gradient (between top of Upper Disaster Falls and bottom of Hells Half Mile); 1,500,000 acre-ft average yearly discharge (below Flaming Gorge Dam).

Maps: Dinosaur National Monument USGS Quad.

Guide: Dinosaur River Guide, Westwater Books, Boulder City, Nev.; *River Runner's Guide and Dinosaur National Monument,* Powell Society, Denver, Colo.

Land Ownership: National Park Service.

Information: Dinosaur National Monument, Dinosaur, Colorado 81610.

The run through Dinosaur National Monument takes two to four days. Although permits can be difficult to get due to heavy demand, there are usually many cancellations, especially late in the summer. The water level fluctuates wildly from day to day and is usually no higher in the spring than in fall. An August or September trip, when cancelled permits are plentiful—often on a day's notice—is recommended.

Migrating waterfowl, raptors, and many bighorn sheep make this an ideal season to float the Green.

The Park Service will supply a booklet of rules, regulations, designated camp spots, maps, and practically everything else boaters might want to know about this finest of multi-day rafting and kayaking runs.

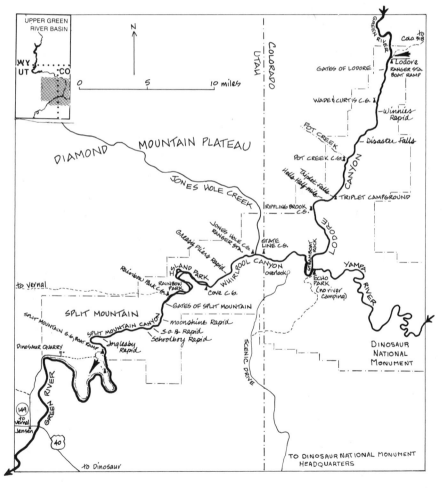

Green River from Gates of Lodore to Jensen, Utah.

Lower Green River Basin

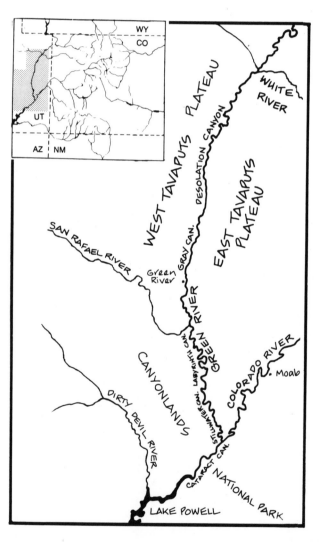

Sometimes the country appeared in its primitive
state as if the Indian still inhabited it.
   —Thoreau, *A Week on the Concord and Merrimack Rivers*

Human Drama Along the Green

South of Dinosaur National Monument on the Green River lie Desolation and Gray, two of the nation's most remote canyons, adored by fluvialists of every ability and in every variety of craft. Over 60 forgiving rapids wait at the mouths of side canyons where boulder fans interrupt the current. Tranquil spaces between rapids offer a chance for recovery in the event of a swamped or capsized boat. At high water, however, the waves grow large and will easily swamp an open canoe. Above Desolation, the Green has picked up the Yampa, White, and Duchesne, each a primary river in itself. The only larger river in the Southwest is the Colorado.

This is a perfect place to beguile a week. Nothing, apart from a ranger station at Sand Wash, spoils the ferity of these canyons. They remain almost as desolate as they were in 1869 when John Wesley Powell, observing the lonely beauty, came up with the name "Canyon of Desolation." Those who go to these canyons will return there.

There is much to catch the boater's attention. Great blue herons stalk the shallows and eddies. Megansers zip over the surface. Turkey vultures glower from their rocky perches. Beaver and muskrat dimple the surface. Bighorn sheep stand camouflaged on cliff faces. Herds of mule deer scamper beside the water. And catfish—innumerable and fat—delight the palate of the discriminating connoisseur. Less friendly rattlesnakes and scorpions also inhabit Desolation and Gray.

Spring is an ideal time to visit these canyons. The ice usually breaks up in early March, but only a handful of expeditions set out before the first of May. The earlier you go the more wildlife you will see. Then deer herds take refuge from the snow-covered Tavaputs Plateau in the warmer depths of the chasm. They are stalked by mountain lions, more abundant here than almost anywhere in the United States. The birds, migrating through this north-south break in the Rocky Mountains, greet boaters at every bend—wading birds, nesting herons, snowy egrets, hundreds of geese, bright tanagers, bald eagles, and millions of colorful warblers flitting in the sage and tamarisk during the day and flying northward at night.

Evidence of the Fremont Culture can be found at Firewater Canyon, where a stone structure stands on a small bench half a mile from the river. Two miles below Firewater, a well-preserved petroglyph panel on a block of Wasatch

Sandstone river-right, 100 feet from the water, was probably made by these elusive people.

The Uinta Band of the Ute Tribe occupied the land surrounding Desolation and Gray when the first settlers arrived. They were quickly forced onto a reservation west of Vernal, Utah. An extension of the reservation borders Desolation Canyon on its east bank between Nutter's Hole and Coal Creek.

D. Julien, the mysterious trapper who left inscriptions all the way downriver through Cataract Canyon, carved his initials on a rock at the mouth of Chandler Canyon in 1836. He was probably the first European to visit Desolation and Gray by boat.

Cattlemen and outlaws infiltrated the canyons in the late 1800s. Preston Nutter established a ranch in Nine Mile Canyon, running his herds in the upper reaches of Desolation. For years he ruled this territory with an iron fist backed up by a fast gun.

Jim McPherson's ranch, today a historical landmark, was located at Florence Creek. McPherson entertained the Wild Bunch on their forays up and down the Green. Apparently he was fond of Butch Cassidy, often remarking that the outlaws were "alot nicer folks than the posse chasing them."

There were those who wished to alter the natural character of these canyons. In 1908 the Denver and Rio Grande Railroad offered $100,000 to anyone who would clear the river of rocks between the towns of Ouray and Green River. If the channel were opened, they reasoned, fruit could be ferried from Vernal to their tracks at Green River. Fortunately for boaters, there were no takers.

Three years later, in the spring of 1911, a survey crew from the Bureau of Reclamation built a stone hut beside Coal Creek Rapid and began reconnaisance for a dam at that site. Because these projects never came to fruition, Desolation and Gray canyons can be enjoyed today by those with a less destructive appreciation of the river.

A Trip Through Tertiary Time

Desolation Canyon divides the forested Tavaputs Plateau into two parts, East and West Tavaputs. The Green eases gradually into its canyon below Ouray, the walls growing taller with every mile. This contrasts sharply with Lodore and Split Mountain canyons upriver, where the Green breaks directly into the upthrust mountains in its path. Within the heart of the plateau, Desolation Canyon reaches a depth of 3,000 feet. The river leaves the canyons in a more abrupt manner than it enters them, emerging suddenly from the Book Cliffs into the broad valley at the town of Green River, Utah. Because Desolation and Gray are cut into the topmost layers of a deep structural basin (the Uinta Basin), the strata visible in the canyon walls are much younger than those in most Southern Rocky Mountain canyons. These strata dip imperceptably upriver. Therefore a trip down the Green takes boaters back through geologic time, beginning 50 million years ago with the Eocene-age Uinta Formation bordering the river below Ouray. Downriver the lighter, buff-colored Green River shales appear in the building walls. The Green River Formation contains a rich oil shale bed, the Mahogany Member, whose exploitation could ruin upper Desolation Canyon. Fifteen miles below Sand Wash the older, redder Wasatch Formation appears at river level below the Green River Formation.

The Green River Formation was deposited in, and the Wasatch on the edge of, a great inland lake—Lake Uinta—which stretched from present-day Glenwood Springs to Salt Lake City during Eocene times. Volcanic ash beds, or bentonite, in the Green River Formation proves the area surrounding Lake Uinta was volcanically active. Fossilized fish, birds, and insects were trapped in the mud at the bottom of the lake.

The Wasatch-supported Desolation Canyon walls crumble near the old McPherson Ranch, forming the Vermillion Cliffs. Downstream, the Green River cuts into the older strata of the Mesa Verde Group in Gray Canyon and finally into the softer Mancos Shale. The river emerges from its canyons at the Book Cliffs. The Mesa Verde, composed of beach sands and coal beds, represents a swampy coastal plain on the edge of the advancing Cretaceous Sea. The ancestral Wasatch Mountains poured mud into the sea, which stretched east past Denver, creating the Mancos Shale.

Long after the retreat of the Cretaceous Sea, the meandering Green River began eroding the gradually rising plateau region, forming antecedent canyons. The river's meandering course became entrenched in the surrounding uplift. In succeeding years the Green was able to break through the necks of most of its meanders in Desolation Canyon and straighten itself out. The attentive river runner will notice these abandoned meanders (rincons) perched at various levels above the river throughout the canyon.

Far into the future, as the Vermillion and Book cliffs continue to recede northward in an upriver direction, the canyons will shorten and ultimately disappear.

Green River—Desolation and Gray Canyons Section

Green River: Ouray to Green River

Physical Data: 128 mi; 560-ft drop; 1 ft/mi average gradient above Jack Creek Rapid, 6.5 ft/mi below Jack Creek Rapid; 4,566,000 acre-ft average yearly discharge at Green River, UT.

Maps and Guides: Utah Multipurpose Maps #2 and #3, Utah Travel Council, Salt Lake City; *Desolation River Guide,* Westwater Books, Boulder City, Nevada; *River Runner's Guide to Desolation and Gray Canyons,* Powell Society, Denver.

Land Ownership: BLM land on right bank through both canyons; Uinta and Ouray Reservation left bank from below Nutter's Hole to Coal Creek and Ouray area. Private land begins 8 miles above Green River, Utah.

Information and Permits: BLM, Price, Utah.

The Ouray launch point is located on the east bank above the Utah State Highway Bridge 28 miles south of Vernal. If you launch during June or July, be prepared for a horde of mosquitos in the Ouray area unmatched anywhere in the west.

The first 34 miles of this stretch lead to Sand Wash in gradually deepening Desolation Canyon. No rapids interrupt the smooth river. Abundant waterfowl, heron rookeries, and cliff nesting sites of raptors offer superb

Sand Wash launch site in Desolation Canyon.

wildlife viewing.

A rough dirt road from Myton leads to the Sand Wash access point. A plaque commemorating Desolation Canyon as a National Historic Landmark and two old cabins used by ferry operators in the 1920s were the only evidence of man at Sand Wash a few years ago. Since 1976, the BLM has hauled into this pristine place an array of mobile homes and trailers for rangers.

The first genuine rapid lies 16 miles beyond Sand Wash at Jack Creek. But there are numerous spectacular sights—Nutter's Hole, Sumners Amphitheater, Rock House Canyon, the grand sweep around Peters Point—and a few tantalizing riffles before Light House Rock marks the approach to Jack Creek Rapid. Evergreen forests are beginning to develop on the ruddy canyon walls. Rapids punctuate the Green every mile or so below Jack Creek. The first big rapid is Steer Ridge (sometimes called Boy Scout because of the tragic drowning of two scouts here in June 1971) above the Rock Creek Ranch. The rapid is half a mile long with a swooping wave at the entrance, a big hole at the exit, and a rocky channel between. Powell's boat was swamped here in 1869.

Around the next corner is Rock Creek and the abandoned Rock Creek Ranch. Boaters can stop to fish in the creek and explore crumbling buildings and abandoned farming implements in the fields, but camping is prohibited here. Rock Creek, flowing from the deeply forested West Tavaputs Plateau, provides clear drinking water. Rock Creek Ranch sits in the lush heart of Desolation Canyon. Evergreen-blanketed canyon walls contrast with the desert vegetation at Sand Wash.

The canyon begins to widen downriver. Beach campsites abound. The rapids get bigger. The walls glow in reds, maroons, purples, and pinks. Desolation ends abruptly below Florence Creek and the old McPherson

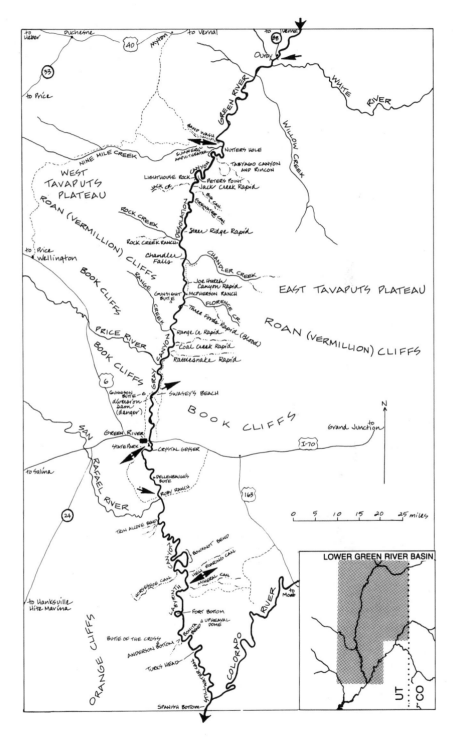

Green River from Ouray to Colorado River.

Ranch. At the canyon's mouth, around a sharp right turn, lies Three Fords or Blood Rapid. It is perhaps the trickiest spot on the river, especially at low water levels. Scout it from the right bank. The open amphitheater below Three Fords Rapid offers spectacular views of the Vermillion Cliffs and Gunsight Butte.

Thereafter, imperceptibly, you glide into Gray Canyon. Gray holds two big rapids, Coal Creek and Rattlesnake. Coal Creek is full of big waves and crashing holes at high water. Be careful not to get pulled too far right. At Rattlesnake, four miles farther down, it is best to stay away from the right wall, as two cabin-sized rocks block the river just below. The dirt road from the town of Green River follows the left bank up to Nefertiti Rapid, two miles below Rattlesnake. This is the uppermost take-out. Beyond the Price River confluence and several more rapids, at the mouth of Gray Canyon, is a wide sandbar bordered by tall cottonwoods. Called Swasey's Beach, it is river-left at the bottom of the last rapid, under Gunnison Butte. Many parties take out here. Others proceed to the boat ramp at the Green River State Park just past the Interstate 70 Bridge. This takeout involves eight additional miles of flat water and a hazardous irrigation diversion dam three miles below Swasey's Beach. Several enterprising ranchers allow cars to be parked on their property (for a fee), river-right above the diversion dam.

One more possibility: Red Tail Aviation in Green River will fly people either to Sand Wash or Ouray. A long shuttle can be avoided by first driving to the put-in and dumping gear. Cars are then driven to Green River and parked, and bodies are airmailed back to the launch point.

Raft crew plunges into Three Fords Rapid. (Mark Buswell photo.)

Green River—Labyrinth and Stillwater Canyons Section

Flat water and spectacular desert canyon scenery characterize this 117-mile wilderness run. Starting in the gray Mancos Shale, the Green cuts gradually down through the Lower Cretaceous Dakota Sandstone, through Cedar Mountain shales and mudstones, and finally into the colorful Morrison Formation. The canyon walls begin to rise as the Green dips into the San Rafael Group—the Summerville, Curtis, Entrada, and Carmel formations. Downriver the upper Triassic Glen Canyon Group—Navajo, Kayenta, and Wingate sandstones—bring these spectacular canyons into full bloom. The Cutler and Rico formations are recorded in narrow Stillwater Canyon near the end of the run. The beauty of this run lies not only in the panoply of buttes, grottos, and yawning gorges but also in the region's remoteness.

Labyrinth and Stillwater canyons are popular for open canoes and rafts. The Friendship Cruise, a fleet of motorboats, makes the run from Green River to the Colorado and up the Colorado to Moab each Memorial Day weekend.

An almost unbroken string of tamarisk bushes lines the banks, but native desert vegetation can be found behind them. Excellent campsites are located where the tamarisk line breaks. Everywhere the quiet river murmurs as it laps against the shore.

Green River: Town of Green River to Colorado River Confluence

Physical Data: 119 mi; 125-ft drop; 1 ft/mi average gradient; 4,566,000 acre-ft average yearly discharge (at Green River, UT).

Maps and Guides: Utah Travel Council Maps # 1 and # 2; USGS topographic map of Canyonlands National Park; *Canyonlands River Guide,* Westwater Books, Boulder City, NV; *River Runners Guide to the Canyons of the Green and Colorado Rivers,* Mutschler, Powell Society, Denver, CO.

Land Ownership: Mostly public land.

Information and Permit: Canyonlands National Park, Moab, UT.

Most parties launch at the Green River State Park boat ramp. A good take-out, unless one plans to go on through Cataract Canyon, lies at Spanish Bottom. From here float boats must be ferried up the Colorado to Hite by motorboat. A 26-mile whiplash dirt road from U.S. Highway 160 north of Moab reaches the river at Mineral Canyon 67 miles downriver from the town of Green River. A take-out here, however, will mean missing 40 miles of spectacular canyon lands.

Small riffles sing over the gravelly river bottom in the first 10 miles below Green River. Then the bottom becomes muddy, with an array of shallow sandbars that can prove a nuisance at low water stages. Boaters learn quickly the art of spotting telltale fluvial signs of a shallow sandbar ahead. Dellenbaugh's Butte, a round, red turret composed of the Summerville Formation, signals the approach to the San Rafael River. (Frederick Dellenbaugh, a 17-year-old member of the 1871 Powell expedition, wrote two of the best books about the river, *The Romance of the Colorado River* in 1902 and *A Canyon Voyage* in 1908.) A road leads south from Green River to the mouth of the San Rafael, providing a second launch point. Across from the mouth of the San Rafael is the old Wheeler Ranch (now the Ruby Ranch), the oasis that saved Frank Kendrick's 1881 expedition from starvation. (See "Early Explorers," Lower Colorado River Basin.) A rough dirt road from Green River reaches the west bank here, providing an alternate put-in.

The walls of Labyrinth Canyon begin to rise beyond the confluence with the San Rafael River. Seven miles past this point, the Green sweeps eastward in a broad curve, Powell's Trin-Alcove Bend. Three side canyons in the Navajo Sandstone meet the river on the right side of the bend. A short hike up the right-hand alcove leads to beautiful pools and cottonwood groves. Dripping rain water has painted the Navajo Sandstone with desert varnish.

Eight meanders beyond Trin-Alcove, the Green begins an eight-mile journey around Bowknot Bend. A moderately difficult scramble over the low point in the neck of the bend can be made by some members of the party while others take the long route on the river. The view from the top of the neck shows the Navajo Sandstone capping distant pinon-clad mesas. Here, the canyon is encased in vertical walls of the massive Wingate Sandstone with the less resistant Chinle Shale forming slopes to river level. John Wesley Powell's name, Labyrinth Canyon, perfectly characterizes the river's serpentine course.

Seven miles beyond the end of Bowknot Bend, entering from the left, is Hell Roaring Canyon. A "D. Julien 1836" inscription is found 200 yards up Hell Roaring on the south side. Two miles beyond lies the Mineral Canyon access point.

The next broad meander, 10 miles downstream, has a ruin on the top of the bluff at its center. The ruin consists of several round, stone towers. With river on all sides, only a narrow strip of land from the east provides easy access to the structure. The meander, called Fort Bottom, gave the Anasazi protection and a commanding view of surrounding canyon country. From here to the Colorado many stone structures were built by the "ancient ones" on ledges beside the river.

North of the Fort Bottom ruin, closer to the water, sits an old log cabin. It is said that Butch Cassidy and the Wild Bunch built the cabin as a stopping point for trips up and down the Green River on the Outlaw Trail.

Downriver from Fort Bottom, Powell's Butte of the Cross comes into view. The two buttes forming this inspiring landmark are composed of Wingate Sandstone. The sharp right turn five miles beyond, Bonita Bend, is a cut-off meander, or rincon. Because the old channel, extending the river by two miles, is situated only about 40 feet above the present river level, the meander was probably cut off quite recently, geologically speaking. The old river channel, called Anderson Bottom, provides several large, flat campsites. Water is found (at last) issuing from the base of the white sandstone cliff across Anderson Bottom 300 yards west of the large campsite at the head of Bonita Bend. The white cliff is composed of White Rim Sandstone, the top member of the Cutler Formation. Anderson Bottom is an excellent place to explore. Dunes of white sand are piled up in the middle of the rincon.

A climb to the top of the White Rim Sandstone offers inspiring views. Candlestick Tower, a needlelike spire of Wingate and Kayenta sandstones, soars like a jet of flame above the mesas and buttes to the east. Cleopatra's Chair and the Orange Cliffs overlook the canyon to the west. The contorted strata surrounding Upheaval Dome can be seen to the north.

Anasazi ruins, with piles of pottery shards in and around them, can be visited river-left around the bend below Bonita. In the middle of the next big incised meander is a huge, triangular block of White Rim Sandstone resembling a turban, aptly named Turks Head. More ruins can be found at its base. The benches around Turks Head are covered with pieces of flint, jasper, agate, and many other varieties of cryptocrystalline quartz. This hard rock was used by the Anasazi and Fremont cultures for arrowheads and grinding stones.

Beyond Turks Head the canyon walls close in, marking the entrance to Stillwater Canyon. Reddish walls of the Rico Formation hold the river tightly as it glides around many curves for 20 miles through the canyon. The Hermosa Formation, which forms the walls of Cataract Canyon downstream, comes up beneath the water and reaches river level 10 miles above the confluence of the Green and Colorado rivers. Powell's name for the canyon is particularly apt, since not a ripple breaks the surface of the tranquil water. But the river is not sluggish. It slips swiftly along past sandbars and ancient ruins to meet the Colorado.

Lighthouse Rock (center) signals first rapid in Desolation Canyon.

White River Basin

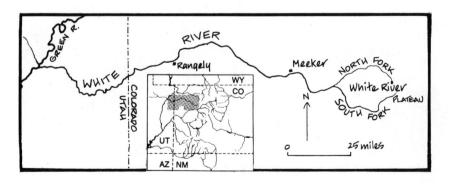

Thou has taught me, Silent River!
Many a lesson, deep and long;
Thou hast been a generous giver;
I can give thee but a song.
   —Henry Wadsworth Longfellow

Battle and Massacre on the White

The first Europeans to venture into the White River Valley were Fathers Dominguez and Escalante in 1776. After crossing the Colorado east of Grand Junction, their expedition ascended the Book and Roan cliffs. They reached the Roan Plateau and continued northward into the White River's watershed. The padres descended by way of Canon Pintado, which they named for Indian paintings on the cliffs. They met the White River at the mouth of Douglas Creek just east of Rangely. Escalante named the river the San Clemente.

After Dominguez and Escalante, mountain men moved into the White River Valley in search of beaver pelts. Because they left few records of their travels, the valley remained shrouded in obscurity.

In the fourth decade of the 19th century, a new kind of explorer suddenly appeared in the Southern Rocky Mountains. In the fall of 1854, this commanding figure stood on the majestic summit of the Gore Range, near today's Vail Pass, and gazed westward toward the White River Plateau and the uncharted peaks, valleys, and rivers extending toward the far Pacific. He was imbued with a broader purpose than his predecessors—that of scientific exploration. His name was John C. Fremont.

This was Fremont's third expedition into the Rocky Mountains. Unlike the small party of padres, he had with him a cavalcade of 60 men. Some of these men, such as Kit Carson and Thomas Fitzpatrick, were to become as well known as Fremont himself.

The expedition followed the Piney River, crossed the Grand (Colorado) River above its confluence with the Piney, and ascended the White River Plateau. After reaching the White's headwaters on top of the plateau, Fremont traveled down the length of the river to the Green. This was the first time the White had been explored from its source waters to its mouth.

For centuries before the explorers came, the White River Valley had been the domain of the Northern Ute Tribe. They called it the Smoking Earth River. With its large herd of elk, the White River Plateau was their prized hunting ground. Because they depended on the plateau for subsistence, the Utes bitterly resented the encroachment of white settlers in the years following the Civil War. As a result, the White River Valley was to become the site of one of the tragic episodes in the history of the pioneer West.

In the summer of 1878 one Nathan C. Meeker had just been appointed Indian agent at White River. An idealist and friend of writers Emerson and Hawthorne, Meeker had long served Horace Greeley as agricultural editor of the New York *Tribune*. Traveling westward to cover the Mormon colonization, he returned to New York with enthusiastic stories about the settlement potential of this vast region.

Meeker later founded the city of Greeley at the confluence of the Cache la Poudre and South Platte. He was instrumental in revolutionizing high-altitude agriculture by building high line canals. Meeker realized more water would be needed for east slope farms than its rivers could supply. Men were sent to the Continental Divide to search for low places where Pacific-bound water could be coaxed to flow down the east slope rivers by way of ditches and tunnels. Here lay the genesis of the great water diversions that today significantly diminish the flow of the Colorado River Basin.

In the meantime, the folks in the Greeley Colony were growing restive under Meeker's leadership. He was accused of being an atheist and an advocate of free love. At the age of 63 he lost his job. Heavily in debt to Horace Greeley, he was desperate for work. His unexpected assignment to the White River Ute Agency rekindled Meeker's quixotic optimism. He planned to lift the savages out of their squalor by introducing the agricultural techniques which had been so successful at Greely.

It never occurred to Meeker that the Utes might prefer their nomadic hunting life to the white man's plows. His crusade to turn the "savage" away from "hunting, horse racing, cock fighting and war dancing, to make him a hard working farmer who will go to school," was doomed from the start.

The Ute Agency was located across the river from the present site of the town of Meeker on a broad floodplain called Agency Park. The Ute Village was six miles downstream. Meeker and his wife, daughter, and several loyal friends from Greeley moved from Agency Park to the Indian village in order to establish his model Ute farm. Old Chief Douglas cooperated with Meeker, but his successor, a younger chief known as Ute Jack, was not interested in the salvation Meeker intended to bring the tribe.

When the track where the Utes raced their horses was plowed for a wheat field, Jack was furious. A couple of warriors roughed Meeker up, and rifle shots began going off around the agency. Meeker soon got the message that the Utes were upset and called for help from Fort Steele at Rawlins, Wyoming, 165 miles north. Major Thomas Thornburg, commander of Fort Steele, left for the White River Agency with 150 men, three companies of cavalry and one of infantry. Ute Jack met Thornburg on the Williams Fork River between the White and the Yampa and pleaded with him to take the soldiers back to Fort Steele. Jack insisted the squabble at the agency was over and military force was unnecessary. Thornburg agreed to leave the troops on Milk Creek at the Ute Reservation boundary and proceed to the agency with only a couple of officers. But on the morning of September 29, 1879, he neglected his promise and marched his troops across the boundary at Milk Creek. Immediately warriors on the surrounding hills opened up with their rifles, catching the column in a deadly crossfire. Thornburg moved out ahead of the column to reconnoiter and was instantly blown from his horse by a hail of bullets. As he lay dying, the Utes attacked the column, killing 15 men and wounding 30 before the troops could barricade themselves behind a circle of wagons and dead horses. The seige continued intermittently for four days. Finally the beleagured troops were rescued by a company of black soldiers from Middle Park.

Nathan C. Meeker (left) and Chipeta. (Denver Public Library, Western History Dept. photos. Right photo by F.S. Balster.)

Meanwhile, a courier from Ute Jack arrived at Powell Flats to give Chief Douglas news of Thornburg's broken promise and the subsequent battle. Without delay, the Utes attacked the White River Agency. All eleven white men were killed save one who escaped to die of his wounds two days later. Meeker received a bullet through the head. The agency was burned to the ground. Women and children were taken hostage and transported south to Chief Ouray's village on the Colorado River. Horrified by news of the massacre, Ouray's wife, Chipeta, rode her horse through the night to the White River Agency to help any survivors. Poet Eugene Field, then a newspaper man in Denver, immortalized her journey in a poem entitled "Chipeta's Ride."

The die was cast. Proponents of the slogan "The Utes Must Go" instantly received support for their campaign. The event chiefs Ouray, Douglas, and Jack feared most came to pass: the Utes were taken from their ancestral lands along the White River to a reservation in Utah. The White River's fertile bottomlands were given over to white settlement. By 1885 the town of Meeker had been founded to support hundreds of new farms and ranches up and down the valley.

Nathan Galloway— First Down the White

When Nathan Galloway set off from the town of Meeker in 1901 to voyage down the White, he sought neither adventure nor fame. A trapper by trade, he merely wanted to make a living. Venturing down a remote river was the best way to improve his chances.

Galloway's stoutly built wooden "cataract boat," which he had perfected several years before, was small enough to be handled by one man. A rockered hull allowed him to turn quickly. With blunt ends and watertight compartments fore and aft, his boat could take the waves head on. Until the advent of the rubber raft, almost all expeditions used the cataract boat on trips through the canyons of the Colorado and Green.

Galloway's method of navigation was also unique. Instead of rowing downstream, his back to approaching obstacles, he pulled upstream on his oars while facing downstream. Thus he could see what was coming and maneuver left or right to slow his momentum and avoid obstructions. Oarsmen have used the Galloway river technique ever since.

Game was probably scarce on the ranchlands between Meeker and the Rangely Trading Post. Below Rangely, however, the Green River Formation loomed up in rugged walls as the White left the last outpost of civilization. This was the territory Nathan Galloway sought. He was one of the last true mountain men in the Colorado River Basin. No one knows the nature of his success on the White, for he kept no record of his ventures, but it is reasonably clear he was the first to traverse the White to its confluence with the Green.

Galloway's competence had great impact on the rivers. In 1895 he made his way from Green River, Wyoming all the way to Lee's Ferry. The following year he repeated this expedition with William Richmond. Upon reaching Lee's Ferry, the two couldn't resist going on through the Grand Canyon to Needles. Since Galloway must have known the Grand Canyon would hold little game, this trip was probably merely for sport. He spent the following years trapping the rivers of the Southern Rockies, often with his sons. In the spring of 1909, with his son Parley, Galloway pioneered the run down the Yampa River. In the fall of the same year, he led a well-publicized Grand Canyon trip with Seymour Dubendorff and the eastern industrialist, Julius Stone. Finally, in 1912, the old navigator hung up his oars and retired to his home in Vernal, Utah.

Oil Production Threatens the White

In recent years, vast reserves of hydrocarbons on the White River have been the region's chief commercial attraction. Many oil and gas fields have been discovered on either side of the river between Meeker and the Green River. The greatest impact on this pastoral valley may come from oil shale production, now in the beginning stages up Piceance Creek south of the White river. The White borders the richest oil shale deposits in the world.

Oil shale development needs water—at least 3.6 barrels per barrel of oil extracted. The White River Canyon, remote in the Utah desert, has been deemed a logical source. The proposed White River Dam would flood 14 miles in the heart of the canyon. The dam would end boating on one of the Southwest's most remote and starkly beautiful canyons. In addition, it would eliminate much of the precious remaining habitat of four endangered fish—the Colorado River squawfish, humped-back chub, bonytail chub, and razorback sucker.

The White River and its northern neighbor, the Yampa, remain the only major untamed rivers in the Southern Rockies. In addition to wildlife protection and wilderness preservation, environmental groups are fighting the White

OIL PRODUCTION THREATENS THE WHITE

River Dam on economic grounds, arguing that its cost far outweighs any possible benefits.

White River

Navigating the gentle White is best accomplished in open canoes during the months of May and June, when the water is high. Rafters and kayakers will find little to challenge their whitewater skills below Meeker.

White River: North, South Fork Confluence to Rangely

Physical Data: 80 mi; 1,720-ft drop; 21.5 ft/mi average gradient; 40 ft/mi maximum gradient (between confluence and Meeker); 450,000 acre-ft average yearly discharge (near Meeker).
Maps: Leadville, Craig, and Vernal 1-250,000 scale USGS Quads.
Land Ownership: Mostly private; some BLM.

A swift run can be made from the South Fork-North Fork confluence for a distance of 12 miles downriver to the Base Line Road Bridge in the upper end of Agency Park. During high water periods some lively haystacks can be found here.

Beyond Meeker the White murmurs across rural pastureland. A pleasant flat water canoe trip begins at the Rio Blanco Lake State Recreation Area at the Piceance Creek confluence and ends at the Roadside Park 20 miles downriver. Here the river wanders away from Colorado Highway 64 into a quiet valley of dusky bluffs dotted with pinon pine. Several small headgate weirs provide the only whitewater.

There are many access points between the confluence and Rangely. However, the river crosses private land along most of the way, and landowner permission should be sought.

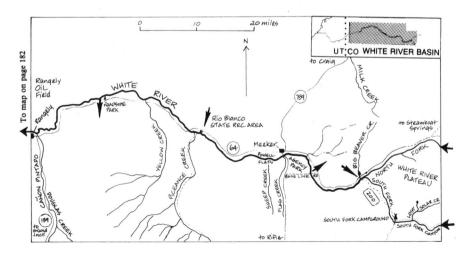

Upper White River, South Fork of White.

White River: Rangely to Green River Confluence

Physical Data: 68 mi; 500-ft drop; 7.5 ft/mi average gradient; 472,000 acre/ft average yearly discharge (near Rangely).
Maps: Vernal and Grand Junction 1-250,000 scale USGS Quads.
Land Ownership: First 5 miles mostly private; last 15 miles Uinta and Ouray Reservation; middle 40 miles mostly BLM.

Beyond Rangely the river steals into the White River Canyon, one of the least known and most scenic canoeing canyons in the Colorado River Basin. Cliffs of Green River shales separate the narrow strip of verdant bottomland along the river from the parched Utah desert beyond. Unfortunately, tamarisk chokes the bank much of the way, but tall cottonwoods and box elders provide shade on many of the bottoms. New natural gas wells are springing up near the rim of the canyon, but most are located out of sight of the river. At low water the White drifts sluggishly. A high water run is vastly preferable. At such times rolling waves, generated by the swift current, punctuate stretches of the run. Campsites are situated at places where breaks in the tamarisk bank provide adequate space. Dirt roads follow both banks for 10 miles below Rangely, providing many access points. The roads then leave the riverside to return only intermittently in the next 50 miles. Utah State Highway 45 crosses the river 25 miles below Rangely, providing good river access. The canyon walls gradually break down about 12 miles above the Green River confluence. At this point a dirt road, reached from U.S. Highway 40 or Ouray, crosses the river. This take-out is preferable to floating all the way to Ouray. A note of caution: swarms of mosquitos in the spring can reduce the pleasure of the White River Canyon for those who are not prepared.

South Fork of the White: Headwater Cataracts—South Fork Canyon

Though the North Fork is undesirable for boating, some technical kayaking can be found in unsurpassed South Fork Canyon near the South Fork's head-

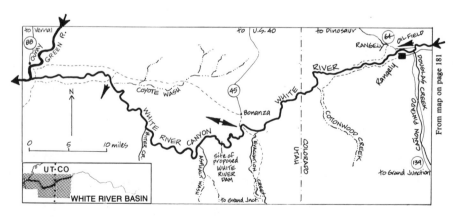

Lower White River.

The gentle art of kayaking. Rick Dukes surfs upstream on a wave.

waters. From South Fork Campground at the end of County Road 200, near the mouth of the canyon, boats must be carried upriver on the pack trail. The thundering river is marginably navigable from a point four miles above the confluence with Lost Solar Creek. Five and six-foot falls with whitewater reaching class V to VI difficulties make this a demanding place to play. Log jams are hazardous, but a lovelier and more isolated setting would be hard to find. The walls plunge over 2,000 feet from the White River Plateau to the narrow canyon bottom. In slicing deep into the upthrust plateau, the river reaches granite basement rock for the first and only time along its course. Lush meadows and colorful walls cloaked with evergreens adorn this beautiful canyon and make it an intriguing spot to while away a day or two.

Yampa River Basin

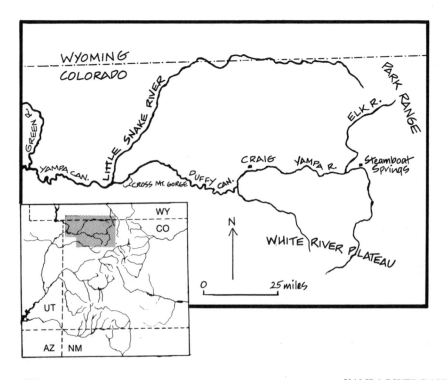

*The rivers are our brothers, they quench our thirst. The rivers carry
our canoes and feed our children. If we sell you our land, you must
remember and teach your children that the rivers are our brothers and
yours and you must henceforth give the rivers the kindness you would
give any brother.*

— Chief Seattle, Suquamish Tribe

The Legend of Ranger McBee

"Not on *my* river you don't," replied Ranger McBee to our request to take
an open canoe down the Yampa River through Dinosaur National Monument.
"Haven't had one death on this river since I've been head river ranger and I'm
not about to let you be the first." McBee, who had achieved almost legendary
status as a river ranger, was a book man. If the regulation said no canoes, that
was that. Of no consequence was the fact that our canoeists had used their
craft on much more difficult rivers than the Yampa.

It was a busy morning at Deerlodge Park, staging area for trips through
Yampa Canyon. Generators ground away. Big trucks loaded with thousands
of pounds of rubber rolled into position by the river. The smell of breakfast
sausage and bacon permeated the still morning air. It was the beginning of the
Memorial Day Weekend and a big day for Ranger McBee. About 250 people
were preparing to launch on "his" river. Like an anxious Napoleon preparing
to send his troops into battle, he marched this way and that shouting orders,
his two lieutenants at his side. A large, middle-aged, somewhat imposing man
with a jovial disposition, it was apparent that he enjoyed his work. His dark
green uniform was starched and creased. His badge gleamed.

He worked efficiently, checking permits and explaining hazards downriver.
He had first-hand knowledge of several of these, having flipped a raft or two
himself.

What Ranger McBee did best, and apparently regarded as his most sacred
responsibility, was to squeeze airtight kapok lifejackets to find leaks. He was
known as the most discriminating squeezer in the West. Not even the tiniest
leak escaped his acute ear. No chamber went untested. We watched nervously
as he went through our lifejacket pile, throwing the rejects into one heap and
those that passed into another. We came up one lifejacket short. "But Ranger
McBee," I pleaded, my ear against a marginal chamber, "listen to this one.
You can barely hear the leak." He squeezed it again and exclaimed, "Son,
that's illeeegal!"

After much haggling, Ranger McBee finally let us go, provided we used the
"illegal" lifejacket as a spare. As we swept away from Deerlodge Park, our
two canoeists grumbled an epithet or two at the clumsy rubber rafts they were
forced to paddle.

The jaws of Yampa Canyon opened and swallowed our little group. We quickly forgot the hectic bustle at Deerlodge Park as we fell under the river's spell.

Our first campsite, a dusty spot in the midst of the beautiful canyon, called Tepee Hole, was easy to see. Six big commercial balonies were lined up there like cattle at a feed trough. We were resigned to the least desirable corner of the sloping site for our camp. We took a hike.

We couldn't wait to get back on the river the following day. The water was swift and the canyon beautiful as always. Only the long lines of charcoal on both river banks spoiled the wilderness quality of the Yampa Canyon this day. The regulations required that all campfire ashes and charcoal be dumped into the river. I suppose they thought the stuff would cleanse the water like a charcoal filter cleanses cigarette smoke. It didn't work. The unsightly mess along the shores forced the authorities to repeal that rule the following season.

Late in the afternoon we passed through thunderous Warm Springs Rapid, met the Green River at Echo Park, and drifted into Whirlpool Canyon. Our camp that night was at Jones' Hole, a pristine campground turned into a crowded slum by bureaucratic policies. There must have been 150 people camped on the small floodplain. A young rangerette greeted us as we pulled into our designated parking position, Jones' Hole #4. "Having a nice trip? Your permit, please." There seemed to be no end to the Park Service's concern for our equipment and permit.

Our last day brought us out of Whirlpool Canyon into Island Park, an open area where the river widens and slows to a snail's pace. Two of us made the mistake of removing our lifejackets for a short swim in the shallow, gentle river. We were unaware that McBee's men had set up an observation post on a high bluff in order to spy through a telescope on unsuspecting river runners. Several miles downriver we were pulled over by a ranger in a pickup truck. He handed us a $50 fine for swimming without lifejackets. More arguments. We refused to pay and took off. He radioed ahead to reinforcements who were waiting for us at the take-out. It was McBee and two pistol-toting lieutenants. They didn't look pleased. "Beautiful river you've got here, Ranger McBee," I exclaimed.

"Pay up or we'll have to send you folks to jail," was his jovial reply.

We paid.

Ranger McBee loved his job.

Land of Cattle, Coal, and Current

The source waters of the Yampa, like those of the White, are found in the Flattops of the White River Plateau. Wide floodplains spread across the upper valleys of both rivers. Both enter canyon country as they approach the Green. The Yampa, however, carries more than twice the volume of the White. Its headwaters lead it in an easterly direction before it arches around the north side of the plateau to follow a westerly course parallel to and north of the White.

Cattlemen were lured to the rich floodplains of the upper Yampa after the Meeker Massacre and removal of the Utes to Utah (see White River Basin). By 1889, three towns—Steamboat Springs, Hayden and Yampa (today called Craig)—had been established to serve the cattle industry. In the following years these towns, in the words of one old timer, "just growed." Ranching was not the sole attraction. Rich coal beds south of Steamboat Springs in Oak Creek Canyon and around Craig brought in the mining industry. Coal production keeps the valley booming today.

*Wreck of the Leakin' Lena in Yampa Canyon. (*Denver Post *photo.)*

Downstream from the grinding noise of powerplants, steamshovels, highways, and busy towns, the Yampa glides into quiet canyon country, first through a series of shallow, still canyons and then into deep, rugged ones with thundering cataracts. These are the canyons eagerly sought by modern river explorers.

There has been considerable discussion concerning the origin of the name "Yampa." Fur traders thought it was the Ute word for bear. As a result, older maps of the valley call the river the "Bear." The name Yampa, however, comes from a plant of that name which grew in abundance along the banks of the river. Settlers called it "squawroot." Its root resembles that of a wild onion, with a spicy flavor, often dried and eaten by the Utes.

The first explorer to venture down the Yampa was probably that turn-of-the-century mountain man, Nathan Galloway. With his son, Parley, Galloway took a single cataract boat from Lily Park, at the junction of the Yampa and the Little Snake, to the Green River in the spring of 1909. Little is known of Galloway's adventures. He kept no records.

When the *Denver Post* sponsored its Yampa River Expedition in August, 1928, it was thought that the river was still unexplored. This most heavily publicized river trip in Colorado history began with great fanfare. The *Post* ran front page headlines about the progress of its expedition. Many other newspapers around the country carried the story. Four men—A.G. Birch; Bert Moritz, Jr.; Charles E. Mace; and Fredrick Dunham—in two open boats, the Leakin' Lena and the Prickly Heat, departed from Lily Park on August 18. The Post party was an inexperienced lot. They tried to paddle the heavy skiffs with only two men per boat. Despite moderate water levels, the inevitable happened. The Leakin' Lena broached on a rock and was lost. Food and cameras were also lost. The *Post* headline read, "Two Barely Escape Death, Pair Pitched From Boat in Yampa Crash." Another headline declared, "Death Faced Many Times by Post's Quartet of Explorers." The four explorers continued in the single boat. Two weeks after their struggles began, the adventurers left the canyon, "glad to get home alive."

Despite its problems, the *Denver Post* trip opened the Yampa to river running. It is probable that the glowing news accounts of the Yampa Canyon's beauty helped persuade President Franklin D. Roosevelt to enlarge Dinosaur National Monument in 1938 to include Yampa Canyon.

Plugging the Yampa

The wide bowls of topography that characterize the Yampa Valley are pinched off in two places by gunsight notches begging to be plugged—Juniper Canyon and Cross Mountain Gorge. Twenty-five years after conservation forces saved Dinosaur National Monument, the Yampa is again threatened. Dam builders now aim for Juniper and Cross Mountain Gorge, with talk of "enhancing the environment" and replacing the equivalent of 600,000 barrels of foreign oil. They suggest that flooding the Yampa Valley will provide lakes for people to recreate on and that river running opportunities will be improved in Dinosaur Monument downstream.

Juniper Canyon Dam and Cross Mountain Dam together would impound slightly less than the river's annual flow. Almost 90 miles of the Yampa would be flooded, much of it in scenic wilderness canyons. The largest free-flowing river in the Southern Rocky Mountains would be harnessed for electrical power. How much power? Only about one percent of the megawattage of the area's two coal-fired powerplants. No foreign oil is used for power production in the Yampa Valley. Local coal reserves are projected to last hundreds of years.

Besides flooding valuable ranchland, the reservoirs would reduce winter range of huge herds of mule deer, pronghorn antelope, and elk. They would eliminate two species of endangered fish from the river—the Colorado squawfish and humpback club. The cottonwood nests of a growing bald eagle population would be drowned. Evaporation from the reservoirs would exacerbate the Colorado's already serious salinity problem.

Impoundment would stop the Yampa's annual spring runoff, which attracts thousands of boaters each year. Extreme daily flow fluctuations would leave boats high and dry one minute and flood campsites the next. Captivating high water runs would be eliminated all the way down the Yampa and the Green. Two magnificent river runs—Cross Mountain Gorge and Duffy Canyon— could be drowned forever unless those who love them speak up for them.

An Anomalous Course

The Yampa River above Craig follows a wide valley between two uplifts, the White River Plateau to the south and the Elkhead Mountains to the north. Thereafter, its course becomes anomalous and confusing. Instead of following its ancient valley west of Craig, the river turns south, cutting the relatively new Duffy Canyon in the Mesa Verde sandstones. Quaternary uplift and stream capture probably persuaded the river to change its course here.

Beyond Duffy Canyon, the Yampa eroded the first of its gorges through a small structural dome of Paleozoic rocks—Juniper Mountain. For 25 miles west of Juniper Mountain it meanders across a wide valley atop the Browns Park Formation, a thick pile of Tertiary volcanic ash, windblown sand, freshwater limestone, and basal conglomerate lying uncomformably on top of older Paleozoic and Mesozoic formations. Almost all the wide valleys in extreme northwest Colorado are filled with the Browns Park Formation including, of course, Browns Park.

Beyond the valley west of Juniper Mountain, a second isolated structural dome sits in the Yampa's path—Cross Mountain. Instead of following the open country around the dome, the Yampa crashes straight into and through it in narrow, tumultuous Cross Mountain Gorge, 1,000 feet deep. Below Cross Mountain, the river joins the south-flowing Little Snake in Lily Park. At the west end of Lily Park the river blasts into the east edge of the Uinta Mountains. It follows a deep canyon route for 45 miles to its junction with the Green in the heart of Dinosaur National Monument. Above this confluence, the Yampa displays one of the Southwest's best examples of entrenched gooseneck meanders.

Why did the river take this course rather than meeting the Green in the wide Browns Park Valley to the north or in the Uinta Basin to the south? These questions, though not fully answered, are the subject of intriguing speculation. One theory (the one espoused by Powell) states that the Yampa is antecedent to the uplifts. The uplifts rose very gradually across the Yampa's path while it chewed its great canyons into them. The problem with this theory is that the Yampa River did not exist when the uplifts first began rising. Another theory (accepted by most geologists after Powell) is that Browns Park Formation was once much thicker than it is today, and the Yampa rode on top of it. As the river slowly stripped away the Browns Park cover, it met the structural domes—Juniper, Cross Mountain, and the east end of Uinta Mountains—buried underneath. This method of canyon cutting is called superposition. There are two problems with this theory: First, the Browns Park Formation would have to have been over 1,500 feet thicker than it is today. Also, the Yampa would have had to singlehandedly strip away this vast amount of fill. Moreover, the uplifts would have to have completed their uplifting by the time the Yampa began slicing into them. The Yampa's sluggishness above these canyons and its steep descent through them suggests that at least some of this uplifting must have occurred quite recently.

The origin of the Yampa canyons probably lies in a combination of antecedence and superposition hypotheses. The river's course was probably established by superposition before the final uplift of the mountains. Recent uplifts of perhaps 500 feet or downwarping of the adjoining basins allowed the Yampa to deepen its canyons by antecedence. This would help explain the river's sluggishness between the uplifts and the fast water in the canyons.

Yampa River— Steamboat Springs Area

Many kayakers and canoeists enjoy the Yampa's easy water through the town of Steamboat Springs. A two-mile run can be made from the sewage ponds south of town to the city park at the west end of town.

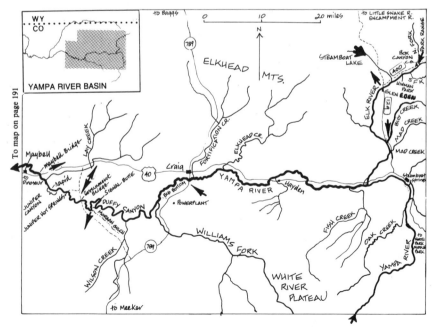

Upper Yampa River and Elk River.

Local kayakers have instituted the "Yampa River Improvement Project" in Steamboat. Constructed in 1981, this project greatly improved the river for boating with the placement of large boulders in the river above and below the Fifth Street Bridge and construction of a kayak race course.

Yampa River—Duffy and Juniper Canyons Section

Yampa River: Big Bottom To Maybell Bridge (Duffy and Juniper Canyons)

Physical Data: 49 mi; 150-ft drop; 3 ft/mi average gradient; 1,120,000 acre-ft average yearly discharge (at Maybell).

Maps: Round Bottom, Horse Gulch, Juniper Hot Springs, Citadel Plateau, and Maybell USGS Quads.

Land Ownership: Mostly public land inside Duffy and Juniper Canyons; mostly private outside the canyons.

One of the best places in Colorado for wilderness canoeing on relatively flat water is Duffy Canyon on the Yampa below the town of Craig. A single, rock-studded headgate weir marks the Duffy Tunnel entrance near the end of the canyon and provides the run's only whitewater. Below Duffy Canyon, the country opens up for 10 miles across marshy ranchland past abandoned Juniper Hot Springs. A mile below the bridge at Juniper Hot Springs, the Yampa abruptly enters Juniper Canyon, a short, three-mile slice bisecting Juniper Mountain. The only sizeable rapid on the run is located at the Maybell Ditch intake in the middle of Juniper Canyon. This rapid, located on a blind left curve, can reach class III at high water stages.

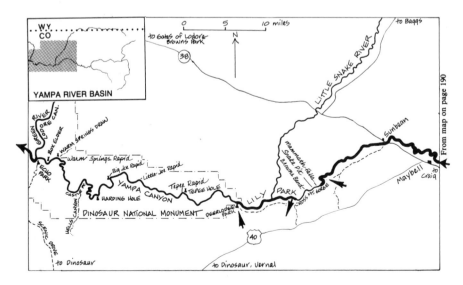

Lower Yampa and Little Snake rivers.

To reach a put-in point, drive straight south from Craig on State Highway 789 in the direction of the massive new power plant. At a point just west of the powerplant, boaters can drive down to Big Bottom, a large willow flat where boats can be launched. An alternate put-in is at the Highway 789 Bridge a few miles upriver.

At the lower end of Big Bottom, the Yampa meets the Williams Fork before entering Duffy Canyon. Canoeists find the 30-mile canyon a most pleasant place. Numerous cottonwood flats provide excellent camping. Wildlife abounds, including nesting eagles and, in the spring, many varieties of water-fowl. Canada geese and cliff swallows nest here, mule deer inhabit side canyons, and bank beavers live in the river. Scrub junipers dot the canyon walls. Mosquitos can be a problem.

In Duffy Canyon the Yampa meanders widely. Near the canyon's end, the river arcs four miles around Signal Butte to cover a half-mile air distance. The bluff sandstone walls are composed of layers of the Mesa Verde Group. In the valley beyond Duffy Canyon, the Yampa crosses the Browns Park Formation.

There are several take-out points in the valley. The first lies just beyond the canyon mouth at Morgan Gulch, the second at the Government Bridge in the middle of the valley, and the third at the bridge adjacent to Juniper Hot Springs. The valley can be reached most easily by driving due south on a dirt road that leaves U.S. Highway 40 at a point 19 miles west of Craig. There should be a sign pointing to Juniper Hot Springs at the road junction. Those proceeding downriver through Juniper Canyon can take out at the Highway 40 Bridge east of Maybell.

In Juniper Canyon, Paleozoic and Pre-Cambrian rocks have been thrust to the surface along fault lines. Pennsylvanian strata exposed in the steep canyon

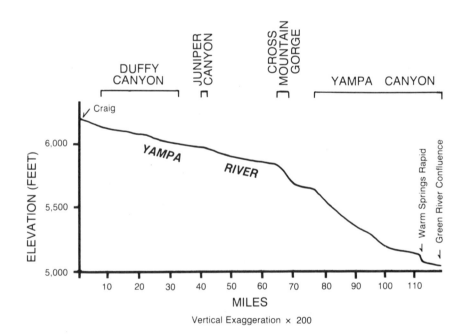

Gradient profile of the Yampa River from Craig to Green River confluence.

walls contain abundant fossils. Formed by a harmonious combination of antecedence and superposition, it is structurally the twin of Cross Mountain Gorge, 25 miles downriver, except that its waters are less ferocious.

Yampa River—Cross Mountain Gorge Section

Although expert kayakers have successfully tackled Cross Mountain Gorge for years, the boulder-choked riverbed was always considered impossible to raft. In the early 1970s, a big Hatch military pontoon entered the gorge. Pieces of the rig and half-drowned swimmers emerged at the mouth.

On May 29, 1974, three boatmen from a local outfitting business—Rob Wise, Rocky Innes, and Alan Easom—decided to attempt the gorge. On that day the river gushed through the narrow slot at a torrential level, 10,000 c.f.s. Every inch of the route was carefully scouted during two days of preparation. The boatmen knew their chances of escaping from the first big drop, Mammoth Falls, were not good—let alone the remaining three miles of leaping whitewater. At the head of the gorge, the raft was loaded with dirt-filled steel boxes for extra ballast, and the mariners put on lifejackets which would float cannons. Spotters were strategically stationed along the route. Anxious friends with a chase boat waited at the end of the run. Bidding defiance to danger, the three committed their 22-foot pontoon raft to the torrent.

They hit the reversal wave at the bottom of Mammoth Falls straight on. All they heard was the sound of the wooden floor cracking and the spare oars being ripped from the side of the boat. The raft folded, shuddering. Their worst fears were realized: The huge backwash sucked the boat back into the falls. The three hung on, as tons of water crashed over them. For five minutes the boat thrashed about at the bottom of the falls. Then, miraculously, it slipped out and the shaken rafters were on their way again. They traded off at the oars. Rowing hard, they successfully passed the Snake Pit, hugged the left wall at Browns Bend, and lost daylight in two more holes. Finally, after 20 minutes in the maelstrom, the river spit them out of the canyon into a happy reunion with their friends, who had given them up for lost.

Yampa River: Cross Mountain Gorge

Physical Data: 3.5 mi; 200-ft drop; 57 ft/mi average gradient; 80 ft/mi maximum gradient; 1,120,000 acre-ft average yearly discharge (at Maybell).
Maps: Elk Springs U.S.G.S. Quad.
Land Ownership: Public; private land above and below gorge.

Cross Mountain Gorge is not a rafting area. At lower water levels (300 to 600 c.f.s.), Cross Mountain becomes a plum of a technical kayak run. The cabin-sized boulders jumbled through the route form a marvelous obstacle course for expert paddlers. Play spots abound. The near-vertical walls of colored strata form a beautiful backdrop to one of the most unique and challenging canyons in the Colorado River Basin.

Despite the run's short length, expert paddlers from far and wide seek the canyon after peak high water, usually during July and August. Boaters can put in at the bridge below Maybell, but the long flatwater stretch above the canyon will be trying. A small dirt road leading north from U.S. Highway 40 on the east flank of Cross Mountain, if not fenced off, will get boaters close to the river near the entrance to the canyon.

Mammoth Falls, just below the entrance, consists of a complex chute above a steep drop. Its massive reversal hole appears only at high water. Below the falls, the river turns southward through the Snake Pit. Careful scouting will avoid a possible broach. The difficulty eases slightly as the river turns westward again. On the next turn to the south, at Browns Bend, lies a difficult drop along a cliff face, river-left. It requires an inspection stop and perhaps a portage. Large boulders continue to clog the riverbed below Browns Bend to the canyon mouth, but additional scouting will probably prove unnecessary. The dark canyon suddenly ends as the Yampa drifts out into the light of broad, gentle Lily Park. The road connecting Deerlodge Park with Highway 40 passes the mouth of Cross Mountain Gorge, offering a convenient take-out.

Yampa River—Yampa Canyon Section

Yampa River: Deerlodge Park To Echo Park

Physical Data: 46 mi; 550-ft drop; 12 ft/mi average gradient; 40 ft/mi maximum gradient (for three miles from top of Tepee Rapid); 1,525,000 acre-ft average yearly discharge (at Deerlodge Park).

Maps: Dinosaur National Monument (1:62,500 scale) U.S.G.S. Quad.

Guides: *Dinosaur River Guide*, Belknap and Evans, Westwater Books, Boulder City, Nevada; *Yampa River Supplement, River Runners Guide to Dinosaur National Monument*, Powell Society, Denver.

Land Ownership: National Park Service.

Information and Permits: Dinosaur National Monument, Dinosaur, CO.

Details of the Yampa Canyon run are provided in the excellent guidebooks listed above. Yampa Canyon is popular with rafters and kayakers of intermediate ability. At high water the current flows speedily and generates big waves, but as the water drops in July, the river becomes more suitable for open canoes. Though rapids abound—Tepee, Five Springs, Big Joe, Little Joe—only one, Warm Springs, is dangerous.

Warm Springs, near the Green River confluence, is an example of how Southwest desert rapids can be formed overnight. When Powell rowed up the Yampa from its confluence with the Green on July 20, 1869, he found only a riffle here. Almost 100 years later, on the night of June 10, 1965, a tremendous flash flood thundered down Warm Springs Draw. Hundreds of tons of rock debris piled up against Warm Springs Cliff, effectively damming the river and creating the most notorious rapid in Dinosaur Monument. The river is flat for six miles above this rapid, backed up by the natural dam of rock debris.

At high water stages, boats must follow the right bank through the upper part of the rapid to avoid being sucked into the converging waves in the main current which will take them directly into the ferocious Maytag Hole. This terrifying hole will flip the biggest rafts at high water; it has done so many times.

Almost the entire river flushes into it. Missing it is a trick. A 15-foot-wide slot on the right will carry you safely by. Another remarkable feature of this rapid is its capriciousness. When the level of the Yampa drops, the holes disappear, and the Warm Springs turns into a common class II rapid.

The geology of Yampa Canyon deserves note. In its first 25 miles, the Yampa incised itself into the Pennsylvanian Morgan Formation composed of interbedded grey limestone and massive reddish sandstone. On top of the Morgan, on the south rim, is the Weber Sandstone, a thick, white, cross-bedded sandstone. The depth of the upper canyon reaches 2,500 feet, the gradient over 17 feet per mile. Beginning at Harding Hole, the canyon's character changes dramatically. The Morgan drops below river level, and massive white walls of the Weber Sandstone dominate the scene. Here the gradient eases to seven feet per mile as the river swings through a series of looping meanders. The Weber has eroded into ice cream domes and spires, including Cleopatra's Chair and Katy's Nipple.

Tall cliffs of Weber Sandstone at Grand Overhang and Tiger Wall plunge into the river. Water falling on the upland plateau cascades over these cliffs. The water carries manganese and iron hydroxides derived from soils above. As the cascades begin to evaporate and trickle down the cliffs, tapestries of black, blue-black, and red stain—called desert varnish—are precipitated from the water. Long stripes of desert varnish adorn the cliffs of Weber Sandstone throughout the lower canyon.

Mary Ann Griffin rows Big Joe Rapid in Yampa Canyon. (Don Grall photo.)

Elk River

The headwaters of the Elk River, a tributary of the Yampa, lie in the Mount Zirkel Wilderness of the Park Range. This is one of the most productive watersheds in Colorado. The Elk runs high in late May and June. Thirty-five miles of the river above Glen Eden have been recommended for Wild and Scenic River status. This would prevent construction of the proposed Hinman Park Reservoir, which would destroy the best kayak run.

Elk River: Box Canyon Campground To Glen Eden Bridge

Physical Data: 8 mi; 560-ft drop; 70 ft/mi average gradient; 242,000 acre-ft average yearly discharge (at Clark).
Maps: Farwell Mountain, Floyd Park, and Clark U.S.G.S. Quads.
Land Ownership: Mostly Routt National Forest; some private land near Glen Eden.

The Elk becomes navigable just below the box canyon above the junction of the river's North and Middle Forks. County Road 400 leads to Box Canyon Campground. The gradient on this upper run is steep but steady, usually about class III in difficulty. At high water, it flushes through big waves at a fast pace with few eddies. A deep forest lines the banks. Many riverside campgrounds provide good access (see map). It is an excellent kayak run at every water level. At moderate levels, rafts can also be taken from Box Canyon to Glen Eden.

Below Glen Eden, the Elk's valley widens as the river slips into ranching

Raft crew struggles past Maytag hole in Warm Springs Rapid.
(Tom Fellows photo.)

Author Doug Wheat kayaks the Yampa. (Don Grall photo.)

country. Although it keeps up a fast pace, headgate weirs, fences, and hostile landowners make this a much less desirable boating stretch than the one above Glen Eden. Under pressure from these landowners, the Routt County sheriff has attempted to close Elk River to boating in recent years.

Approximately 12 miles below Glen Eden is the town of Mad Creek. A second popular kayaking area begins at the park two miles above Mad Creek, down to the town. Here, for a short distance, the valley narrows, and National Forest once again protects the river corridor. This run usually earns a class I to II rating.

Below the town of Mad Creek, the Elk proceeds in a slow, meandering pace through pasturelands down to the Yampa confluence.

Little Snake River

The Yampa's second northern tributary is the Little Snake. It begins in the Sierra Madre Mountains, follows the Colorado-Wyoming border past Baggs, Wyoming, and then turns southward toward the Yampa. Although this river carries an average of over 400,000 acre-feet of water each year, people rarely boat it. Its gradient is low. There are no rapids on the river below Baggs. In the late spring however, the Little Snake offers 70 miles of pleasant, flat canoeing water between Baggs and the Yampa River confluence at Lily Park. The countryside is scenic, with bluffs of white and buff Green River shale rising here and there from arid bottomlands. Remote campsites are abundant and ranch buildings few and far between.

Part III

Rivers of the East Slope

Kayakers carefully pick their way down Encampment River.

North Platte River Basin

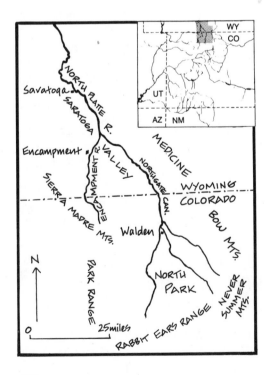

*The river called. The call is the thundering rumble of distant rapids,
the intimate road of white water, the whisper of wind through tall
pines, the music of night produced by the elemental instruments of
wind, rock and water. It is the compelling call of great spaces, of
wilderness beauty, of soul satisfying serenity, inspiration, freedom and
wholesome thrilling adventure—a primeval summons to primordial
values.*

— John Craighead

A Whimsical River

From encircling mountain ranges—the Medicine Bows to the east, the Never
Summers to the northeast, the Rabbit Ears to the south, and the Park Range to
the west—a thousand streams pour their bounty into the northernmost island
park in Colorado: North Park. North Park is smooth as a dance floor amid
the rough mountains. The Utes called it the "Bull Pen," because it held large
herds of buffalo. It was known by the trappers as New Park, probably because
it was the last to be discovered.

After coalescing in North Park, the chorus of mountain streams becomes
the North Platte River. On his 1844 expedition, Fremont the Pathfinder was
much taken with the place, describing it in glowing terms. No river, he observed, could ask a more beautiful orgin than that granted the Platte. The
Mallet brothers, French explorers, gave it the name Riviere de Plat, the flat
river. But there are canyons in its upper reaches where it is anything but flat.
Below North Park, where the North Platte leaves the basin, it tumbles through
Northgate Canyon. The hush of a tranquil river gives way to lively rapids. Its
major tributary, the Encampment, sports a classic whitewater run through a
deep, north-trending canyon in the Sierra Madre Mountains.

Both rivers evolved in a most peculiar way. Beyond the neck of North Park,
the North Platte defies logic. Instead of following the flat Saratoga Valley between the Medicine Bow and Sierra Madre Ranges, it carves a steep canyon
parallel to the valley in the flank of the Medicine Bow Range (see cross section,
page 207). The river, once at a higher level, was flowing on the east side of its
broad valley when it encountered the metasediments and metamorphic rock of
the Medicine Bow Mountains hidden underneath and began cutting into this
hard rock. At this point the river became trapped in harder rock and could not
escape to the soft gravels of the Saratoga Valley nearby. The river continued to
carve its canyon as the Medicine Bows slowly rose, entrenching itself still
deeper. Thus, Northgate Canyon was formed by a combination of superposition and antecedence.

The Encampment River, west of the North Platte, was once a mightier
stream than it is today. It began in the lofty Sawtooth Range, coursing northward to meet the North Platte. During the last Ice Age, however, the Encampment's headwaters were captured by a Colorado River tributary and redirected

from the East Slope to the West Slope. A large glacier had its source in the high country at the head of the Encampment, between the Mt. Zirkel Massif and the Sawtooths. The glacier, moving westward, found it difficult to turn south and follow the Encampment's riverbed. Instead it continued in a westerly direction at the base of the Sawtooths, where it met the headwaters of the North Fork of the Elk River. As the Ice Age progressed, this glacier cut a deep, U-shaped canyon. When it finally melted, the Encampment River had been beheaded.

Today boaters can stand in Encampment Meadows at the headwaters of that river, look southward up the valley toward the towering Sawtooth Range, and never realize that the glacier-hewn gorge of the North Fork of the Elk drops below their feet.

Tie Drives

It is March, 1903, in the high country along the Colorado-Wyoming border. A spring snow drifts down upon this empire of spruce and fir, sagging their branches under a white burden. The winter's accumulation has climbed 10 feet up the trunks. All is quiet.

A sudden crack followed by a loud boom breaks the stillness. A Douglas fir has met its end behind the powerful blows of the broad axe of a burley Swedish woodsman—a tie hack, "bull of the woods." The trunk is sawed into sections, each section neatly squared off. Horse drawn sleds pull newly cut piles of railroad ties to the bank of the Encampment River in Hog Park.

As April arrives, the Carbon Timber Company's tie hacks throw down their broad axes and take the month off. The mushy, melting snowpack is unsuitable for tie cutting and sledding. Next month, as the spring melt gains momen-

Tie hacks break a jam on Encampment River near Grand Encampment, Wyoming. (Grand Encampment Museum photo.)

tum, the men will pick up their pike poles and pickaroons and be transformed into river rats.

With the prospect of a month's respite, tie hacks from surrounding valleys head for Commissary Park, where the river flows gently through a wide, treeless valley at the head of its thunderous canyon. Some men travel the 20-mile road to the downstream town of Grand Encampment. Up at Commissary Park the bars—Robbers Roost and Hackers Delight—run "full blast with a double force of bartenders," says the *Grand Encampment Herald*. The newspaper relates boisterous activity at the tie camp this year:

"Nothing of an exciting nature happened except a couple of cutting affairs followed by a duel with shotguns between two noted desperadoes named Missouri Jack and Red Nose Pete. Owing to a poker chip getting into the muzzle of Missouri Jack's gun and splitting the charge, Red Nose Pete lost both ears while Missouri Jack received the full charge from Pete's gun. Missouri was immediately dropped into an old prospect hole and by way of variation in the days of celebration a lynching bee was formed with Pete as the central figure, hanging him from the limb of a pine.

"The lynching was followed by a dance in the camp hall, which lasted until midnight, when all returned to their homes filled with patriotism and enthusiasm. Everyone present at the tie camp's celebration felt that life is well worth living under the flag of the free whether in the center of civilization or in the heart of the Rocky Mountains."

The men at Commissary Park are filled with more than patriotism—many of the newly arrived immigrants are homesick. They decide to call this hodgepodge of cabins, stores, and bars "Sweden."

As April passes, half a million ties sit neatly stacked on the banks of the East Fork, Main Encampment, and Hog Park Creek. On many smaller creeks, flumes are ready to carry ties down to the river. Over on Douglas Creek, a northern tributary of the North Platte spilling out of the Medicine Bow Mountains to the east, another quarter million ties have been cut. It has been a good year for the Carbon Timber Company—so far.

An early May sun beats down on the snow-covered forest, bringing the river to life. For the tie hacks, the party is over. Hundreds of men go to their stations along the Encampment River and its tributaries. At the optimal moment, ties will be released to the river by the thousands to begin a journey through tumultuous Encampment Canyon to Grand Encampment. There, a boom across the river will catch them before they are sent en masse northward to the Platte River and the Union Pacific rail line at Fort Steele, Wyoming.

Timing is crucial to the drive. High water must be avoided because if the river drops, thousands of ties will be stranded on the banks and wedged in jams. The water should be rising, almost but not quite peaking. A slight miscalculation of snowpack or weather could mean financial ruin for the Carbon Timber Company.

When the signal finally comes, hundreds of tie hacks-turned-river-rats heave thousands of ties into the boiling Encampment River. Downstream, at narrow falls and constricted rapids, other men keep the drive going by breaking jams and rounding up strays (ties stranded in eddies) with their pike poles. It's dangerous work. If a jam should break loose unexpectedly, men on the rocks downstream could get swept into the river and crushed.

The drive of 1903 went well. There were few serious jams as the river kept rising during the drive. The better part of a million ties reached the Union Pacific tracks. But this was to be one of the last good years. Coming dry years would mean fewer ties reached their destination. Irrigation diversion dams were springing up on the river below Grand Encampment, causing the drivers great difficulty. Finally, a problem arose which was to have a fatal impact: On December 8, 1911, a headline in the *Grand Encampment Herald* read, "Carbon Timber Company Abandons Operations at the Tie Camp at Hog Park. Tie Drive Will Be A Thing of the Past." The reason:

"It is not that there is any lack of suitable timber, but that the present government policy is to let it stand for future generations or to be consumed in forest fires, rather than let it be used to aid the present prosperity and development of the country."

"The tie camp has been a considerable factor in the business interests of Encampment...for the past 10 years. Several million ties have been shipped out...but your Uncle Sam has written 'finis' to this industry for the present."

Thus ended the Encampment River tie drives.

Today little remains of the days of tie drive glory. The buildings at Commissary Park are gone. Only a few weathered remains of tie hack cabins can be found along the banks of tributary creeks.

North Platte River—Northgate Canyon Section

North Platte River: Routt Launch Site to Pickaroon Campground

Physical Data: 18 mi; 470-ft drop; 22 ft/mi average gradient; 40 ft/mi maximum gradient (for 4 miles above Six Mile Gap); 310,000 acre-ft average yearly discharge (near State Highway 125 Bridge).
Maps: Northgate, Horatio Rock, and Elkhorn Point USGS Quads.
Land Ownership: National Forest.
Information: North Park Ranger District, Walden, Colorado.

Since its discovery by river runners in the late 1960s, increasing numbers come yearly to court Northgate Canyon's tumbling descent. The river usually peaks twice: once in early May when the lowland snowfields of North Park melt; and again in June, when the encircling ranges release their pent-up waters. Extreme caution is advised above Six Mile Gap at high water. By mid-July in an average runoff year, although the water has dropped too low for rafting, kayakers can still get through. Canoes are prohibited.

The put-in is located a quarter-mile east of Colorado State Highway 125 (Wyoming State Highway 230), 12 miles north of Cowdrey, just downstream from the Platte River Bridge. A satisfactory take-out can be a problem. The intermediate take-out is located 12 miles downriver at Six Mile Gap, at the end of County Road 492. A steep, 200-yard hike is required from the river to the Six Mile Gap parking lot. Heavy rafts are not advised. The Pickaroon take-out is even harder to reach. A rough dirt road leads northeast toward the river from Big Creek, four miles north of the Six Mile Gap Road. A four-wheel-drive vehicle is recommended. Snow usually keeps this road closed until late May. Beyond Pickaroon, landowners block all access to the river for 16 miles, until Bennett Peak Campground.

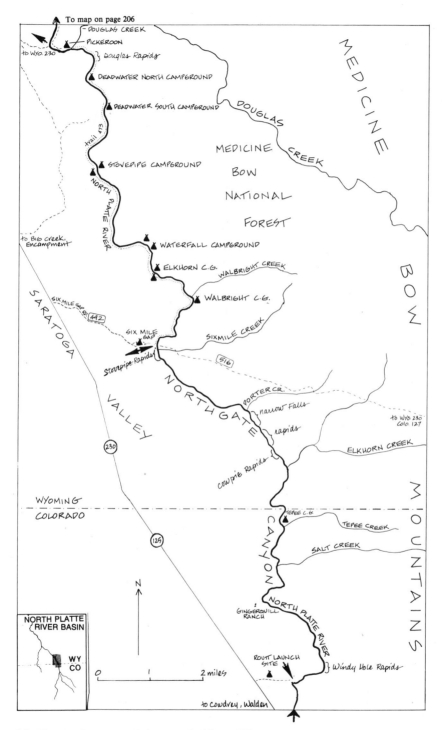

To map on page 206

DOUGLAS CREEK

PICKEROON

to Wyo. 230

Douglas Rapids

DEADWATER NORTH CAMPGROUND

DEADWATER SOUTH CAMPGROUND

DOUGLAS CREEK

MEDICINE

BOW

NATIONAL

FOREST

MEDICINE

BOW

NORTH PLATTE RIVER

Trail 473

STOVEPIPE CAMPGROUND

to Big Creek, Encampment

WATERFALL CAMPGROUND

ELKHORN C.G.

WALBRIGHT CREEK

WALBRIGHT C.G.

SIX MILE GAP

442

SIX MILE GAP

SIXMILE CREEK

Stovepipe Rapids

516

SARATOGA

VALLEY

NORTHGATE

PORTER CR.

narrow Falls

rapids

to Wyo. 230
Colo. 127

ELKHORN CREEK

230

Cowpie Rapids

WYOMING

COLORADO

125

CANYON

TEPEE C.G.

TEPEE CREEK

SALT CREEK

MOUNTAINS

N

NORTH PLATTE RIVER

GINGERQUILL
RANCH

NORTH PLATTE
RIVER BASIN

WY
CO

0   1   2 miles

ROUTT LAUNCH
SITE

Windy Hole Rapids

to Cowdrey, Walden

Northgate Canyon of the North Platte River.

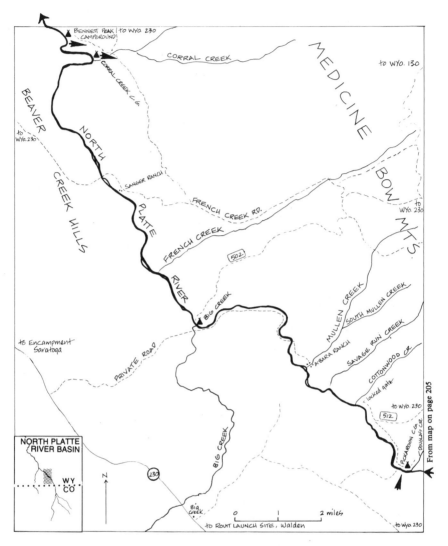

North Platte from Pickaroon to Bennett Peak Campground.

The first rapid, Windy Hole, is situated on the first curve below the Routt Launch Site. The next five miles contain only small rapids and riffles. Then, four miles above Six Mile Gap, at Cowpie Rapid, the heavy stuff begins. Bus-sized boulders clog the channel, and the gradient steepens considerably. The rapids in the mile between Cowpie and Narrow Falls tend to blend together, especially at high water. Beyond Narrow Falls there is a slight respite before Stovepipe Rapid, which is just above the Six Mile Gap access point.

Between Six Mile Gap and Pickaroon, the North Platte moderates considerably. The scenery, however, continues to be magnificent in this wild canyon. The boater's only regret will probably be that Northgate Canyon is too short. Many parties take a two-day run to Pickaroon, choosing one of the many

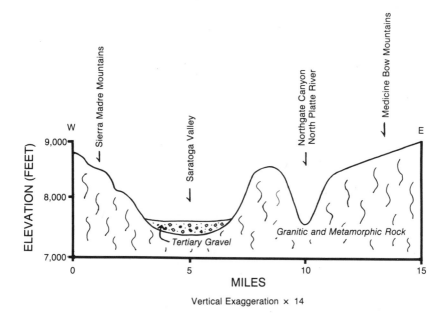

Cross section of Northgate Canyon and Saratoga Valley just north of Six Mile Gap.

splendid, forest-draped campsites along the way. Others continue on the flat water to Bennett Peak Campground.

The Forest Service requires a permit for Northgate. Private boaters can obtain permits at the put-in. During the prime high water season the river tends to be crowded on weekends, but solitude can be found on weekdays.

Encampment River

To my knowledge, Don Grall and I were the first to run the Encampment. There is good sport in this forested canyon if the water is neither too high nor too low. When we started down the Encampment in 1978, the water was too high. We knew we had found the paradigm of technical wilderness streams, but at flood stage its difficulty placed us in the lunatic fringe. Each section had to be carefully evaluated from the bordering trail, and in several places we had to carry our boats. Perhaps, we thought, the entire section could be paddled without portage at a lower stage.

We returned on July 18 of that year with three others to find out. At a moderate level, the answer to our question was a resounding yes—though plenty of elan had to be mustered at Entrance Falls, Damnation Alley, and S-Turn Gorge, all of class V difficulty.

Encampment River: Commissary Park to Encampment

Physical Data: 20 mi; 1,240-ft drop; 62 ft/mi average gradient; 130 ft/mi maximum gradient (Box Canyon Creek to Cascade Creek—3 miles).

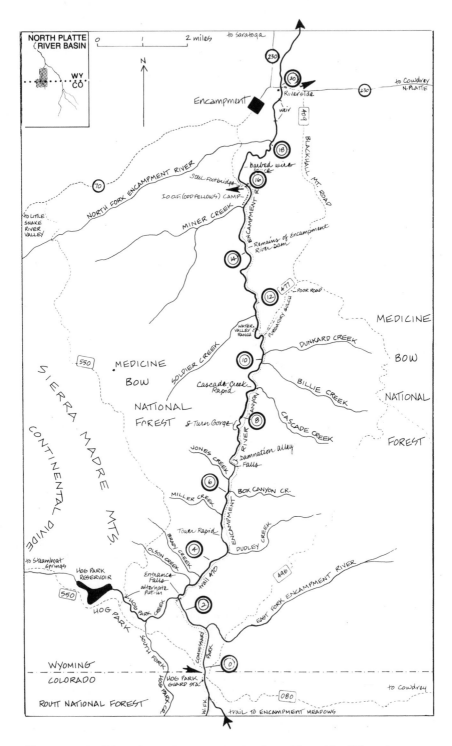

Encampment River from Commissary Park to Riverside, Wyoming.

Maps: Dudley Creek and Encampment USGS Quads; Medicine Bow National Forest Map.

Land Ownership: National Forest; BLM; Private land at Water Valley Ranch, I.O.O.F. Camp, and last mile above Wyoming 230 Bridge.

The source of the Encampment River lies in the Sierra Madre Mountains north of Steamboat Springs. It becomes navigable in the alpine meadow known as Commissary Park on the Wyoming-Colorado border. From here the Encampment dashes into a deep, wilderness canyon flowing due north for 20 miles to the town of Encampment, Wyoming. Below Encampment it joins the North Platte.

The river is without question too difficult for rafts, but for expert kayakers no finer technical water exists in the Southern Rocky Mountains. The continuous class IV water, punctuated with class V drops, hardly lets up for a distance of 10 miles, nor do the deep seclusion and lush beauty of the fringing forest.

The put-in at Commissary Park below the Hog Park Guard Station can be reached by driving south from Encampment on Forest Road 550 west of the river, or from Riverside on Blackhall Mountain Road east of the river. There are also good roads to the put-in from Cowdrey, Colorado on Forest Road 080 and Steamboat Lake on Forest Road 550. At high water levels an alternate put-in spot can be found on Hog Park Creek below the reservoir.

The run can be made in one long day. It seems a shame not to linger in the magnificence of this wild, granite canyon, but carrying overnight gear requires a heavier boat—take your choice.

One mile below the put-in at Commissary Park, the river nearly doubles in size with the addition of the East Fork. In another mile Hog Park Creek again adds to the flow volume.

The exciting action begins below the footbridge at the Hog Park Creek confluence. The trail following the right bank of the river (Trail #470) provides good scouting access. There are hundreds of difficult slalom-type moves in the next ten miles. Boaters must be capable of quick, accurate appraisal of the river ahead.

At mile four, above Dudley Creek, the gradient eases a bit as the river makes a sharp turn to the west. Boaters will find good campsites at the mouth of Dudley Creek. An old broken-down flume once used by tie hacks can be found along the banks of Dudley Creek. Numerous fairy slipper orchids adorn this part of the canyon in June and early July.

A half-mile below Dudley Creek the Encampment turns north again. Here the boating becomes very technical for half a mile.

Below Box Canyon Creek the Encampment steals into a precipitous gorge filled with boiling rapids. Near the end of the gorge, a six-foot navigable falls marks the approach of Damnation Alley (mile 6.8). A stone's throw below the falls, the river drops out of sight. Stop and scout from the trail river-right. Damnation Alley is a technical chute 200 yards long with a gradient of 250 feet per mile. At high water it consists of a series of big stopper holes. As water level drops it becomes narrow and technical. At flood stage it is an unnavigable, frothing morass. Damnation Alley is reminiscent of Pine Creek Rapid on the Arkansas.

The Encampment lets up very little as it turns north again below Damnation Alley. The next mile consists of continuous class IV water. A herd of bighorn sheep often haunts this area on the west side of the canyon.

S-Turn Gorge is next. A low falls marks its entrance at mile 7.8. Here the river swings to the right through a series of steep drops before turning back to the left and crashing into a cabin-sized mid-river boulder.

Below S-Turn Gorge the river continues to be demanding. A last big rapid lies at the Cascade Creek confluence, mile 9.1. Below Cascade Creek the difficulty begins to ease past Purgatory Gulch and the Water Valley Ranch. The brushy alders which have lined the riverbank for miles give way to groves of tall cottonwoods. The south-facing canyon slopes are covered with sagebrush, but patches of evergreen forest still cling to the north-facing slopes.

At mile 14.1 two broken-down wooden structures rise from each bank, and the river swoops through a big wave between. This is all that remains of the North American Copper Company's Encampment River Dam. Built in 1902, the wooden dam was 18 feet high. A pipe four feet in diameter led from the dam downriver to an electrical generating plant at the big smelting works in Grand Encampment.

The best take-out is just beyond the I.O.O.F. (Odd Fellows) Camp at a new steel footbridge, about two miles past the old dam site. A two-mile dirt road going south out of the town of Encampment leads to the public footbridge and the I.O.O.F. Camp.

One-half mile past the footbridge, a river-spanning barbed wire fence requires caution. Two diversion weirs farther down produce small rapids. The last take-out is at the Wyoming State Highway 230 Bridge in Riverside.

As you pass through the outskirts of Encampment note the red, green, and yellow soils on the flats beside the river. This was the site of the Grand Encampment Copper Smelter. Around the turn of the century, the world's longest aerial tram supplied copper ore to the smelter from the Ferris-Haggarty Mine on the Continental Divide 16 miles to the west. Before the big copper strikes, the townsite, known as Camp le Grande, was a favorite rendezvous of Indians and trappers.

The problem with the Encampment is that of scheduling a trip on this small river at a moderate level. The river is quite dangerous at very high levels and drops to unnavigable levels by late July. The U.S. Geological Survey does not monitor the river daily, so there is no way to phone for the water level unless you know someone in the town of Encampment. Because it is a free-flowing river, however, a fairly accurate judgement of the water level on a particular date can be made in advance. During high water years, snow blocks the access roads to Hog Park in May and early June when the river is on the way up, so

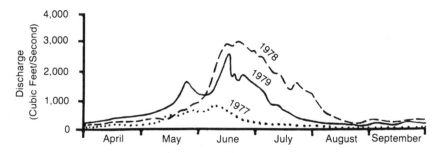

Hydrograph of Encampment River near Encampment, Wyoming (approximately one-half this flow at Commissary Park put-in).

John Hough in Damnation Alley.

catch this run while the river drops. This is almost always during the first two weeks in July (see hydrograph, page 210). In a year with average snowpack, the river will usually be navigable between the first of June and the first of July. In a low year it becomes navigable for only a short time, usually early to mid June. Obtain the *Water Supply Outlook for Wyoming,* published and distributed free by the Soil Conservation Service, the winter prior to your trip. With this tool you can accurately appraise the coming runoff pattern and plan your trip for the optimum time. Ask for the publication from the Snow Survey Supervisor, Soil Conservation Service, P.O. Box 2440, Casper, Wyoming 82601.

A substantial trans-Divide water project is underway which will affect the Encampment River's flow. The dam on Hog Park Creek is being raised to accomodate a big new diversion tunnel from the Little Snake River drainage. In a few years this diversion will substantially enhance the Encampment's flow below Hog Park. The Forest Service has worked hard to insure minimal damage to the river habitat in Encampment Canyon. Dam operators will be required to release only the natural flow during the high water season. As the level drops, water from the Little Snake River Basin will be released. The project should provide a longer boating season on the Encampment. Say goodbye to the Little Snake.

South Platte River Basin

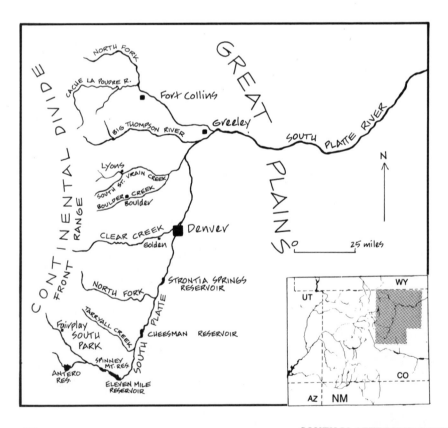

*A river is more than an amenity;
it is a treasure.*
   —Justice William O. Douglas

The Many-Fingered River

The tributaries of the South Platte spring from the Front Range like the fingers of a great hand, the tip of each finger pointing skyward to the Continental Divide. All of these rivers are short, small, with steep gradients, roaring defiantly, confined by high granite walls. All have unnavigable sections where they tumble over cascades. When they emerge from the mountains, it is as though a thunderstorm has just passed. Suddenly they calm, sparkle placidly across the plains, and coalesce between Denver and Greeley.

There are no long runs in these mountain canyons. The drop from the Divide to the plains is a short one. Tumbling descents and narrow river beds generally preclude rafts. These rivers are suited to nimble fiberglass kayaks, whose enthusiasts flock to their scenic reaches each spring and summer.

The canyons provide easy routes from population centers on the plains up into the high country. Accompanying roads offer abundant access points and scouting opportunities. Occasionally, floodwaters wreak vengeful destruction on bank-side roads, as happened in the canyon of the Big Thompson River in 1945, 1951, and 1976.

The best paddling in the South Platte Basin can be found on those tributaries whose flow is enhanced by trans-Divide diversion tunnels—the Cache la Poudre, Clear Creek, and North Fork of the South Platte.

Cache la Poudre River

Originating in Rocky Mountain National Park, the Cache la Poudre—known to its devotees simply as the Poudre—flows in a northerly direction for 25 miles. Then, as if sensing its ultimate destiny as a Great Plains river, it abruptly turns eastward. Gathering momentum and bulk, it carves a twisting canyon 40 miles long into the granitic and metamorphic rocks of the Front Range. The river walls flare out near Fort Collins, and the Poudre moves off across the flatlands to meet the South Platte. Its vicissitudes range from meadowy parks to short, boulder-studded gorges.

As its name "hide the powder" implies, the river has enjoyed a colorful history. Exactly who hid the powder has never been established with certainty. The first to record the name was Colonel Henry Dodge on a mission west from St. Louis to make friends with the plains Indians. His journal notes that on July 18, 1835, they "passed the mouth of the Cache de la Poudre, a stream emptying into the Platte."

Several accounts concur that the cache in question was made by trappers caught in a snowstorm at Pleasant Valley just below the mouth of Poudre Canyon. It seems probable the trappers were William Ashley's party making their way up the Platte to the Green, the successful navigation of which made Ashley the West's first river runner (see Upper Green River Basin). Several members of Ashley's party mentioned a cache. The expedition was made in the winter months, which would explain accounts of a snowstorm. It is most likely that while the men spent several days probing the mountains to find a satisfactory route westward, they hid their valuable powder to protect it from thieving Indians. After scouting a route west, they probably dug up the cache and continued their journey.

Whether or not Ashley's trappers made the famous cache, his party was almost certainly the first to enter the Poudre's mountain gate. The route up the main fork was blocked by snow, and the men turned up the North Fork, an easier trail around the Medicine Bow Range. This route to the northwest from the plains later became known as the Cherokee Trail.

In 1860, when rumors circulated that the coming Transcontinental Railroad would use the Cherokee Trail route, a covey of speculators rushed to the Poudre and established the Laporte Townsite Company in 1860. The company claimed 1,280 acres along the river just north of the site of present-day Fort Collins.

Unfortunately for the speculators, the Cherokee Trail route was not the one chosen. Years later, however, another railroad, the Burlington Northern, brought men to the Poudre's upper reaches. Over a million railroad ties were cut around Chambers Lake at the head of the canyon and floated down the Poudre to the plains while the railroad was being built.

In the 1870s, Nathaniel Meeker brought life to the dry but fertile plains around his newly formed Greeley Colony through a series of high ditches which trapped the Poudre near its canyon mouth (see White River Basin). Since the snow-fed river carried excess capacity for irrigation in the late spring and an inadequate flow by mid-summer, Meeker and his cohorts built small reservoirs near the headwaters to store water until it was needed. In addition, they originated methods of augmenting the river's total volume. A landslide hundreds of years before had blocked the Poudre's western neighbor, the Laramie River, where it straddles the Divide. The outlet of the resulting lake (named Chambers Lake for Robert Chambers, killed by Indians there in 1858) took a new channel into the Poudre River by way of Joe Wright Creek. Meeker's first project was to dam the outlet of Chambers Lake. Water could then be released from the lake at will. Ditches were built from the Colorado and North Platte watersheds through La Poudre Pass and Cameron Pass, bringing water into the Poudre River by gravity feed. The most ambitious diversion project, the Laramie-Poudre Tunnel built in 1906, tapped the Laramie River through a two-mile tunnel.

Today agricultural interests demand more water from the Poudre. The result is the Bureau of Reclamation's planned Grey Mountain Project, a complicated system of dams, tunnels, and conduits that would still 30 miles in the Poudre Canyon. On the other hand, the Forest Service has recommended 67 miles of the Poudre for the National Wild and Scenic River System, making it the only river in the Front Range to be so recommended. River runners, canyon residents whose homes would be inundated, and fishermen are lining up against the proposed water project. Anglers often call the Poudre the "trout route" because of its plentiful bounty. The popularity of the canyon is such that the battle should prove particularly fierce.

Cache la Poudre River: Laramie-Poudre Tunnel to Second Headgate

Physical Data: 43 mi; 1,650-ft drop; 38 ft/mi average gradient; 140 ft/mi maximum gradient (for 2 miles through Big Narrows); 300,000 acre-ft average yearly discharge.
Maps: Kinnikinnik, Rustic, Big Narrows, Poudre Park, and Laporte USGS Quads.
Land Ownership: Alternating strips of private land and National Forest.
Information: U.S. Forest Service, Fort Collins, CO.

The Poudre reigns as one of Colorado's premier kayaking rivers. Although a staircase profile precludes lengthy runs, the river boasts dozens of short runs. Meadowy stretches give way to impassable cataracts. Confined in a granite canyon, the Poudre has few stretches for beginners. For intermediates and experts, good sport can be found if water is not too high. In late May and early June, caution is advised. During high water periods, the Poudre will put the kayaker to his mettle. The large granite boulders clogging the riverbed produce awesome holes.

Paved State Highway 14 skirts the river in Poudre Canyon, providing ample scouting opportunities. Numerous National Forest picnic sites and campgrounds make access plentiful.

The Poudre is navigable between the Laramie-Poudre Tunnel and the headgate dam above Ted's Place at the mouth of the canyon. Permits, obtained from the local sheriff's office, are sometimes required, especially during high

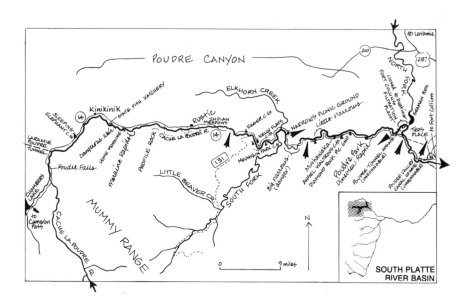

Cache la Poudre River Canyon.

water periods. Starting upstream, the following are the more popular stretches:

• *Kinikinik Run:* Sleeping Elephant Campground to below State Fish Hatchery, novice, 6 miles. Dangerous diversion weir below Fish Hatchery. The river is backed up by Home Moraine.

• *Rustic Run*: Home Moraine to the bridge at Indian Meadows, expert, 8 miles. Difficult water at Moraine Rapids at the top of the run. Considerable private land in this stretch.

• *Race Course Run*: Bridge at Indian Meadows to Narrows Picnic Area, advanced, 9 miles. Many access points. Slalom and downriver races are held in the stretch during the last weekend in May.

• *Big Narrows:* One-half mile below Narrows Picnic Area for a distance downriver of 2 miles. Danger, class V and VI rapids.

• *Mishawaka Run:* Campground below Big Narrows to Diamond Rock Picnic Area, advanced, 5 miles. Passes Little Narrows.

• *Bridges Run:* Base of Pineview Rapid (class IV to V) below Poudre Park to Poudre Tunnel Headgate, intermediate, 3 miles. Below the headgate the river is closed where it passes another small dam, the Fort Collins Filtration Plant, and the North Fork confluence.

• *Beginner Run:* Put in 1 mile below Poudre Tunnel Headgate and run to the big bend above the Poudre Valley Canal Headgate (unnavigable), beginner-novice, 3 miles.

South and North Forks of the Poudre

The plummeting South Fork and tiny North Fork have occasionally been paddled. Both are scenic runs, marginally boatable. The South Fork is especially hazardous. In its final 10 miles it drops 1,350 feet for a nearly impassable average gradient of 135 feet per mile. Numerous portages are required. In addition, it reaches a navigable stage of about 300 c.f.s. only in June in high water years. Its wild, forest-cloaked canyon holds many log jams. It is strictly for those with a taste for adventure.

A seven-mile run can be made on the North Fork from the Livermore Bridge on the Red Feather Lakes Road to the Seaman Reservoir. Upstream diversions take much of the river, but when it flows, the North Fork Canyon offers a good intermediate run.

Big Thompson River, St. Vrain and Boulder Creeks

This trio of tiny rivers south of the Poudre has adequate water for boating only at peak levels in high water years. Nevertheless, at such seasons they provide some notable runs.

The Big Thompson is the largest. Its flow leaves the riverbed near Estes Park and is taken through a series of pipes down to the plains. In June of a heavy runoff year, however, some good, expert-level boating may be found between Drake, at the North Fork confluence, and the Narrows, five miles downstream. Its gradient here reaches 120 feet per mile. The river can be scouted

Narrows of the Poudre River as they looked in the early 1900s. The Narrows haven't changed much. (Denver Public Library Western History Dept. photo.)

from U.S. Highway 34, which skirts the river in the bed of Big Thompson Canyon. Access is available from Highway 34.

The mountain stretches of the North and South forks of the St. Vrain River plunge precipitously through unnavigable canyons. The two forks meet at the town of Lyons, set between the hogbacks at the base of the mountains. For several miles above Lyons, in the transition zone between the granite canyons and the plains, both forks become navigable. During June in a heavy snow-pack year, some intermediate- to expert-level kayaking can be found here. Roads providing access follow both rivers above Lyons.

Boulder Creek has marginally navigable water in the last five miles of its granite canyon above Boulder. In some years it captures an adequate flow for paddling into July. In drier years it lacks sufficient water at any time. Boulder Creek is a steep and hazardous run, for experts only. The gradient approaches 200 feet per mile in places. Obstacles include logs, debris in the water, and small dams. It should be carefully scouted and evaluated from the skirting canyon road, Colorado State Highway 119. Access is available from this road.

Clear Creek

Much is hidden in the bends of Clear Creek's canyon, where the river rocked thousands of sluice boxes for the early gold and silver miners. In the 1850s, Central City on North Clear Creek became known as the "Richest Square Mile on Earth." Stories of wealth, luxury, privation, and poverty flowed from the mouth of Clear Creek Canyon into Denver during the mining era.

The stream was originally named the Vasquez Fork. The name was ironical-ly changed to Clear Creek just before its waters were turned into mud by the countless placer operations set up in its bed. "The stream had been full of trout that would rival any of their speckled cousins from the White Mountains or the Adirondacks but the dirt drove them away," lamented Thomas Knox in *Frank Leslie's Illustrated Newspaper* in 1871. Today, as mining activity dies away, Clear Creek is once again becoming worthy of its name.

A note for trivia buffs: west of Idaho Springs the Fall River enters Clear Creek from the north. This may be one of the few places in the world where a river flows into a creek.

In the 1950s, a century after the gold rush, kayakers discovered Clear Creek. A six-mile stretch from Idaho Springs to the junction of U.S. Highways 6 and 40 was once the site of an annual slalom and downriver race, held each June. With the coming of Interstate 70 the races were abandoned, but this short stretch is still occasionally used by intermediate boaters. There are no other intermediate stretches on Clear Creek.

Above Idaho Springs the river is impassable. From a point seven miles downriver of Idaho Springs to Golden, Clear Creek is a lunging boat and back breaker. Each June some people try their luck on the river in tubes and flimsy rubber rafts. Each June reports of drownings in these tumultuous waters hit the newspapers. The tragic stories immediately induce the local sheriff to close the river. This is unfortunate, for there is good sport for kayaks and decked canoes on Clear Creek's wildhorse current. But it should be tested only by experts. Most of the river can be scouted directly from Highway 6. Careful evaluation is a necessity. Roadside rest areas provide plentiful access points. Enhanced by West Slope water, Clear Creek exceeds 1,000 c.f.s. during June in an average runoff year. During this period the river should be considered extremely hazardous, with only short boatable stretches. The best months for paddling are May, before high water, and July, after high water. Inadequate flow at other times precludes boating.

Clear Creek: I-70 Junction to Above Golden

Physical Data: 15 mi; 1,550-ft drop; 103 ft/mi average gradient; 160 ft/mi maximum gradient (for 2 miles in middle of run above and below double tunnel); 117,000 acre-ft average yearly discharge (near Golden).
Maps: Squaw Pass, Evergreen, and Golden USGS Quads.
Land Ownership: Mostly highway right-of-way and private land.

An upper put-in can be made at the Clear Creek Inn below the junction of Interstate 70 and U.S. Highway 6. The next three miles, past Tunnel #6 and Tunnel #5 to the State Highway 119 Junction, hold class III and IV water with several riverside campsites.

The river eases for three miles below Highway 119. Boulders and gravel have been removed from the riverbed and piled in mounds along the shore by abandoned large-scale placer operations. The paddler should not be lulled into complacency on this class II and III water, because below the tailings piles, Clear Creek gets nasty. The next four miles are the most difficult on the river. Several class V rapids, some produced by log jams, lead past Tunnel #3 to the bridge below Tunnel #2. Immediately below the bridge a class V or VI rapid—narrow, twisting, and tricky—greets paddlers brave (or crazy) enough to tackle it. Another class V to VI rapid with three drops and big holes sits just above the next bridge. In the two miles below this second bridge, the river eases slightly to class IV and V. Vertical walls and river-choking boulders of

Idaho Springs gneiss offer little relief in Clear Creek's relentless plunge to the plains.

A dangerous four-foot-high weir just above Tunnel #1 is a mandatory portage. Lives have been lost in the backwash beneath this dam. A gage here marks the water level. Below Tunnel #1, Clear Creek's difficulty gradually eases as boaters approach Golden. There are several take-out points along U.S. Highway 6 just above the city limits.

South Platte River

The North Fork of the South Platte spills off Mt. Evans, flowing due east through a series of canyons to meet the South Fork. The South Fork gathers in South Park, where it meanders sluggishly across willow flats to the edge of the Front Range. Here it knifes through Eleven Mile Canyon, then Cheesman and Platte canyons, where the two forks meet. The augmented river then traverses Waterton Canyon before its granite walls flare out and it meets the plains southwest of Denver.

As early as the 1850s, miners used the canyons of the South Platte as a route to the gold fields of South Park. The corridor served the historic mining towns of Fairplay and Alma. One of Colorado's first mountain narrow-gauge railroads—the Denver South Park and Pacific—was built through Waterton Canyon and up the North Fork in 1876. It brought life to the timber industries and mining towns of South Park and was later extended to Leadville at the headwaters of the Arkansas.

Although the railroad was removed in 1938, it left behind many historical sites. Stations such as South Platte, Buffalo Creek, Pine, and Bailey remain as small resort communities on the North Fork. Others, such as the Strontia Springs Resort in Waterton Canyon and Crossons in the narrow canyon above Pine, lie in ruins along the abandoned grade. Crossons was established as a lead bullion refinery, the only works of its kind in Colorado. In its heyday,

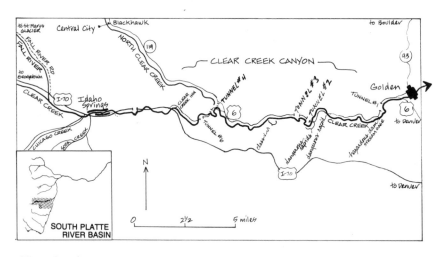

Clear Creek.

Crossons refinery was capable of treating 200 tons of lead ore per day.

As Denver's main water supply, the South Platte has long been a target of ambitious water projects. The Denver Water Board's first impoundment came in the early 1900s with construction of the Cheesman Dam and Reservoir. Later, two other reservoirs were built in South Park—Antero on the west side and Eleven Mile on the east where the river begins its canyoned descent. In the early 1960s, Dillon Reservoir was constructed on the Blue River. The 25-mile-long Roberts Tunnel brought the Blue's bounty from Dillon through the Continental Divide to the North Fork of the South Platte. In 1980 the Spinney Mountain Dam was built in South Park just above Eleven Mile Reservoir. After a fierce battle, the Water Board was recently authorized to build Strontia Springs Dam and Reservoir. This most recent project eliminates most of much-loved Waterton Canyon. The blasting and flooding of once-wild Waterton is taking its toll not only on whitewater enthusiasts, but on one of Colorado's last herds of indigenous bighorn sheep. This herd, once comprising 65 sheep, is dying at an alarming rate and for unexplained reasons: perhaps because of stress and trauma related to construction.

The Water Board's next target is the top of Waterton Canyon just below the confluence of the North and South Forks: the Two Forks Dam site. This will be the Board's most ambitious project to date. The high dam will back the river's water up the scenic North Fork seven miles to Foxton and up the South Fork 15 miles past Deckers Resort. Two Forks Reservoir would be the largest in the Colorado mountains. To fill it would require much more water from the West Slope than is presently being exported, resulting in more tunnels through the Divide and more destruction of the West Slope watershed.

But Two Forks Reservoir is not a sure thing. Fishermen, canoeists, and recreationists are mobilizing to protect their beloved South Platte canyons. No other place in the country exhibits such a diverse ecological character or so much lush beauty so close to a major metropolitan area. When it comes to a choice, Denver residents will choose the canyons.

North Fork of the South Platte River: Bailey to Pine

Physical Data: 11 mi; 950-ft drop; 86 ft/mi average gradient; 200 ft/mi maximum gradient (for 2 miles half a mile into the canyon); 100,000 acre-ft average yearly discharge.
Maps: Bailey and Pine USGS Quads.
Land Ownership: National Forest in canyon; private above and below canyon.
Flow Information: Denver Water Board Public Relations Dept., Denver, CO.

Enhanced by the Roberts Tunnel from Dillon Reservoir, the North Fork maintains an adequate boating flow (250 to 800 c.f.s.) not only in the summer months, but well into the fall. It is one of the few technical rivers close to Denver that has good water late in the season. When the North Fork is high, the South Fork is usually low and vice versa. The Water Board alternately turns on one river or the other to meet Denver's needs.

The stretch between Bailey and Pine holds the only wild, navigable canyon on the North Fork since the damming of Waterton Canyon. It is one of the finest highly technical runs in Colorado. Only expert paddlers should venture into it. Clear, cold water tumbles beneath steep slopes covered with ponderosa pines. July and August are the best months for a run.

Boaters have sometimes run into problems with landowners around the put-in and take-out. Caution and courtesy are advised. Once in the canyon you will be on National Forest land.

A good put-in is found at the first bridge downriver from Bailey. If the gage one mile downriver exceeds two feet, you will find hazardous boating ahead. A short, class II to III canyon is followed by a second mile of private ranches before the river turns north and abruptly enters the sheltered gorge.

Class III and IV rapids come one after another through the length of the canyon, but three major drops (class V to VI) stand apart from the rest. These three major drops are portaged by most paddlers. The old Denver South Park and Pacific Railroad grade, overgrown in places, makes scouting and portaging easy.

The first portage, at Four Falls, is reached half a mile into the canyon. One mile of marvelously technical water below Four Falls leads to Super Max, a huge drop and the second portage. A little over a mile beyond Super Max, just beyond the Deer Creek confluence, lies the last portage past Deer Creek Rapid. A massive chunk of granite, slumped off the right wall, marks the entrance to the rapid. Passage through Deer Creek Rapid is blocked by a piece of cut timber, probably from the railroad. At higher water levels it might be possible to sneak down the right side past the timber.

A quarter of a mile beyond Deer Creek Rapid, the ruins of Crossons are seen on the riverbank. After another two miles or so of class III and IV water the canyon gradually opens up. This land belongs to the Pine Valley Ranch; its magnificent lodge can be seen ahead. Upstream from the lodge a small dam will probably require a short carry. Beyond the ranch, the river holds three more good class IV drops before reaching Pine. A good take-out is found at

Super Max, a class VI rapid in canyon between Bailey and Pine. Rick Dukes in foreground. (Don Grall photo.)

the bridge below State Highway 126 just upriver from Pine. A gage is fixed to the underside of the bridge. Between eight inches and 1.5 feet on the gage marks a good level for boating. Cars should be parked on the highway above and boats carried quickly away from the private land around the bridge.

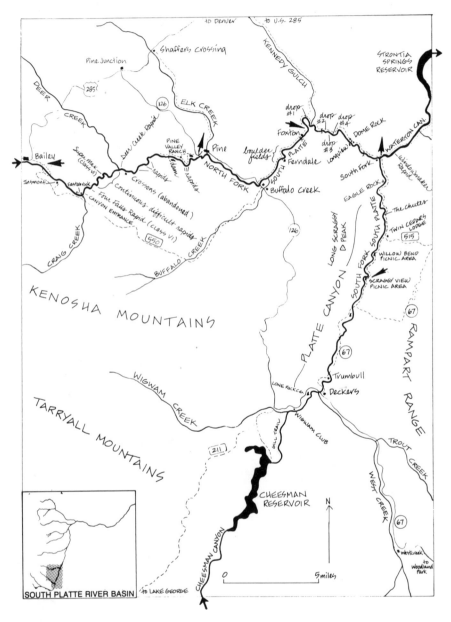

North and South forks of the South Platte River.

SOUTH PLATTE RIVER

North Fork of the South Platte River:
Buffalo Creek to South Fork Confluence

Physical Data: 10 mi; 610-ft drop; 61 ft/mi average gradient; 110,000 acre-ft average yearly discharge (at South Platte).
Maps: Pine and Platte Canyon USGS Quads.
Land Ownership: Alternating private and National Forest.
Flow Information: Denver Water Board Public Relations Dept., Denver, CO.

Below the town of Buffalo Creek, the North Fork again provides boating opportunities. The river can be scouted from the dirt road which skirts its north side. Numerous roadside access points lie along the route. Where the river crosses blocks of private land, fences may prevent access. Picnickers, fishermen, and campers enjoy the canyon along with kayakers and a few rafters.

Technical rapids begin one-half mile above the resort cabins at Ferndale. Cabin-sized blocks of granite choke the riverbed and offer a complex maze of chutes and drops above and below Ferndale. The North Fork quiets down past Foxton, then makes a sharp turn to the east. For five miles past this corner, it plunges over a series of steep drops. Log jams can be a hazard here. Drop number one lies just past the corner. One mile beyond the corner is a low bridge. The next three drops are encountered in the next mile beyond the low bridge. Each of these reach class IV difficulty at higher water levels. Beyond them the river passes broad campsites and a huge cut stone beside the river called the Westall Monument. A message on the stone reads, "Tell my wife I died thinking of her." The small towns of Dome Rock and Longview are passed in the next mile below the Westall Monument. Watch for a low bridge at Longview. In the last two miles above the South Fork confluence, the river eases to a class II to III level.

Below this confluence lies Waterton Canyon. The upper part of the canyon, with its lunging rapids, may be opened by the Denver Water Board down to the new Strontia Springs Reservoir. Below the dam the river will probably be dewatered much of the time.

South Fork of the South Platte River:
Eleven Mile and Cheesman Canyons

Unnavigable rapids prevent an extended run through Eleven Mile Canyon. Short stretches of boatable water, however, offer interesting play spots.

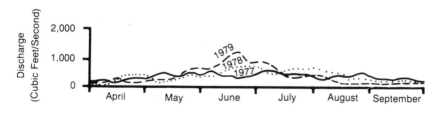

Hydrograph of North Fork of the South Platte River above South Fork confluence.

Below Lake George, where the river passes under U.S. Highway 24, the South Platte enters a wild canyon which ends at Cheesman Lake Reservoir. Impassable cascades and places where the river tunnels beneath piles of huge boulders hinder passage through this canyon.

If you can get down to the river at the base of Cheesman Dam (this is Denver Water Board property), there is a wild, three-mile canyon with rapids approaching class IV that leads past the private Wigwam Club (permission required). A small dam creates a steep class IV rapid adjacent to the club buildings. A take-out is found at the Lone Rock Campground off State Highway 126 one mile past the private resort. This is one of the most popular fishing stretches in Colorado—flies only, catch and release.

South Fork of the South Platte River: Deckers to North Fork Confluence

Physical Data: 14 mi; 300-ft drop; 21.5 ft/mi average gradient; 113,000 acre-ft average yearly discharge (below Cheesman Dam).
Maps: Deckers and Platte Canyon USGS Quads.
Land Ownership: Alternating private and National Forest.
Flow Information: Denver Water Board Public Relations Dept., Denver, CO.

Below Deckers, the South Platte Canyon is a favorite resort and fishing area. Although the rapids are generally light, landowners have thrown up fences and "No Trepassing" signs in several places along the route. Access points for short runs are available at riverside campsites and picnic grounds, Adequate flows from the upstream reservoirs arrive sporadically through the summer months.

A good class I to II run in Platte Canyon goes from Scraggy View Picnic Area (six miles from Deckers) to Willow Bend Picnic Area (eight miles from Deckers). The last four miles to the North Fork confluence is also readily accessable and contains some interesting water. You can put in across from the Twin Cedars Lodge. One mile downstream lies the Chutes, a steep slot popular with inner tubers but recently closed by the Water Board. Placid water beyond the Chutes leads to a sharp left curve around Eagle Rock. Class II rapids ripple in this vicinity.

The two forks differ markedly in the last miles above their confluence. The North Fork is steeper and more boulder clogged. The banks are choked with twisting alders. The South Fork has many sandy beaches, and willows, not alders, inhabit the area.

South Platte River: Below Chatfield Dam

Emerging from the mouth of its canyon, the South Platte stills behind Chatfield Dam. Below the dam the river enters the Denver urban area. Here the South Platte is used for disposal of junk, industrial waste, and treated sewage. Its gradient is concentrated behind a myriad of small dams. It is not particularly attractive for boating. The Greenway Foundation of Denver, however, is beautifying the river corridor and installing boating facilities. They built a permanent slalom course at Confluence Park. Chutes are being installed at many of the dams to allow safe passage. Future plans include a boating center with showers, lockers, and a concession for raft, kayak, and canoe rental and instruction.

Raft crew heads into Widowmaker Rapid in Waterton Canyon. (Tom Fellows photo.)

Two runs in the Denver corridor are noteworthy. The first begins at the Chatfield dam and ends five miles downstream at Bellview Avenue. The city of Littleton is presently building parks along this run. The second stretch starts at Frog Hollow, the 8th Avenue Boat Launch. This is probably Denver's most popular run. A concrete chute allows boaters to get past the fabric dam at the Zuni Powerplant half a mile down the run. Confluence Park, where Cherry Creek meets the South Platte, is reached two miles downstream. A handy slalom course chute gets paddlers past the falls here. Several more artificial rapids greet boaters down to a good take-out at the Globeville Landing just upriver from the Interstate 70 Bridge.

The next 10 miles past the north outskirts of the Denver metropolitan area are not recommended due to stockyards and oil refineries. Farther from Denver many attractive, tranquil canoe runs are possible. Irrigation dams every few miles may require portaging. From below Denver to the Nebraska border, the South Platte flows on private ranchland, and permission to float should be sought from landowners.

Arkansas River Basin

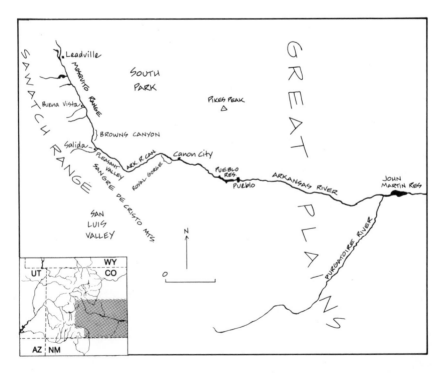

Leadville

SAWATCH RANGE

MOSQUITO RANGE

SOUTH PARK

Buena Vista

PIKES PEAK

BROWNS CANYON

Salida

PLEASANT VALLEY

SAN GRE DE CRISTO MTS

ARK R CAN

ROYAL GORGE

Canon City

PUEBLO RES.

PUEBLO

ARKANSAS RIVER

JOHN MARTIN RES

GREAT PLAINS

PURGATOIRE RIVER

SAN LUIS VALLEY

N

WY

UT CO

AZ NM

*Rivers are roads that
move and carry us whither
we wish to go.*
—Pascal

Geologic History of the Arkansas

The Arkansas comes to life in a broad, timberline basin between the Sawatch and Mosquito ranges surrounding Leadville, Colorado. Here the evening shadows of Colorado's highest peaks—Massive, Elbert, and La Plata—creep across the young river as it picks up momentum and bulk. It is fed in its early stages not only by streams from the flanking mountains, but by a score of ditches and tunnels originating in the West Slope drainages of the Eagle, Fryingpan, and Roaring Fork rivers. However, it is unique among Colorado rivers in that it has no river-sized tributaries. Where the Arkansas passes Buena Vista at the mouth of Cottonwood Creek, the granite monarchs of the Collegiate Range—Oxford, Harvard, Columbia, Yale, and Princeton—tower above its waters.

Below Buena Vista the Arkansas enters granitic Browns Canyon. Beyond Browns Canyon, near Salida, the river encounters the northern end of the Sangre de Cristo Range and is forced eastward, paralleling the Sangre de Cristos. At the head of Wet Mountain Valley it makes an unexpected turn to the northeast and begins a precipitous descent through the Arkansas River Canyon. Finally, near the end of the river's life in the mountains, rock walls close in suddenly and the river enters the Royal Gorge, "Grand Canyon" of the Arkansas. After eight miles in the gorge's depths, it emerges above Canon City to begin a long, flat passage across the Great Plains to the Mississippi.

The course and character of the Arkansas River have been shaped by an elaborate panoply of geologic events.

The river's upper valley, between the towns of Leadville and Salida, follows the Rio Grande Rift, a downthrown trough in the earth's crust extending southward into northern Mexico. The headwaters of the Arkansas mark the northern end of the Rio Grande Rift. A broad arch or anticline once stretched from South Park on the east to the Aspen area on the west. The central part of the anticline began to collapse in mid-Tertiary time along north-south fault lines bordering the upper Arkansas Valley on the edges of what later became the Mosquito and Sawatch ranges. Streams from these highlands gathered in the trough to form the embryonic Arkansas River.

Through the ages, as the trough's bottom continued to drop, sediments from the surrounding highlands poured into it. The resulting fill, called the Dry Union Formation (for Dry Union Gulch, five miles south of Leadville) has a thickness of 1,000 to 1,500 feet in the valley of the upper Arkansas between Leadville and Salida.

The ancient river glided southward on the surface of the Dry Union Formation. It continued beyond the Salida area, following the rift into the emerging San Luis Valley to join the Rio Grande. Later, east-west trending faults thrust up the Dry Union Formation between the northern Sangre de Cristo and southern Sawatch ranges, blocking the ancient route of the Arkansas. The river's course was forced eastward toward the Great Plains.

Still later, floods of outwash debris from the higher Sawatch Range to the west shoved the Arkansas against the edge of the less lofty Mosquito Range on the east side of the rift. During renewed downcutting, the river exposed the latter range's granitic edges, which had been covered by the Dry Union Formation. The Arkansas superimposed itself into this resistant rock and carved short, narrow canyons—Granite, Wildhorse, and Browns—on the east side of the rift. Today the upper Arkansas continues in this course, crossing parks or basins of Dry Union shales and outwash debris between confining canyons in granitic rocks on the western flank of the Mosquito Range. Broad, sloping terraces covered with Dry Union shales dominate the landscape of the rift valley to the west of the Arkansas. The terraces slope toward the river on several levels from the Sawatch Mountain front.

During the last million years (the Pleistocene Epoch), another profound event altered the character of the upper Arkansas River: the Ice Age. Deep glaciers accumulated in the canyons of the Sawatch Range. During successive stages they moved eastward toward the mouths of the canyons and finally into the wide rift valley. In the upper portion of the valley, north of Buena Vista, the Lake Creek, Clear Creek, and Pine Creek glaciers slid eastward across the rift, shoving their terminal moraines into the path of the Arkansas.

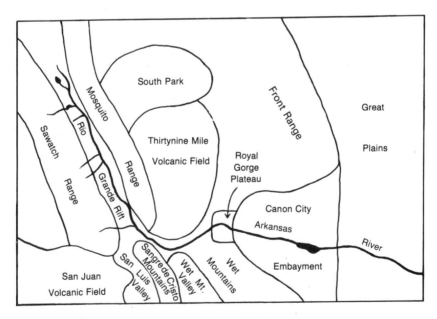

Physiographic map of Arkansas River vicinity.

The moraine at the snout of Pine Creek Glacier had an especially important effect on the river. This massive mound of glacial debris crowded the Arkansas against a steep wall of Mosquito Range granite, forming a dam behind which the river was impounded. On at least two occasions the glacial dam broke, releasing catastrophic floods downriver. The floods carried large boulders which were deposited on riverside terraces below. "One Through Six" rapids on the present-day Arkansas were formed by such torrents. Broad, boulder-studded outwash fans at the mouths of the short granite canyons downstream also formed when the glacial dams broke. These rocky terraces are below Wildhorse Canyon (the Buena Vista area) and below the mouth of Browns Canyon.

As the Pine Creek Glacier retreated, the river attacked its terminal moraine on the edge of the granite wall. It gouged out a narrow, boulder-studded chute which is today's Pine Creek Rapid. Other glaciers and the rock load they left behind in the river channel are partly responsible for making the Arkansas a technical whitewater river of the highest order.

Although the glaciers continued a general retreat, they occasionally renewed their advance for short periods, raising additional moraines across their valleys. Small lakes, such as Twin Lakes, filled the valleys behind the blockading moraines. The Bureau of Reclamation has used these moraines as a foundation on which to build greater impoundments, such as Twin Lakes Reservoir, Clear Creek Reservoir, and Turquoise Lake Reservoir.

Below Salida the Arkansas turns southeastward, following the trough of a syncline between the Thirtynine Mile Volcanic Field to the north and the northern extremities of the Sangre de Cristo Range to the south. This stretch, sometimes called the Pleasant Valley Basin, is the only place along the mountain Arkansas where the river crosses Paleozoic-age sedimentary rocks. Exposed in places beside the river in this section are the layers of Leadville Limestone and Minturn Evaporites. Above these, in the area around the Badger Creek confluence and downriver at Red Rock Rapids, the ubiquitous Permian Red Beds appear. In this region the Red Beds are called the Sangre de Cristo Formation.

In Pleasant Valley, the Arkansas has once again been pushed sideways by outwash debris. This time the source of the debris is the Sangre de Cristos, towering over the valley to the south. Crowded against the northeast side of its valley, the river encounters the much less imposing Thirtynine Mile Volcanic Field. Sloping terraces sweep down on several levels from the high mountains and are particularly well exposed south of Howard.

Lava and tuff from the volcanic field overlie the Sangre de Cristo Red Beds. In places both the Red Beds and their cap of lava dive beneath river level and the adjacent bluffs are composed of outwash gravel.

The natural extension of the Arkansas River's southeastward course below Pleasant Valley would have led into the Wet Mountain Valley. This valley's elevation is only 500 feet above the river's present elevation. Undoubtedly the Arkansas flowed at this higher elevation in the past. Could the river have continued southeastward through Wet Mountain Valley a few million years ago? Why does it turn so abruptly to the northeast at the head of the valley? Why does it choose to entrench itself in the hard rocks of the Arkansas River Canyon instead of the much softer rocks composing the bottom of Wet Mountain Valley? If the river had once occupied the Wet Mountain Valley, its route to the Great Plains would have been on a gentle slope about 60 miles in length. Its present path to the plains through the Arkansas River Canyon and the Royal

Gorge is only 30 miles long. Possibly a smaller, steeper stream growing headward from the Canon City area captured the ancient river, offering it a shorter route to the plains. It would then have become superimposed on granitic and metamorphic rocks along its new course.

The answers to these questions are not yet fully resolved. Geologists know only that the Arkansas quickly leaves Pleasant Valley, bypasses Wet Mountain Valley, and begins a journey through the longest hard rock canyon along its course. The depth of the Arkansas River Canyon approaches 2,000 feet. Its walls are composed of granite with contorted bands of schist and gneiss. The basaltic rocks of the Thirty-nine Mile Volcanic Field can be seen high on the west rim of the canyon. Broad terraces, so common upriver, are absent here. There is only room for a narrow floodplain about 20 feet above river level.

Below the Arkansas River Canyon the river once again emerges into an open area known as Webster Park. Here, folded Mesozoic sedimentary rocks have been exposed. The Great Plains lie only eight miles to the east, but the river must assault a final granitic barrier in order to reach them. This is a somewhat isolated block called the Royal Gorge Plateau. Geologists believe this block uplifted in the relatively recent geologic past as part of the final upheaval of the Rocky Mountains. The Royal Gorge cuts through essentially the same rocks as in the wider Arkansas River Canyon upstream, but the gorge's perpendicular walls imply a much shorter period of canyon erosion. Maintaining its already established easterly course, the Arkansas ground the great Royal Gorge chasm as the plateau slowly rose around it. In the gorge's central por-

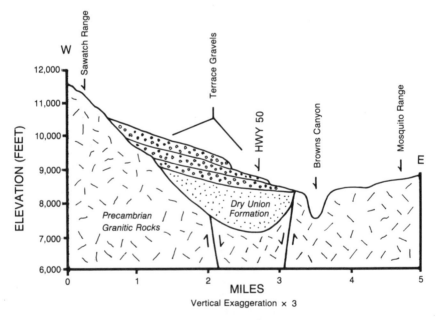

Cross section of Arkansas River at Browns Canyon.

tion, where the river attacked hard granite, the walls are nearly vertical, and not even the tiniest floodplain is present. Farther downstream, lenses of schist appear in the walls. Here the canyon widens somewhat where clefts have been eroded in the weaker schist.

As the Arkansas emerges from this titan of canyons, it greets the flanking hogbacks of Paleozoic and Mesozoic rock tilted upwards by the rising granitic block of the Royal Gorge Plateau. The river easily breached these hogbacks. Within a distance of two miles the Arkansas emerges from its mountain canyons to begin its long journey across the Great Plains. The initial section of Great Plains that the river traverses is a westward tongue that has followed an inroad into the mountain front, like a bay on an ocean coastline. Geologists call it the Canon City Embayment. Beyond Florence the river is still engaged in downcutting through layers of strata. Harder layers of the Niobrara limestones support the rim of shallow, gentle Swallows Canyon above Pueblo.

Pike Discovers the Source of the Arkansas

Juan de Ulibarri, a Spaniard from Santa Fe who made the first visit to the canyon mouth of the Arkansas in 1706, called the river the Napestle, Indian name for "red water." His journal praises the valley around the site of Pueblo for its fertility and beauty. A strikingly different opinion was expressed by Stephen H. Long of the 1820 American Exploring Expedition. Long pronounced the area "dreary and disgusting" and "almost wholly unfit for cultivation." He coined the phrase "Great American Desert." History proved the Spaniard's assessment to be the more accurate of the two.

In 1806 a young army officer, Zebulon Montgomery Pike, was sent into the recently purchased Louisiana Territory "to ascertain the direction, extent, and navigation of the Arkansas and Red Rivers." The first of these rivers had been given the name of a tribe of plains Indians. The location of the second river was something of a mystery, but it was supposed to mark the boundary between Spanish Mexico and the territories newly acquired from the French.

Pike left St. Louis in July with 22 men. In November, after a long trek westward, the expedition reached the Rockies, cold and weary and at precisely the wrong time for further exploration. Where Fountain Creek meets the Arkansas near the site of present-day Pueblo, Pike found a "defensible situation," and erected a small fort. (Pike's journal was recorded in his *Account of Expeditions to the Sources of the Mississippi and Through the Western Parts of Louisiana to the Sources of the Arkansaw, Kans, LaPlatte, and Pierre Juan Rivers* in 1810.) In order to view the surrounding country, he proposed to climb the "grand peak" he had seen to the north, "which we conceived would only be one day's march" from camp. His attempt to climb the mountain, later to be given his name, ended in failure. "I believe no man could have ascended to its pinical [sic]" he said.

On November 30, the party continued up the Arkansas in a violent snowstorm. They encountered the Royal Gorge on December 7. Turning away from the impassable gorge, Pike headed across the divide to the northwest and into South Park. Here, Pike reported, the party "...fell on a river 40 yards wide, frozen over; which after some investigation, I found ran northeast. This was the occasion of much surprise, as we were taught to expect to have met with the branches of the Red River, which should run southwest. Quere. Must it not be the headwaters of the river Platte? If not [this branch of] the Missouri must run much more west than is generally represented; for the Platte is a small river by no means presenting an expectation of so extensive a course.''

Pike was correct in his assessment of the Platte's source. Still eager to find the elusive Red River, he turned westward from South Park. On December 18, the party struck the Arkansas again, probably in the vicinity of Buena Vista, and assumed it to be the long-sought Red River. Pike traveled upriver 12 miles, to where he accurately described Pine Creek Rapid: "the river continuing close to the north mountain and running through a narrow rocky channel.'' The next day, he continued up the Arkansas for an additional 13 miles.

At that point, Pike thought he had discovered the source of the Red River. In fact, he had found the source of the Arkansas. He turned the expedition around in order to trace the river in a downstream direction. After some days, during which he described his difficulties in Browns Canyon and correctly observed that he should have led the expedition over the smoother country to the west, Pike reached "the entrance with the most perpendicular precipices on both sides, through which the river ran and our course lay.'' He had come upon the entrance to the Arkansas River Canyon. Sleds were constructed and, with great difficulty, the party hauled them down the frozen river. The horses fell so often they had to be pulled over the ice. In the canyon Pike first expressed doubts about his bearings. "The river turned so much to the north, as almost induced us to believe it was the Arkansaw.''

Pike climbed the canyon wall and saw Webster Park, the open area just above the Royal Gorge, eight miles ahead. The news that they would soon be out of the difficult canyon "gave great joy to the party.'' It took two more days to escape the Arkansas River Canyon, during which three horses became so bruised and battered they had to be shot.

Finally, on January 4th, the party reached Webster Park. Here Pike sent several groups in various directions to look for game while he and two men continued downriver into the Royal Gorge. Fortunately, Pike managed to find one of the narrow ravines leading out of the gorge to the south. He ascended it with "the utmost difficulty and danger.'' At the top he found one of his hunting parties which had been without success. Hungry and fatigued, they all returned to the camp in Webster Park.

"I then took a double barrelled gun,'' wrote Pike, "and left them, with assurances that the first animal I killed, I would return with part for their relief. About ten o'clock I rose to the highest summit of the mountain, when the unbounded space of the prairies again presented themselves to my view, and from some distant peaks, I immediately recognized it to be the outlet of the Arkansaw, which we had left nearly one month since!

"This was great mortification, but at the same time I consoled myself with the knowledge I had acquired the source of the La Platte and Arkansaw rivers.''

Pike took his men across the river near Parkdale and proceeded to their old camp north of the rediscovered Royal George. "We felt comparatively happy,'' he said, "notwithstanding the great mortifications I experienced at having been so egregiously deceived as to the Red River.''

By now Pike's horses were unable to travel farther and supplies were short. But he was indefatigable in his search for the elusive Red River. He and his men, with heavy packs on their backs, again turned toward the mountains, this time toward the south with the intention of crossing the Sangre de Cristos.

At the summit of the range, the wide San Luis Valley lay before them, with a shining ribbon of water meandering across its level floor, "which we hailed with fervency as the waters of the Red River." It was the Rio Grande. The party passed the site of Alamosa and camped on the north bank of the Conejos River (which Pike may have thought to be the main branch of the Red River) five miles west of its confluence with the Rio Grande. Here the expedition built a stockade of cottonwood logs. From a tall cottonwood in the midst of the stockade the Stars and Stripes flew jauntily in the breeze.

But alas, Pike had erected his fort on Spanish soil. In February, 1807, hundreds of Spanish troops arrived. The Americans were forcibly escorted to New Mexico where they were detained for several months before being released on the border of the Louisiana Territory.

Pike has been portrayed by some historians as a bumbling knucklehead. However, he deserves more credit than has generally been bestowed upon him. The 29-year-old pathfinder had nothing but misinformation to go on. The Red River actually lay hundreds of miles southeast of where he was sent, along the north Texas border. He was the first American to enter the mountain front of the Southern Rockies. He discovered the Royal Gorge and the mountain valley of the Arkansas. He found the sources of the South Platte—which was never expected to lie so far to the west—and of the Arkansas. He gathered valuable information about the Rio Grande. He accomplished all of this in the midst of winter, leading a brigade of 22 men without a single casualty. He was resourceful, intelligent, and daring. His journals accurately describe his route. He deserves to be considered one of the foremost river explorers in Colorado history.

As for his failure to reach the summit of relatively gentle Pike's Peak (for which he has been made the butt of many a joke), few explorers would not have turned back from such a goal in winter snowstorms, with no trail and no support group save a band of inexperienced men surviving on what game they could shoot.

Thirty years after Pike, the federal government ordered another exploration of the route into the Southern Rockies by way of the Arkansas River. Its leader was the famous Captain John C. Fremont. On this, his third expedition to the west, Fremont was well aware of Pike. He followed Pike's route to the mouth of the Royal Gorge, then northward into South Park, and again westward to rejoin the Arkansas near Buena Vista. He then followed the Arkansas to its headwaters. Unlike Pike, Fremont had the advantage of warm summer weather and the assistance of the finest scouts in the West, including the legendary Kit Carson. The rigors of Pike's journey bear no comparison to the ease of Fremont's.

The Daring Run of Hank Myers

Ironically, the first recorded navigation of the Arkansas River was accomplished on its most treacherous stretch, in the heart of the Royal Gorge. Young Hank Myers and his friend (mentioned in records only as Todd) did not brave the chasm for fame, exploration, or adventure. They only wanted to make a buck.

In 1871, construction of the Rio Grande Railroad was proceeding southward to Pueblo from Colorado Springs. Railroad ties cut on the mountain banks of the Arkansas were floated downriver through the Royal Gorge. That fall, the construction crews noticed that, of all the ties that entered the river above the gorge, few showed up at its mouth. No man could be found who would venture into the depths to solve the problem.

The following spring, the railroad offered one dollar per tie to anyone who would break the jam in the Royal Gorge. Seeking this bounteous reward, Myers and Todd found a boat, filled it with provisions, and set off from the present site of Parkdale. "The way the water rushed into that hole in the rock," Myers related in a 1902 story in the Cripple Creek *Times,* "would have scared anyone who had sense enough, but with dauntless bravery born of ignorance, we never hesitated."

The boat flipped in the first big rapid. "By the time we got ourselves collected and began to size up the situation, the boat must have been near the outlet," said Myers. The two were stranded on a tiny gravel bar walled in above and below. The only thing they had managed to save was one coil of rope. "The roar of whitewater was anything but music to our ears."

Gathering some driftwood timber, they managed to fashion a crude raft with the aid of the rope. They hung on for dear life as the raft rolled, pitched, and crashed through the Royal Gorge's many cataracts. Finally it stuck on a rock, but they were able to get to shore. They salvaged the rope and built another raft.

Five days later, soaking wet and weak with hunger, the young argonauts walked out of the canyon. Everything had been lost. They hadn't thought much about railroad ties.

"The sun never shone in there," Myers told the folks in Canon City. "That's gonna be my last boat trip."

The Royal Gorge War

The canyons in the Southern Rocky Mountains were first opened to travel by Colorado's great railroad builder, General William J. Palmer. Fresh from the Civil War—in which he had served with distinction—General Palmer constructed the Kansas Pacific Railroad from Kansas City across the plains to Denver. Here the General gazed upon the shining mountains to the west and set his mind on creating a railroad system into and through them.

Palmer incorporated the Denver and Rio Grande Railroad on October 7, 1870. His concept was daring. In 1870 the only transcontinental railroad was the Union Pacific. Its route lay to the north of Colorado across gentle South Pass. General Palmer's scheme was to build a north-south line following the eastern base of the mountain chain. Smaller branch lines would then be constructed westward into the adjacent mountains, with their timber and precious metal resources. The rivers had already graded many pathways to the high country. Palmer believed he could follow their narrow, twisting canyons with narrow-gauge tracks.

The result of General Palmer's genius was a vast railroad system penetrating many gorges of the Southern Rockies. In the Rio Grande's heyday, its tracks ran through the menacing canyons of the upper Colorado and Eagle rivers. They invaded the Black Canyon of the Gunnison, the Toltec Gorge, and the deep canyon of the Animas. Branch lines followed the San Miguel and Dolores canyons. Another line went up the Roaring Fork to Aspen. Few Southern

Camp of the Denver and Rio Grande Western army in the Royal Gorge. (Colorado Historical Society photo.)

Rocky Mountain canyons escaped Palmer's engineers.

Today most of these historic railroads are gone. Overgrown grades, scarcely visible, are all that remain of once busy lines. Some tracks, like the Silverton-Durango route, have been preserved as tourist attractions. Others were regraded and equipped with standard gauge rails that today carry freight between Denver and Salt Lake City.

Perhaps the young railroad magnate's greatest challenge was the Arkansas River, with its impassable Royal Gorge. The challenge came not only from the gorge's vertical walls but from a competing railroad, the powerful Atchison, Topeka and Santa Fe. In 1878, as Palmer's little railroad pushed southward from Pueblo toward Trinidad and Raton Pass, the Santa Fe's tracks reached the border of Colorado from Kansas City. Raton Pass was an objective of the Santa Fe as well. The stage was set for a clash.

The Santa Fe arrived at Raton Pass first. Five hundred armed men were garrisoned on the summit to stop the advancing Rio Grande. Palmer scouted the

Santa Fe position. The general's military experience told him that his men could not defeat the Santa Fe's superior force. He retreated. He switched his objective to the Royal Gorge—to the entrance of which his Rio Grande tracks had already been laid. But Santa Fe scouts also had their eyes on that chasm-like breach in the mountain wall.

The Rio Grande readied its construction crew to begin grading the gorge while a Santa Fe official, W.R. Morley, hurried to get a blockading force into position. At Pueblo, Morley boldly attempted to charter a Rio Grande locomotive to Canon City. The suspicious Rio Grande officials refused. April 20, 1878, was the day of Palmer's expected move into the canyon, and it was already three o'clock in the morning of that day. Morley was desperate. As a last resort he hired a fast horse and galloped toward Canon City, 45 miles distant. Three miles short of his destination the horse fell dead of exhaustion. As dawn broke, Morley ran on foot into Canon City, raised a force of 150 men, and proceded to the mouth of the gorge.

The Rio Grande was unpopular with Canon City residents. General Palmer had initially delayed his move toward the Royal Gorge, and the citizens of Canon City felt jilted. They believed a route through the gorge ought to be the beginning of a great, transcontinental railroad line. They were apparently glad to have an opportunity to even the score with the Rio Grande.

Accordingly, when the Rio Grande crew reached the gorge on the morning of April 20, they found themselves facing Morley's force. This time, however, Palmer did not intend to retreat. The route was his property. The Royal Gorge War was about to begin.

The Rio Grande men marched north and west to the rim of the gorge near the present day bridge. Using ropes, they descended the steep walls to the bottom and built a rock fort. Here they hoped to stop the advance of the Santa Fe, which was cutting and blasting its way up the river. Above this fort the Rio Grande crew began constructing its own grade. Each side hired reinforcements. Santa Fe riflemen advanced up the gorge only to be repelled by Rio Grande snipers.

Meanwhile, General Palmer went from the battle front to the courts to gain an injunction against further construction of the Santa Fe roadbed. The Santa Fe did the same. Arguments, writs, briefs, and injunctions boiled in courtrooms as battles continued in the depths of the gorge. The federal courts finally ruled that both railroads were free to build lines up the Arkansas. Neither could obstruct the other. Despite the ruling's apparent equity, there was barely room for one railroad in the Royal Gorge. Unless someone could shut off the river, two sets of tracks would never fit.

Palmer was dejected. His finances were running painfully short. Creditors and bondholders were demanding some return on their investments. He decided to bow, temporarily, to the stronger railroad, leasing all of his track and rolling stock to the Santa Fe for a period of 30 years. The Santa Fe in turn agreed to maintain the tracks and trains and not raise rates or discriminate against Colorado shippers.

This lease arrangement turned out to be a terrible mistake for Palmer. No sooner had it been signed than the silver boom began at Leadville. Hauling the ore over muddy passes to smelters in Colorado Springs by horsedrawn wagons proved cumbersome and costly. Leadville needed a railroad.

Rio Grande stockholders were furious that their Arkansas River route to the silver mines was soon to be taken over by easterners. It was agreed that the Rio Grande must somehow repossess the route. Claiming they were being discriminated against by the Santa Fe, Colorado shippers joined General Palmer in a court fight to get the route back.

As the lawyers for both sides sparred in the courtrooms, Palmer quietly sent his forces back into the Royal Gorge to harass the Santa Fe construction crews. This time he commissioned one of his ablest engineers, James De Remer, another Civil War veteran, to command his men. De Remer, following Palmer's earlier tactics, took his men on a flanking maneuver around the canyon's fortified mouth and down its sheer walls. They reoccupied old forts and prepared to stop the Santa Fe. The competing railroad, however, had kept the loyalty of the Canon City population. A large force, complete with sheriffs, deputies, and Santa Fe riflemen, marched up the canyon to De Remer's position. "We've got a warrant for your arrest, De Remer," yelled the sheriff. "Come on up and get me," was the reply. The Royal Gorge exploded in gunfire. The deputies retreated to Canon City, where a reward was placed on De Remer's head: ten thousand dollars, dead or alive.

Outnumbered ten to one, De Remer turned to guerilla warfare. He used both guns and rocks to hound Santa Fe work parties. Track layers would hear a rumble and look up to see boulders crashing down upon them from the canyon rim. Track laying slowed to a snail's pace.

Meanwhile the sheriff, with plenty of Santa Fe money at his disposal, hired able-bodied men for five dollars a day. The ever-crafty De Remer sent some of his men into Canon City to join the Santa Fe forces and learn their plans.

One Rio Grande employee was recognized and arrested. De Remer decided to free the man himself and boldly rode into Canon City under cover of darkness. As he was bailing his partner out of jail, the Rio Grande captain was spotted and the news relayed to the sheriff. Just as the sheriff opened the jailhouse door, the two Rio Grande men leapt out a window, mounted their horses, and fled down the main street pursued by a shooting, yelping posse. When they reached the rim of the gorge, the posse close behind, they abandoned their horses and slipped to safety amidst the clefts and crags.

The following day, Rio Grande scouts spotted a Santa Fe force outflanking them upriver at Stonewall Point. Realizing they were about to be boxed in, De Remer decided to swim the river and get above the enemy. He pleaded with his men to leap into the foaming torrent. "I'll give twenty dollars to every man who swims the river," he shouted (as quoted by Clyde Davis in *The Arkansas*, Farrar and Reinhart, 1940). There were no takers. "All right, I'll go it alone."

He plunged in and was quickly swept into a boulder field. The men watched helplessly as their leader was washed against the rocks and disappeared in a hole. Finally they saw a hand gripping a boulder on the far side of the river. Like a soaked puppydog, De Remer crawled from the water. A cheer went up from the opposite bank, but he didn't hear it over the noise of the river. He found a cleft and began climbing toward the rim. At this point, Santa Fe riflemen spotted him and began shooting. De Remer's men saw puffs of pulverized rock cracking all around their boss as he scrambled up the rock chute. But De Remer reached the rim, and an instant later a hail of boulders crashed down on the Santa Fe men. Down the gorge they fled with the Rio Grande party returning fire from across the river. De Remer had won the day at the battle of Stonewall Point.

Despite such successes, De Remer was slowly pushed upriver by the Santa Fe's superior force. Near the western entrance to the gorge, at a point recognized as the "20 mile limit," De Remer decided to throw up a barricade and draw the line. A railroad tie marked "Dead Line" was placed in the Santa Fe's path. Rio Grande forces hastily erected several stone forts as Santa Fe work crews continued to advance, grading and laying track ever nearer the "Dead Line." (The overgrown forts can still be seen half a mile downriver from Parkdale.

"Don't you cross the line," came De Remer's voice from behind a row of Winchesters lined up on one of the rock parapets. When a Santa Fe laborer was ordered across the line by his boss, he turned and said "Listen, if you want to cross the line, go ahead and do it yourself."

One of the Santa Fe's lawyers came to the front and yelled, "By what authority do you stop the United States mails?"

"The Santa Fe Railroad isn't hauling mails through this gorge. Not yet it isn't," was De Remer's reply.

"By what authority do you try to stop construction of this railroad?" returned the lawyer.

De Remer thought a minute, then shouted, "By authority of the United States Supreme Court."

Not knowing whether the Supreme Court had given anybody authority to do anything, the Santa Fe men went back to Canon City to consult the rest of their lawyers. De Remer had fooled them again. Santa Fe tracks never advanced beyond Twenty Mile Post.

Meanwhile, far from the scene of battle, General Palmer had found a sympathetic judge in San Luis, Colorado. On June 9, 1879, the judge ruled that the Santa Fe was violating its lease with the Rio Grande and ordered local sheriffs to repossess the railroad. Encouraged by this ruling, Rio Grande sympathizers joined railroad men and sheriffs in repossessing station after station from Denver to Pueblo.

"Don't you cross that line!" shouted De Remer from behind a row of Winchesters. (Colorado Historical Society photo.)

But the federal courts didn't side with the Rio Grande. On June 23, 1879, they declared the state decision null and void and ordered the Rio Grande to return the repossessed property to the Santa Fe.

Finally, in 1880, the long war between the two railroads was terminated by a compromise. The Rio Grande agreed not to build its proposed line to Santa Fe and El Paso. In return, the Santa Fe agreed not to construct its line up the Arkansas to Leadville. The lease was cancelled, and the Rio Grande agreed to pay the Santa Fe for the track it had constructed in the Royal Gorge. On March 27, 1880, the Santa Fe abandoned the gorge. Thus ended one of history's longest and most bitterly contested railroad wars.

After the compromise, General Palmer quickly resumed construction of his railroad to Leadville. By July, 1880, the tracks had reached the booming silver city at the headwaters of the Arkansas. Salida became the main station along the Rio Grande Route between Canon City and Leadville. Several branch lines were built from Salida toward the south and west. In 1881 Palmer built a narrow gauge line over Marshall Pass into the valley of the Gunnison. His tracks entered the Black Canyon and eventually were completed as far as Salt Lake City.

No history of railroading in the Royal Gorge is complete without reference to the famous "hanging bridge" in the narrowest part of the gorge. The bridge never actually hung. In 1879, when the Santa Fe first built the structure, it was constructed of wood, supported by rock. A flash flood washed away this first structure, after which the Rio Grande built a new bridge with steel overhead beams anchored to the solid rock wall to help support the vulnerable bed. In the 1880s the bed was reinforced with large boulders, making the overhead beams useless. Nevertheless, the historic structure retains the name "Hanging Bridge of the Royal Gorge" today.

Arkansas River

The Arkansas from below Leadville to the Pueblo Reservoir, a distance of approximately 150 miles, is a rubber rafter's and kayaker's paradise. It is not wilderness, since roads and small towns are set along its banks and the Denver and Rio Grande Western Railroad follows its length. A rocky, small, clear mountain stream, it contrasts sharply with the muddy torrents that sweep down the Green and Colorado to the west. As with the Green and Colorado, however, the Arkansas beckons boaters from around the world. Swirling, twisting, and diving through granitic canyons, it offers many superb runs varying in difficulty from intermediate to expert.

The Arkansas can be dangerous during June high water. Its volume holds up reasonably well during July and August due to a partially regulated flow and releases of West Slope water.

Permits are not required. Care should be taken, however, to avoid private land in gaining access to or camping along the river. Courtesy to private property owners will insure continued use of the river.

Arkansas River: Granite to Pueblo Reservoir

Physical Data: 129 mi; 4,100-ft drop; 32 ft/mi average gradient; 75 ft/mi maximum gradient (from Pine Creek to Rapid Six), 60 ft/mi (through Royal

Gorge); 268,000 acre-ft average yearly discharge (at Granite), 518,000 acre-ft (at Canon City).

Maps: Pueblo and Montrose USGS Quads (1-250,000 scale); San Isabel National Forest Map; BLM Arkansas River Map.

Land Ownership: Alternating BLM and private land.

Information: BLM, Canon City, CO.

Flow Information: State Irrigation Engineer, Pueblo, CO.

Granite to Mt. Harvard Estates Bridge

The Arkansas in this stretch tumbles through the most difficult whitewater on the river outside the Royal Gorge. An average gradient of 60 feet per mile and a channel filled with granite boulders make this poor rafting water. It is suitable only for advanced-to-expert boaters in kayaks and decked canoes.

Within these 13 miles lie several short, forested canyons, one of the most notorious rapids in Colorado at Pine Creek, and a boulder-filled series of rapids known as "One Through Six." This stretch has seen many slalom and wildwater races, including the national championships.

A wide variety of plant life hugs the riverbank. The most abundant varieties include blueberry, buffaloberry, mountain mahogany, chokecherry, hawthorn, mountain gooseberry, baby's breath, and alder.

The put-in is just off Highway 24, a stone's throw south of the town of Granite. Excellent water begins immediately. The river pours down a big drop in a class III rapid one mile below the put-in, then twists through slender, forested Granite Canyon, emerging in a pool behind a small dam. A fallen railroad bridge may require a short portage here. The dam is a class VI drop with nasty steel reinforcing bars lying in the rubble of concrete.

The Clear Creek Reservoir spillway enters the Arkansas below the dam. Another short, hidden canyon lies beyond. At high water be careful of the low footbridge at mile 2.6. A tricky rapid in a field of huge boulders marks the end of this mini-canyon. Beyond is a short stretch of open country.

As the current picks up speed around the wide left curve, a large anvil-shaped rock overhangs the river on the right (mile 4.7). This rock marks the beginning of Pine Creek Rapid, a fast, twisting torrent of whitewater. There is an easy portage on a small dirt road east of the river. Pine Creek Rapid is long, about 300 yards. It is full of holes and stoppers. At the entrance, the current accelerates, giving the boater little time to maneuver. Eddies are difficult to catch. The rapid does not end in a pool but eases into a class IV boulder field. Paddlers forced to swim in Pine Creek Rapid have been battered severely by rocks and have had difficulty reaching the bank. This section is extremely dangerous at high water levels. At moderate to low water, however, Pine Creek Rapid is an excellent run for expert kayakers and decked canoeists.

Mile 7.2 is the beginning of rapids "One Through Six." This is class IV whitewater for advanced boaters only. There is a good campsite on the east bank at Rapid One.

Rapid One requires complex maneuvering. It ends at a dilapidated wooden bridge next to Scott's Bridge. A boater's gage is found at the base of Scott's Bridge near the west bank.

The river pools below the bridges then sweeps into Rapid Two at mile 7.6. Rapid Two has a big hole at the base of the first drop, a moderate section in the middle, and a delicious staircase at the end.

Rapid Three (mile 8.1) is short but contains some boat-breaking rocks.

Rapid Four can be very tough at high water. It starts in a straight, narrow

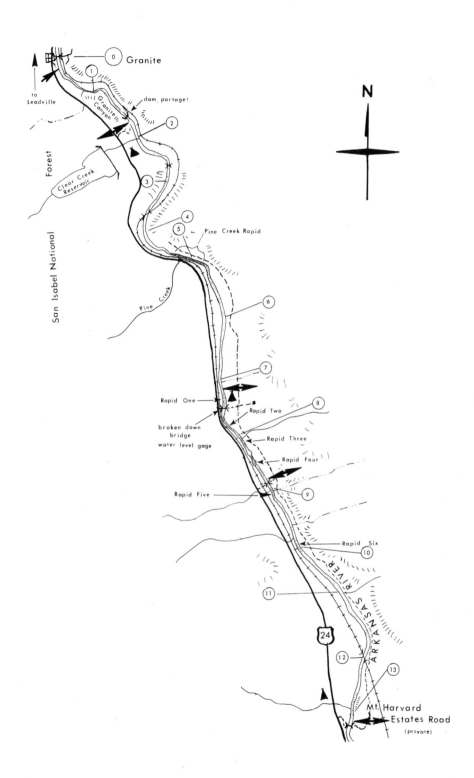

Granite to Mt. Harvard Estates Road.

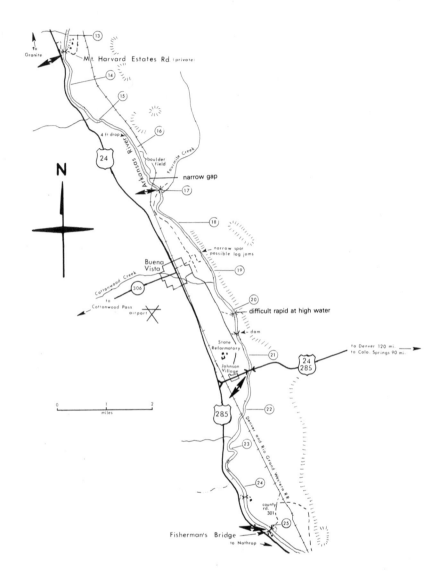

Mt. Harvard Estates Road to Fisherman's Bridge.

chute with good-sized standing waves. After about 50 yards it quickly widens into a shallow field of smaller boulders. At high water a huge hole develops at the point where the narrow chute widens into the boulder field. From here to the bridge at mile 8.9 is a delightful run through rounded granite boulders. Play spots are numerous.

Rapid Five is demanding at any water level. A difficult approach to a four-foot fall is followed by some gnarly hydraulics.

Rapid Six at mile 10 is on a left curve. From here to the Mt. Harvard Bridge at mile 13.2 one encounters fine kayaking water. Holes and surfing waves, bounded by an attractive forest, make this an excellent run for experienced boaters. Two class III-IV rapids lie just above the bridge.

A preliminary take-out can be found just off the dirt road east of the river at mile 10.3. A second take-out is at Mt. Harvard Bridge. This is a private road. Permission for access can sometimes be obtained at the first house at the top of the hill overlooking the river on the east. Cars should be left on nearby U.S. Highway 24. One mile downriver from the bridge, Highway 24 comes close enough to the water to provide a good alternate take-out.

Mt. Harvard Bridge to Ruby Mountain Campground

This run is excellent for intermediate and advanced boaters. There are several good put-in and take-out spots east of Buena Vista which are not marked on the map.

Below the Mt. Harvard Bridge, the Arkansas winds through wooded country away from the highway. Many rounded, granite rock formations stand guard along the river's course.

The four-foot drop at mile 15.7 has a tricky entrance and should be scouted. From mile 16 to mile 17.2 the water picks up speed, widens, and flows through an enjoyable 500-yard boulder patch, rated class III, pooling below a 12-foot-wide notch. This shallow canyon above Buena Vista is sometimes called Wild-horse Canyon.

The next 1.5 miles contain several class III rapids leading to a spot where granite walls constrict the river. A large bedrock block lies in the middle of the streambed, forming two narrow chutes on either side. Drift logs tend to jam in this narrow place, producing an additional hazard. Neither side of the middle rock is easy to run, and the difficulty can vary greatly with water volume. Careful scouting is necessary. A somewhat strenuous portage is available on the west bank.

The small dam at mile 20.5 is a dangerous class IV-plus drop and should be scouted. There is an easy portage on the right.

There is good novice water from the Highway 24 Bridge at mile 21.3 to the Ruby Mountain Campground. In this stretch, the rapids are typically class I and II. Fisherman's Bridge, halfway down the run, is an alternate access point and can be easily seen from State Highway 285 three miles south of Johnson Village.

Ruby Mountain Campground to Highway 291 Bridge (Browns Canyon)

Browns Canyon holds a unique wilderness run. The Arkansas leaves the out-wash gravels of the Sawatch Range and cuts a narrow canyon through the pink-hued granite. Boaters prize this canyon for its quiet beauty and the pleasure of its waters. An interesting variety of drops, boulder fields, and (at higher water levels) standing waves make this an enjoyable run for advanced kayakers and rubber rafters.

Turtles and ducks are occasionally seen. The most commonly observed bird is the whitewater-loving dipper. In the heart of the canyon, green with ponderosa and pinon pine, only an occasional train on the skirting Denver and Rio Grande tracks disturbs visitors.

Intermediate boaters will find Browns Canyon a constant challenge. At higher levels (above 1,000 c.f.s.) Browns is an exhilarating but technical stretch. The water flows rapidly, and rafts must be guided through agonizingly

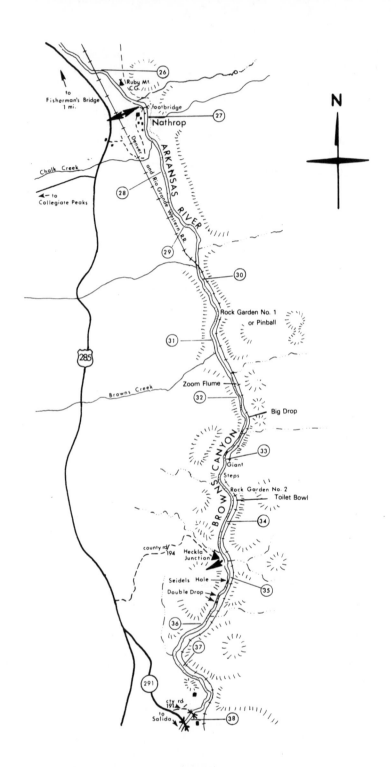

Ruby Mountain Campground to Colorado 291 Bridge.

narrow slots with boat-broaching boulders all about. The water becomes too thin for rafts at levels below 600 c.f.s. At these levels even the best oarsmen and paddle crews will have trouble bouncing off rocks.

Commercial raft companies discovered Browns Canyon in 1978. Since then increasing numbers of paying passengers have been ferried through. At the height of the season a virtual string of rafts fill the river, but boaters can avoid the crowds by planning a morning or late afternoon run.

Almost all of Browns Canyon is public land. The BLM has proposed wilderness protection for the area.

Fisherman's Bridge at mile 25 is a good put-in for a day in Browns Canyon. Ruby Mountain Campground, several miles downriver opposite Nathrop, is the most popular put-in. Class II water for the first couple of miles allows plenty of warm-up time.

From Nathrop the river passes the mouth of Chalk Creek, then flows through relatively open terrain for three miles of largely class II water. Note the springs gushing into the river from the broad outwash fans to the west. Just below the railroad bridge, the canyon begins. A tight, boulder-choked rapid, called Rock Garden Number One, or Pinball, is found at mile 30.6. At low water rafters must portage this spot.

Soon after passing Browns Creek at mile 31.2, the river drops away in a class III to IV rapid called Zoom Flume, or Staircase. This can be one of the most difficult drops in Browns Canyon and should be a good barometer of how well a boater will do through the remainder of the canyon. Staircase should be scouted and portaged if necessary.

From here to mile 36 the river averages a relatively steep 38 feet per mile, with lots of action for the energetic boater. Between mile 33 and 34, three steep drops into pools have been named Giant Steps. Below Giant Steps, Rock Garden Number Two is encountered, with Marble Rapid following. The Heckla Junction Campground at mile 34.7 makes a good alternate take-out. A dirt road leads to this area from Highway 285.

At high water levels small rafts should take out at Heckla Junction. About half a mile downstream lies Seidels Suckhole. A large, rectangular boulder straddles the stream at the base of a steep drop causing a deep, vicious hole. This hole has flipped many rafts and caused more than a few kayakers an unpleasant back end-over-end spin. The hole can be a keeper. Below 500 c.f.s. the rectangular rock is exposed and can be skirted on the right.

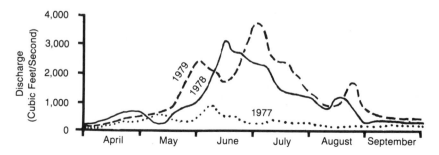

Hydrograph of Arkansas River at Salida.

Double Drop, a pair of steep drops in quick succession, is reached about 100 yards below Seidels Suckhole. From the second drop to the State Highway 291 bridge, the difficulty eases to class I and II.

A take-out at the stone bridge one-half mile upstream from the Highway 291 bridge has been closed in recent years. The highway bridge take-out also has been closed.

Highway 291 Bridge to Stockyards Bridge (Salida Run)

In this stretch, the Arkansas slips across private land bounded by low floodplains and bluffs. The only discernable rapid, Squaw Creek Rapid, lies two miles below the Highway 291 Bridge. At mile 44.5 a six-foot dam requires a portage. Below the dam the river passes a state fish hatchery and continues under two bridges into Salida. Boulders have been placed in the channel above the bridge in the middle of town for the Fibark Slalom Races. Access points below Salida are found at a BLM site and the Stockyards Bridge.

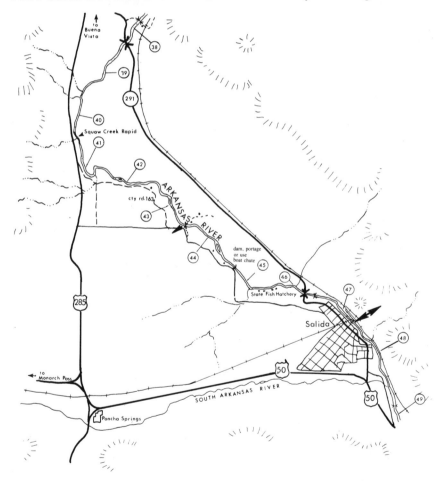

Stockyards Bridge to Cotopaxi (Pleasant Valley)

Beautiful views of the Sangre de Cristo Mountains and pleasant rural country characterize this intermediate section of the Arkansas. It is also the course of the historic Fibark Downriver Race each June. Numerous access points are scattered through the run. The most difficult rapids are found at Bear Creek Rapid (mile 50.6), Flume Rapid at the Badger Creek confluence (mile 58), Tincup (mile 63.2), Red Rock (mile 64), Railroad (mile 67), and Cottonwood (mile 69).

The watercourse leaves Pleasant Valley and enters the Arkansas River Canyon at Cottonwood Rapid. This rapid has achieved fame for its big waves, which flip many racers during the Fibark Downriver competition.

Cotopaxi to Parkdale (Arkansas River Canyon)

This run lies in the heart of the Arkansas River Canyon. U.S. Highway 50 hugs the river, providing ample scouting opportunities. Hordes of rubber rafts clog the river here during the tourist season. Numerous access points can be found along the way.

The initial section from Cotopaxi (Hebrew for "shining pile") to Texas Creek has the easiest water. Below Texas Creek the difficulty increases substantially. At very high water levels it can be treacherous.

Texas Creek Rapid, just below the bridge at Texas Creek, is rated class III. A sharp four-foot drop is found on a right curve at mile 81.6. Above Echo

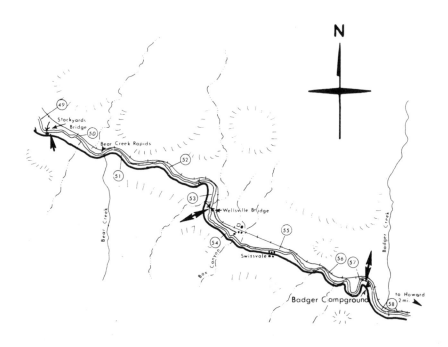

Mile 49 to Badger Campground.   *Continued on next page.*

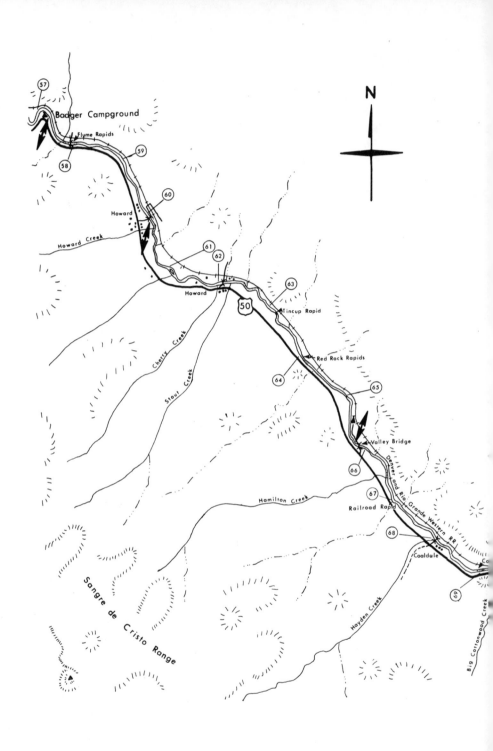

Badger to Mile 70.

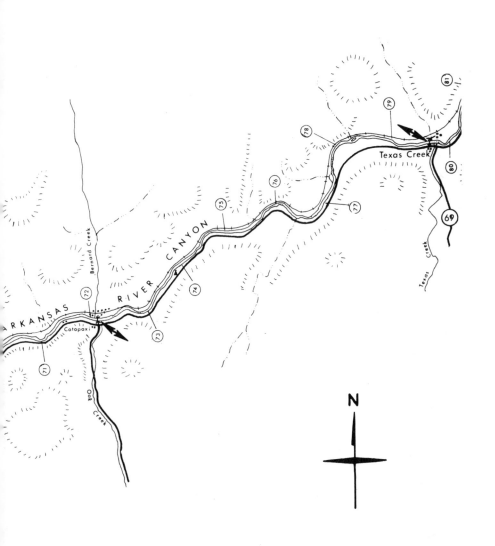

Mile 70 to Texas Creek.

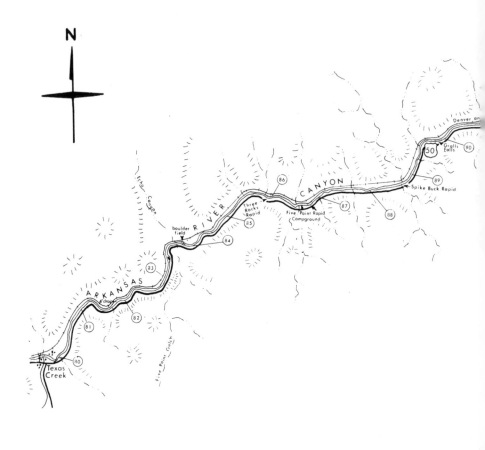

Texas Creek to Mile 91.

Canyon (mile 83.6) still water provides some relief. Below this side canyon, however, the river breaks into three channels. At low water levels this can be a difficult spot. The right channel is recommended. In the next mile, several difficult rapids signal the approach of the trickiest drop in the Arkansas River Canyon, Three Rocks (mile 86). At any level this boulder-peppered rapid provides a challenge. At high water it flips many rafts. Three Rocks lies on a blind left curve and can be scouted from the left bank.

One-half mile of flat water beyond Three Rocks leads to the Five Points Campground (no river access) and Rapid (class III). There are numerous easy rapids in the river for two miles beyond Five Points. Then the river slips into Spike Buck, a 50-yard, boulder-choked rapid (class III to IV). One mile beyond Spike Buck is a steep chute next to the highway known as Gralls Falls

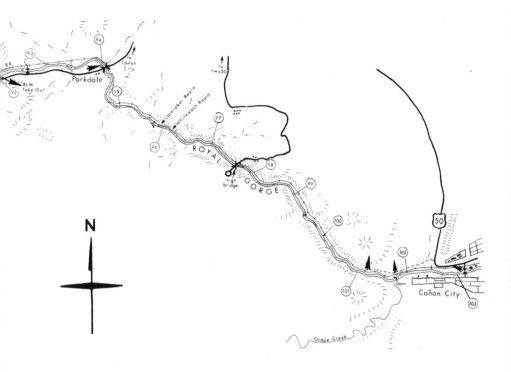

Mile 91 to Canon City.

or The Tube (class III). Two more miles of moderate drops and dancing waves convey boaters to a BLM take-out point (mile 92). Here, rafts must be carried up a steep staircase to the highway.

Below the BLM take-out the river drifts out of the Arkansas River Canyon into Webster Park. The country opens up in this short, flat-water stretch across private land.

Parkdale to Canon City (The Royal Gorge)

Apart from the "One Through Six" area, the Royal Gorge holds the most challenging water on the Arkansas. The sun shines for only a few hours each day at the bottom of the gorge, where a continuous series of thunderous rapids tests the kayaker's skill.

In 1980 the U.S. Army dynamited the only dam in the Royal Gorge after two soldiers drowned at its base. Since then a few commercial raft companies have taken passengers through, but only at prime water levels (1,500 to 2,500 c.f.s.). At low water the many boulders and narrow chutes make raft control impossible. At high water the risk of capsizing is great. Even at ideal levels the Royal Gorge can be a hazardous run for rafts. Numerous broken-down footbridges dangle dangerously close to the water.

Kayakers can put in below the U.S. 50 Bridge at Parkdale. From here the river quickly steals into the chasm. One-half mile below the Highway 50

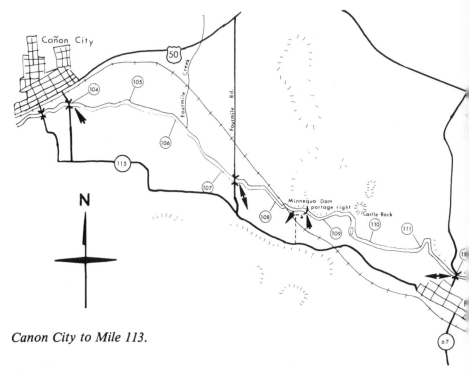

Canon City to Mile 113.

Bridge, just upriver from the first rapid, note the rock forts and breastworks used by Rio Grande forces during the Royal Gorge war. These remnants of Colorado's dramatic railroad history are located on the left side of the river across the tracks.

The gorge's trickiest rapid, Caretaker, lies two miles beyond the bridge, just past the unoccupied house where the Canon City Waterworks caretaker once lived. The rapid consists of two drops about 100 yards apart. The second drop of about four feet has a very difficult entrance and requires a perfect approach line. One-half mile below Caretaker, a huge whitewashed boulder sits in the river on the right. This marks the entrance to Whitewash Rapid, the gorge's second most difficult drop. Scout it carefully from the railroad tracks. Huge waves develop here at high water. Low water requires complex maneuvering. A second steep drop against a vertical granite wall lies just below Whitewash. Then the river calms for a mile before entering the heart of the gorge.

A white cement structure river-left carries a side canyon creek over the railroad tracks at mile 97. Below this structure the river tumbles down a series of steep drops between a granite wall on the right and the railroad grade supported by pieces of steel track on the left. There are no take-outs here and few eddies. Rebar and wire in the river offer constant hazards.

Below this narrow section is the "Hanging Bridge" of the Rio Grande Railroad where the incline railway meets the river. A short pool gives boaters a chance to wave at tourists who have ridden down the steep incline railway before Bridge Rapid. Bridge Rapid must be run on a left curve against the granite wall on the right. Many paddlers have found themselves unexpectedly crashing into the wall as the current pulls them to the right. Boaters should

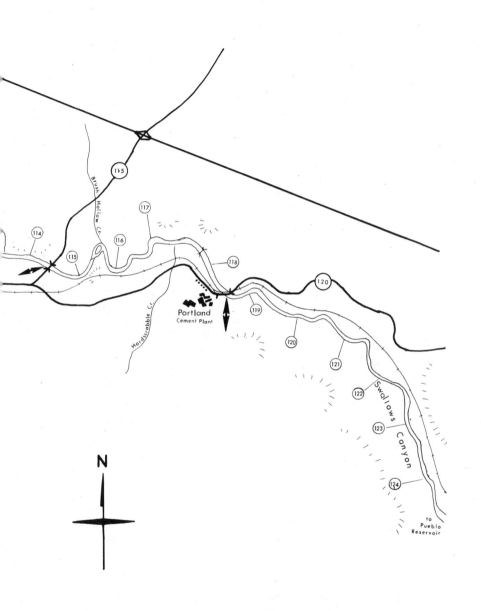

N

Mile 113 to Swallows Canyon.

Royal Gorge in 1910. Canon City waterworks pipe on right, hanging bridge in distance. The high bridge, which spans the gorge in this area, had not been built. (Denver Public Library Western History Dept., George L. Beam photo.)

proceed quickly through this rapid, since some numbskull in the flock of tourists on the Royal Gorge Bridge nearly 1,000 feet above might try "bombing" the tiny specks below with a penny or small stone. Several boaters have reported near-misses.

Bounding rapids continue below the high bridge. About one mile downriver a jumble of big boulders produces perilous holes at high water and tricky navigating at low water. A rapid, through which it is difficult to execute a clean run, is situated below the old waterworks pipe crossing the river at mile 99.5. Below this crossing, the river's difficulty lets up for the remainder of the way to the mouth of the gorge.

The first take-out is at the end of the Tunnel Drive dirt road two miles upstream from the mouth. Another take-out lies just below the mouth past the Grape Creek confluence. A dangerous four-foot headgate dam spans the river a quarter-mile below this confluence. It is possible to take out at the first bridge in Canon City next to the powerplant.

Canon City to Pueblo Reservoir

Upon leaving the mountains, the Arkansas calms. Only minor rapids punctuate the stretch below Canon City. For the first time the Arkansas extends its bounty to beginners, but only during low water periods. Sweepers, driftwood piles, bridge abutments, and small headgate dams are strewn throughout this run; extreme caution is advised at high water. The Minnequa Dam four miles below Canon City requires a portage.

A pleasant two-mile run can be made from the bridge at Florence to the State Highway 115 Bridge. Another short, easy run lies between the Highway 115 Bridge and the State Highway 120 Bridge at the Portland Cement Plant.

A gentler stretch still, and one that offers some wild country, is the ten-mile run in Swallows Canyon below Portland to the Pueblo Reservoir. Open canoeists take advantage of this delightful canyon's flat water and quiet solitude. Cottonwood groves line the river. These tall trees are the homes of great blue herons, ospreys, and eagles. In the spring migrating ducks and geese take refuge in the canyon. Walls of gray Niobrara limestones and shales, 200 feet high, border the floodplain.

A popular take-out is found at the Oasis Marina on the north shore of Pueblo Reservoir. If boaters don't wish to paddle on the reservoir, fishermen's access roads from State Highway 96 can be found near the head of the still water.

Rio Grande River Basin

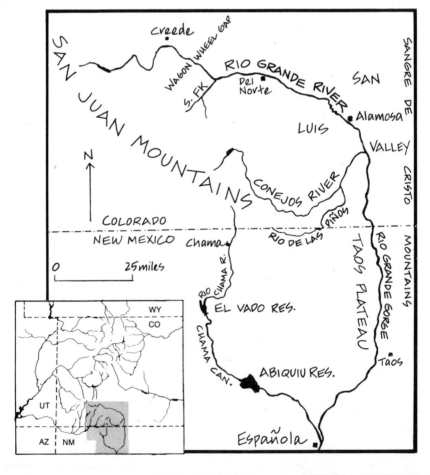

An iron race the mountain cliffs maintain,
Foes to the gentler genius of the plain.
—Thomas Gray

The Grand River From the North

Heralded by Spanish explorers as the "Rio Grande del Norte"—the grand River of the North—this mercurial stream holds an important place in the life and legends of the Southwest.

Thirty years after Columbus discovered America, explorer Cabeza de Vaca wandered through the upper Rio Grande region. To New Spain he brought tales of riches, of the wondrous Seven Cities of Cibola, and of the Land of the Grand Quivira.

Inspired by de Vaca's fables, Don Juan de Onate, a wealthy citizen of New Spain, obtained in 1598 an official contract to "conquer and occupy" the lands north of the Rio Grande Del Norte. Instead of wealthy cities with gold-paved streets, Onate and his conquistadors found bands of fierce natives—the Comanches, Utes, Pueblos, and Jicarilla Apaches. He pushed on with determination, reaching the confluence of the Rio Grande and Rio Chama, where he claimed for Spain the entire area "from the leaves of the trees in the forests to the stones and sands of the river."

Despite Indian danger, the lust for gold continued throughout the 18th century to provoke Spanish exploration in the Southern Rockies. Father Francisco Torres, accompanying a party of gold seekers, first saw and named the San Luis Valley, through which the Rio Grande flows after it emerges from the San Juan Mountains. Here, the Indians guiding the party revolted, driving the Spaniards down the east side of the valley to San Luis Lake where the beleagured party escaped on a hastily built raft. Father Torres had been mortally wounded during the skirmish. As the sun sank that evening, the dying priest on the drifting raft watched the mountains to the east turn to crimson. Exalted, he pointed to the ruddy peaks crying "sangre de Cristo, sangre de Cristo!" Father Torres's vision of the blood of Christ gave this lofty range its name.

In 1779, the newly appointed governor of Santa Fe, Don Juan Bautista de Anza, led a small army into the San Luis Valley to quell the unruly Comanches. Hoping to surprise the Indians, he marched up the west side of the Rio Grande rather than taking the normal route through Taos. On this march Anza crossed, and is credited with naming, several of the Rio Grande's major tributaries: the Conejos (rabbit), LaJara (wild rose), and Alamosa (cottonwood) rivers. His army crossed the Rio Grande near present-day Del Norte at

"El Paso de San Bartolome." Here, Anza wrote, the river originated in a large spring-fed marsh. The springs, he said, were filled by "the melting of snow from some volcanos which are very close."

Anza went on to defeat the Comanches near the banks of the Arkansas River east of Canon City.

The first official visit to the Rio Grande by a United States emissary came in 1807, by the youthful explorer Zebulon Montgomery Pike (see Arkansas River Basin).

Forty years after Pike's visit, the Treaty of Guadalupe Hidalgo formally ceded the upper Rio Grande territory to the United States. In 1848 Captain John C. Freemont was sent on an expedition (his fourth) into the new territory to survey a southern transcontinental railroad route to the west. Fremont hoped to recruit his trusted scout, Kit Carson, but Carson was ill. Fremont was forced to rely on Parson Bill Williams, then aged 61, to lead his party across the mountains.

John C. Fremont, the Pathfinder (right), with his friend and scout, Kit Carson. (Colorado Historical Society photo.)

It was December when Fremont's expedition crossed the Sangre de Cristo Range, circumvented the dunes of the San Luis Valley, and crossed the Rio Grande at El Paso de San Bartolome. Fremont recorded the following: "We found ourselves to the north of the Del Norte Canon where the river issues from the St. John Mountains, one of the highest, most rugged and most impractical of all Rocky Mountain Ranges; inaccessible to hunters and trappers even in summer time.

"Across the point of this elevated range, having still great confidence in his [Bill Williams's] knowledge, we pressed on with fatal resolution."

On the expedition's westward trek, Williams, instead of routing the party up the Rio Grande or over Cotchetopa Pass to the north, led it toward the Continental Divide via Embargo Creek, northwest from near the South Fork confluence. The party trudged for days through deep snow. Obstacles increased daily. Many of the men became frostbitten, and the mules began to die. Snow fell continuously. By the time they reached the vicinity of the Continental Divide, the snow was too deep for travel, and the party was reduced to eating frozen mule meat. With starvation setting in, Fremont was forced to leave his men in camp and attempt to get back to civilization to put together a rescue party. Bill Williams set out separately to seek help. Williams was killed by Indians in the San Luis Valley, but Fremont managed to reach Taos, where Kit Carson assisted him in rounding up a rescue team. On his return, he found his men already struggling out of the mountains. Thirteen of the original 33 had died. Fremont's fourth expedition ended a disastrous failure.

In 1860, after being ejected from their camp near Durango by Ute Chief Colorow, a prospecting party under the leadership of Charles Baker became the first to find the headwaters of the Rio Grande. With the Utes on their tail, the prospectors moved northward up the Animas River to Baker's Park (later the site of Silverton). Here, demoralized, they broke into factions and separated. Baker's group turned eastward toward the Continental Divide at what is now Stony Pass. Just over the pass lay the source waters of the Rio Grande. The party moved down the river, finding an abandoned wagon at a narrow spot. Baker named this passage Wagon Wheel Gap. The party eventually reached Leadville on the Arkansas, where its members spread stories of paydirt in the San Juans. More prospectors came to the upper Rio Grande canyons, and it was not long before rambunctious mining towns such as Creede were established.

In later years, General Palmer's Denver and Rio Grande railroads invaded the San Luis Valley and the upper Rio Grande River, reaching as far as Creede. By 1874, the Stony Pass Trail had become a hoofbeaten thoroughfare between Creede and Silverton. As the metallic wealth dwindled, ranching became the principal occupation along the river and remains so today.

Ancient Cataclysms Alter The River's Course

The San Juan Range began its long period of upthrusting at the beginning of the Tertiary Period. Alternating lava flows and bursts of ash poured from volcanoes in the region of present-day Silverton. Warping of the earth's crust, accompanied by a vast accumulation of volcanic debris, raised a broad, symmetrical dome, known to geologists as San Juan Dome, about 75 miles in diameter. On this great dome's slopes, the ancestral Rio Grande was born. In its youth, it flowed to the south of its present course, joining the ancestral Pecos River in northeastern New Mexico.

During middle Tertiary time, the Sangre de Cristo Mountains were upthrust. Concurrently, the Rio Grande Rift—extending in a north-south direction from the upper Arkansas Valley through the San Luis Valley and the Taos Plateau—was dropping along bordering fault zones. Each upward movement of the San Juan Dome was accompanied by sinking of the rift valley. These events changed the course of the ancestal river. It began flowing eastward from the San Juan Dome toward the rift valley. The newly formed Sangre de Cristo Range, east of the Rio Grande Rift, blocked the ancient route of the Rio Grande and separated it from the Pecos River drainage. Instead of continuing in a southeast direction, the river was turned southward, following the rift valley. At the same time, the Arkansas River's course continued south of the Salida area into the ancient San Luis Valley where it joined the Rio Grande.

For a long period thereafter, the San Juan Dome quieted down. This gave the Rio Grande, as well as rivers flowing westward off the Dome, time to do their erosion work. For millions of years the rivers gradually reduced the dome's massive crustal bulge. Thick beds of sand and gravel from the eroding highlands were dumped into the Rio Grande River Valley by the Rio Grande as well as by streams flowing from the Sangre de Cristos to the east. A deep pile of sediment filled the ancient San Luis Rift Valley. Today, this fill is known as the Santa Fe Formation. The artesian quality of the San Luis Valley results from the Santa Fe Formation's porosity.

As the great San Juan Dome was reduced to a gentle plain, the Rio Grande, its work nearly done, meandered sluggishly on top of the Santa Fe Formation. But the river was not to enjoy a peaceful old age. At the close of the Tertiary period, during a time known as the Hinsdale Volcanic Epoch, volcanic and crustal warping of the San Juan Dome began anew. No longer could the Rio Grande follow its old path across the gentle lowlands. With new vigor resulting from its increased velocity, it began again the long task of downcutting the east side of the reawakened San Juan Dome. Again it deposited its sediments in the sinking rift of the San Luis Valley. Meanwhile, extensive outpourings of basaltic lava of the Hinsdale Epoch flooded hundreds of square miles. Some of this lava poured into the Rio Grande Rift south of the San Luis Valley, filling the rift, lapping up against the Sangre de Cristos to the east, and producing the Taos Plateau. The Rio Grande was effectively dammed, and a lake formed in the San Luis Valley.

About this time, an east-west section of the crust was uplifted along faults in the north end of the San Luis Valley, blocking the southward-flowing Arkansas River from the Rio Grande and turning it eastward toward the Great Plains.

At its outlet, the huge new lake in the San Luis Valley vigorously attacked the lava dam, entrenching a channel in the basalt flows. As the escape trench deepened, sedimentation gradually raised the level of the lake bed, and the lake eventually disappeared. It is probable that this same trench provides the Rio Grande with its present escape from the San Luis Valley and has given us the beautiful box canyons of the Taos Plateau.

In the highlands to the west of the Taos Plateau, another dramatic event helped shape the Rio Grande drainage. About a million years ago, in the early stages of the Pleistocene Epoch, glacial ice began filling the high valleys. Throughout most of the Pleistocene, the San Juan Dome continued to rise, providing cold, wet highlands ideal for the accumulation of glacial ice.

Three glacial stages have been recorded. First came the Florida stage, then the Durango. The last stage, during which the glaciers achieved their greatest advance, was the Wisconsin. Glaciers dramatically altered the gradients and character of the canyons they filled, giving them steep walls and broad floors. During the Wisconsin, the entire upper drainage of the Rio Grande was covered by a sheet of ice a thousand feet deep. Glacial tongues advanced from the mother sheet down many of the tributary valleys. Two of these glaciers, occupying the present valleys of the Alamosa and Conejos rivers, almost reached the San Luis Valley. About 15,000 years ago the dominent glacial tongue, known as the Rio Grande Glacier, finally ceased its forward motion some ten miles upriver from Creede, Colorado.

During the next 10,000 years, as the ice masses retreated, their effects on the upper section of the Rio Grande continued. Behind blockading terminal moraines, the valleys filled with sediments, producing broad flats. Below these moraines the rivers did not have the energy to carry away the glacial debris; therefore the debris was dumped in the valleys. The heavily loaded rivers formed braided patterns on top of the deposits that they had laid down. When the glaciers finally disappeared, the rivers, freed from their sediment loads, began incising into these deposits, producing shallow canyons. In places where the downcutting process was particularly pronounced, narrow slots were carved into the broad bottoms of once glacier-filled valleys. These slots and canyons are the joy of today's river runners.

The Rio Grande drainage has evolved over the past seventy million years, since the beginning of the Tertiary period. It has been an awesome achievement. Four noble geologic processes shaped the present river and will undoubtedly continue to shape it in the future—crustal warping, volcanism, rifting and, finally, glaciation.

A River to Embrace

Flowing 1,887 miles from its headwaters in the San Juan Mountains to the Gulf of Mexico, the Rio Grande is the second longest river in the United States. Only the Missouri-Mississippi system is longer. The Rio Grande's source lies along a westward bulge in the Continental Divide at the crest of the San Juan Range. At first, it flows northeastward through a glacial trough bounded by walls of volcanic rock. Its canyon was once blocked just above the mouth of Squaw Creek by a large landslide which formed an ancient lake. In more recent times, a dam was built on the same landslide, creating the present Rio Grande Reservoir.

A short distance below the dam, the river enters a box canyon seven miles in length. Escaping the confines of this canyon, the river abruptly turns southward on a mile-wide, flat upland valley where the tumbling cascade dies to a meandering crawl. After wandering for nine miles through this upland valley, the river reaches the terminal moraine of the ancient Rio Grande Glacier. Here it turns northeastward again, cutting a shallow canyon through broad terraces produced by outwash gravels from the glacier. The gradient increases to about 25 feet per mile in this shallow canyon, where groves of tall Douglas fir cling to the slopes. The canyon gradually ends as the river approaches Willow Creek, flowing southward from the old mining town of Creede.

The broad upland river valley terminates in the picturesque notch known as Wagon Wheel Gap. Unusually resistant lavas forced the river to carve this gap, in which there is barely room for the bordering railroad and highway. Below the gap, for a distance of twelve miles, the river continues in a narrow V-shaped canyon to its confluence with the South Fork.

The South Fork Canyon once housed a glacier that reached a terminal point only four miles above its confluence with the main stem. High, boulder-studded terrraces of outwash from this glacier surround the vicinity of the confluence, which marks the end of the river's long confinement in the San Juan Mountains. (This upper portion of the Rio Grande will hereafter be referred to as the Headwaters Section.)

Enhanced by the South Fork, the Rio Grande crosses broad alluvial fans marking the borderline between the San Luis Valley and its flanking ranges. The gradient slows to about 10 feet per mile, and a meander pattern develops. Pines and firs of the riparian habitat upstream give way to thick cottonwood groves. In the vicinity of Del Norte, the gradient diminishes to only one foot per mile. Here, the headgates of the Rio Grande Canal, followed by the Farmer's Union, Monte Vista, and Empire canals, bleed off most of the river. Below the canals, during most seasons, the riverbed is dry across the relatively featureless San Luis Valley.

Large watercourses enter the northern part of the San Luis Valley and turn southward toward the master river. These include the Saguache River,

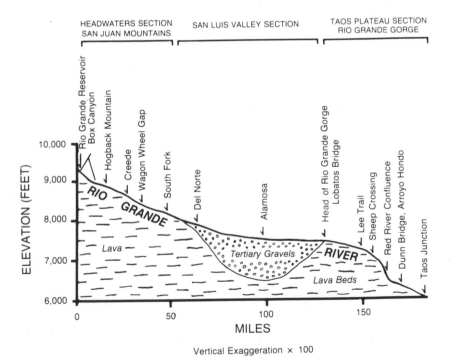

Gradient profile of the Rio Grande from Rio Grande Reservoir to Taos Junction.

originating in the La Garita Mountains north of Creede, and the many creeks issuing from the Sangre de Cristo Mountains to the east. None of these reach the Rio Grande. They are all absorbed in the porous sands, over 1,000 feet deep, that fill the San Luis Valley. This valley, the size of Massachusetts, is Colorado's largest artesian basin.

Below Alamosa the riverbed turns southward. The Conejos River enters from the west, and Trinchera and Culebra creeks join it from the east. Once more, the Rio Grande becomes a river. Below Culebra Creek, the stream begins, almost imperceptibly at first, to eat into the flat lava flows which block the southern end of the San Luis Valley. A narrow trench develops which, at the Colorado-New Mexico border, has deepened to over 100 feet and eventually cuts through a 20-mile-wide plateau of thick basalt sheets between the Sangre de Cristo and San Juan mountains. (This section of the river will hereafter be referred to as the Taos Plateau Section.)

Below the Colorado-New Mexico border, the Rio Grande is protected as a Wild and Scenic River. It deserves such designation. A more striking canyon, or one with a greater variety of wildlife, would be difficult to find. This is the birdland of Southern Rocky Mountains rivers. The pockmarked canyon walls produce ideal nesting sites for a wide variety of raptors. Canada geese, ducks, and shorebirds nest on the riverbanks. In the spring, large flocks of sandhill cranes are seen heading for the San Luis Valley. Almost every species of riparian bird can be found in large numbers within the walls of this narrow gorge.

Rio Grande Raft Race, scramble start at Wagon Wheel Gap.

In addition to birds, the river hosts muskrats, beavers, and otters. Mule deer, elk, antelope, black bears, and mountain lions find shelter in the canyon. Numerous reptiles live along the river.

Lichens of red, orange, yellow, and green color the black canyon walls. Solitary pinon and juniper trees cling to patches of soil. An occasional ponderosa pine is seen among clumps of sagebrush. Along the banks, willows sink their roots into the water table. A narrow border of alluvium supports rabbit brush, apache plume, mountain mahogany, occasional cottonwoods, and scrub oak. Yucca and numerous varieties of cactus are common on the slopes and benches.

As the river approaches the vicinity of Taos, the gorge walls reach their grandest height, over 600 feet. The gradient is only about 10 feet per mile in the upper part of the gorge. About 30 miles below the San Luis Valley, however, huge blocks of the canyon wall—two or three hundred feet long and up to 100 feet wide—have slumped into the river channel. These produce rapids of awesome declivity. Above the Red River confluence, the Rio Grande's gradient exceeds 120 feet per mile. It roars over falls and thundering cataracts. Below the Red River, additional slumping has produced more major rapids, but they are nothing like those above.

South of Taos the river continues to follow the broad Rio Grande Rift, but the canyon widens. Soon the river emerges from its many canyons and continues its long journey to the Gulf of Mexico.

Rio Grande—Headwaters Section

Rio Grande: River Hill Campground to Fern Creek Bridge (Box Canyon)

Physical Data: 9.5 mi; 280-ft drop; 30 ft/mi average gradient; 45 ft/mi maximum gradient (in Box Canyon); 153,000 acre-ft average yearly discharge (below Rio Grande Reservoir).
Maps: San Cristobal and Bristol Head USGS Quads.
Land Ownership: National Forest and Weminuche Wilderness first seven miles; mostly private land last three miles.

This marvelous 10-mile stretch begins two miles below the Rio Grande Reservoir. Just beyond the put-in lies a narrow box canyon, thick with spruce and fir. It has been included in the Weminuche Wilderness. The gradient approaches 50 feet per mile. Many class III and a few class IV rapids accent the descent. Secluded campsites abound. The fishing is superb, since this sheer-walled canyon is inaccessible except by river craft.

Unfortunately, Box Canyon is short. After six miles of technical water, the broad upland valley of the Rio Grande approaches. As from darkness into light, the river glides out of the forest and turns placidly south. Three miles below the canyon, a take-out is reached at the Fern Creek Road Bridge, off State Highway 149. To reach the put-in campground, go west in the direction of the Rio Grande Reservoir from Highway 149. Box Canyon run is highly recommended for its beauty and challenging rapids.

From below Fern Creek Bridge to Hogback Mountain, the river meanders slowly across private ranchlands. This stretch is not recommended for boating.

Rio Grande: Hogback Mountain to State Highway 149 Bridge

Physical Data: 15 mi; 360-ft drop; 24 ft/mi average gradient; 300,000 acre-ft average yearly discharge (near Creede).
Maps: San Cristobal, Bristol Head, and Creede USGS Quads.
Land Ownership: Alternating private and National Forest land.

In this stretch the river cuts a shallow, fir-lined canyon in the outwash plain created by the ancient Rio Grande Glacier. The rapids are mostly class II, with a few rated class III.

Finding a good put-in is difficult. State Highway 149 skirts the river just upstream from its big north bend at Hogback Mountain, with Antelope Park across the river to the south. A fence must be crossed at this access. Below Hogback Mountain the canyon begins. Alternate put-ins are found downriver on County Road 523, opposite Hogback Mountain, and at Rio Grande Campground. Alternate take-outs lie at the Marshall Park Campground, the Fivemile Bridge west of Creede, and the bridge one mile upriver from the Highway 149 Bridge above the fish hatchery. Dancing waves, abundant access (with the exception of the upriver put-in), and the relative seclusion of the shallow canyon make this a good stretch for intermediate boaters.

The next stretch, from the Highway 149 Bridge to Wagon Wheel Gap, crosses a wide valley with private ranches and is not recommended.

Rio Grande: Wagon Wheel Gap to South Fork

Physical Data: 12 mi; 260-ft drop; 21.6 ft/mi average gradient; 30 ft/mi maximum gradient (in Wagon Wheel Gap); 363,000 acre-ft average yearly discharge (at Wagon Wheel Gap).
Maps: Creede, Spar City, and South Fork West USGS Quads.
Land Ownership: Alternating private, National Forest, and state land.
Information: Rio Grande Raft Race Committee or the U.S. Forest Service in Creede, CO.

This is the most popular rafting stretch and the crowning canyon in the Headwaters Section of the Rio Grande. It is also the site of one of the biggest annual raft races in Colorado: the Rio Grande Raft Race. Held the second weekend in June, it is a lively affair. On Saturday a variety of races are held—the Amateur Scramble, Ladies Scramble, "Professional" Scramble, a mixed doubles, and kayak race. The scramble races start with a free-for-all of two-person teams all scrambling to their boats at the same time. On Sunday, the affair becomes serious. This is the day of the "World Championship." As much as $500 is awarded to the winners of this event.

Put-ins are located at the Phipps Bridge on State Highway 149 just above the upper gap, the Goose Creek Road Bridge one mile downriver, and the old train depot (private land). A dangerous railroad bridge crosses the river half a mile below the Phipps Bridge. The biggest rapid on this stretch begins less than one mile below the old train depot in Wagon Wheel Gap. Below this rapid, and just above Blue Creek, the river swings left and flows swiftly through narrow spaces between the steel supports of a small bridge. This can be a dangerous spot.

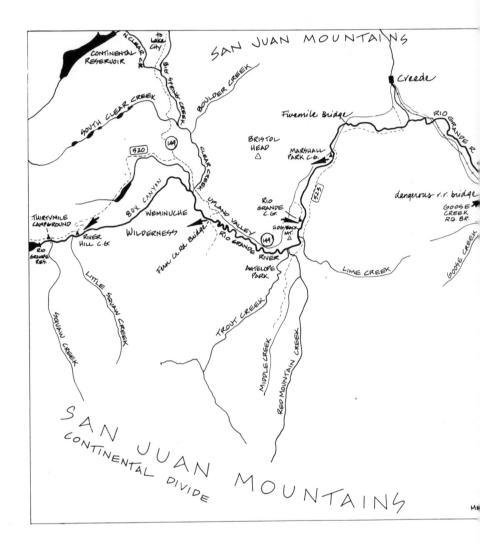

Rio Grande River, headwaters to Del Norte. South Fork of the Rio Grande.

Below the Blue Creek confluence the gradient decreases to about 20 feet per mile. The river widens. Smooth sailing is found the rest of the way to South Fork. Take out at the Highway 149 Bridge above South Fork.

South Fork of the Rio Grande: Park Creek Campground to South Fork

Physical Data: 9 mi; 300-ft drop; 33 ft/mi average gradient; 150,000 acre-ft average yearly discharge.

Maps: Beaver Creek Reservoir and South Fork West USGS Quads.
Land Ownership: Alternating private and National Forest land.

The tiny South Fork offers some marginal intermediate-level kayaking during high water season. A large part of the run can be inspected from U.S. Highway 160. Put-in points are found at the Highway Springs Campground six miles above the town of South Fork and at the Park Creek Campground farther upriver. The best take-out is situated at the County Road 360 Bridge, one mile above the town of South Fork.

Rio Grande—San Luis Valley Section

Rio Grande: Town of South Fork to Del Norte

Physical Data: 18 mi; 300-ft drop; 17 ft/mi average gradient, 650,000 acre-ft average yearly discharge (at Del Norte).
Maps: South Fork West, South Fork East, Indian Head, and Del Norte USGS Quads.
Land Ownership: Private, but open to fishing.

After emerging from its mountain canyon, the Rio Grande must cross the San Luis Valley. Before its waters are absorbed in the big canals crossing the valley, there is a scenic run for beginners and novices. Many riffles, a few class I to II rapids, and low rock weirs break the predominantly flat water.

This part of the run has recently been recognized as a "gold medal" fishery by the Colorado Division of Wildlife. Gold Medal waters by definition "provide outstanding angling success for large trout" (in this case, brown trout). Although the river crosses private ranchland, it has been opened to public fishing through lease agreements between landowners and the Division of Wildlife.

The agreements provide access to the river at several locations. Two miles east of South Fork, a bridge connecting the North River Road and U.S. Highway 160 makes a good put-in point. Take-outs are found five miles downriver at the Granger Bridge on County Road 18, and nine miles downriver at State Bridge on County Road 17. If you go all the way to Del Norte, you must portage at the headgate of the Rio Grande Canal located near the base of a lava cliff one mile above town.

Rio Grande: Below Alamosa

Boaters will probably find only a trickle of water in the riverbed below Alamosa. During high water periods, however, a portion of the flow may get past the headgates above town, providing a pleasant flat water run through the southern San Luis Valley.

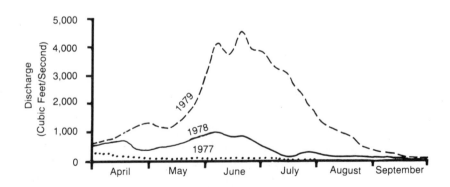

Hydrograph of Rio Grande at Colorado-New Mexico state line.

Put in at the Alamosa National Wildlife Refuge southeast of town. After the first ten miles, the addition of the Conejos River from the west enhances the flow substantially. From here the river passes along the east side of the San Luis Hills. Access points are located at the State Highway 142 Bridge and eight miles farther downriver at the Lobatos Bridge west of Mesita.

Rio Grande—Taos Plateau Section

The south-flowing Rio Grande begins eating into the Taos Plateau just north of the Colorado-New Mexico border. A narrow, rugged canyon carves through layers of basaltic lava. For the next 56 miles, this is one of the most inaccessible canyons in the Southern Rocky Mountain region. A few rough trails enter the gorge. Road access to the river is found at only one place: the Dunn Bridge north of Taos. The canyon cracks the level Taos Plateau so abruptly that standing 100 yards from the edge, one would never know the chasm was there. The Rio Grande Gorge is a paradise for those who seek wildlife and wilderness.

The difficulty of the river ranges from flat to impassable water. The floating season usually begins in mid-April with high water in mid-June.

Rio Grande: Lobatos Bridge to Lee Trail

Physical Data: 23.5 mi; 160-ft drop; 6.8 ft/mi average gradient; 248,000 acre-ft average yearly discharge.

Maps: Kiowa Hill, Sky Valley Ranch, Ute Mountains, and Sunshine USGS Quads.

Land Ownership: In Colorado—private and BLM; In New Mexico—public National Wild and Scenic River.

Information: BLM, Santa Fe, New Mexico; Wild and Scenic River Visitor Center near Cerro, New Mexico.

Flow Information: Ralph Pike of the National Weather Service in Albuquerque, NM gives daily flow at the state line.

This first run in the Rio Grande Gorge offers excellent water for beginner and novice kayakers and intermediate open canoeists. The rough, 500-yard carry-out at Lee Trail precludes heavy rubber rafts. Numerous class I and II rapids are scattered throughout the run. The more difficult ones come near the take-out.

The run is usually done in two days. Excellent camp spots on narrow benches are numerous.

To reach the Lobatos Bridge, drive west on Colorado State Highway 248 off Colorado State Highway 159 through Mesita. Just past Mesita the road turns to dirt and jogs to the south. Take the first road due west past the south jog and drive six miles to the bridge.

To reach the Lee Trail, drive due west off New Mexico State Highway 3 on the marked Sunshine Valley Road. Continue west on this rough road for five miles to a point about one mile short of the canyon. Here, a branch road goes south along a fence line. Follow this road about four miles until it ends at the rim of the gorge and the start of the Lee Trail. The round trip shuttle takes about two hours.

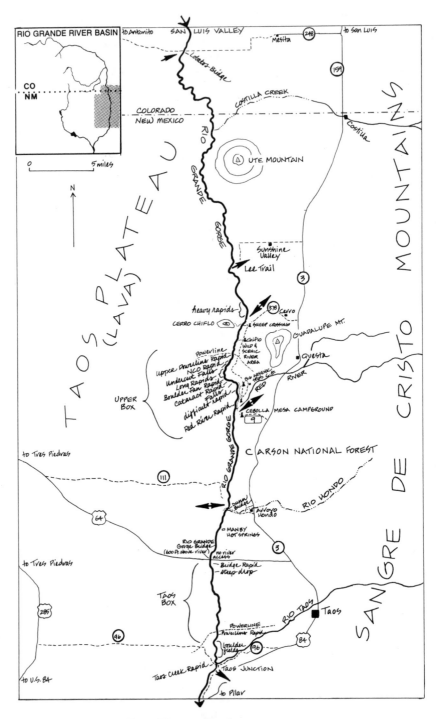

Rio Grande River, Taos Plateau Section.

Below the Lobatos Bridge the gorge walls begin to rise and the San Luis Valley is left behind. Once in the canyon you are in a unique world of wild beauty untouched by man's influence. During an April or May trip, abundant bird life soon becomes apparent. Only infrequent stops should be made, as stops will disturb the nesting Canada geese. Downy yellow goslings hide in the brush along the bank while concerned, honking parents try to lure you away. Please be considerate of these feathered friends.

Near the state line the broad, symmetrical dome of the Ute Mountain, around which the gorge winds, can be seen ahead. Its forested slopes provide a stark contrast to the canyon's desert vegetation.

Costilla Creek meets the gorge from the east about 10 miles downstream. Below Costilla Creek, junipers begin to dot the canyon walls and floodplain. Rapids become slightly steeper and more numerous.

The gorge walls continue to increase in height. Freshwater springs bubble up along the banks, providing clear drinking water. Near the Lee Trail, the canyon walls have reached a height of 200 feet. Here the rapids are more difficult. At lower water levels, some of these could be rated class II.

The Lee Trail is well marked with several signs. Don't miss it. Big rapids lie below.

Rio Grande: Lee Trail to Sheep Crossing

Expert kayakers might wish to continue downriver for another five miles through some big rapids to Sheep Crossing. There, they can be picked up by those in their party who climbed out at Lee Trail. Slumping of the gorge's sides about one mile above Sheep Crossing has produced half a mile of continuous, very complex class IV rapids. A sign warning of the cataracts ahead marks the trail at Sheep Crossing.

This run offers an exciting climax to a trip through the upper Rio Grande Gorge.

Rio Grande: Sheep Crossing to Red River Confluence (Upper Box)

This nine-mile stretch is the most difficult in the Rio Grande Gorge. Its bone-crushing rapids and falls make it suitable for expert kayakers only. Rafts will meet with great danger and difficulty. A permit is required, obtainable at the Wild and Scenic River headquarters.

To reach the put-in, turn west off New Mexico State Highway 3 at the Wild and Scenic River Area sign just north of Questa, through Cerro to the Sheep Crossing trailhead. The canyon is about 300 feet deep here.

As the slotlike canyon makes a broad S-curve to the east, massive slumping of its walls into the river have produced a series of long, steep, and complex rapids. The gradient reaches a steep 120 feet per mile. Above 2,000 c.f.s. the stretch can be exceedingly hazardous and many carries will be required. As the water level drops, fewer carries will be necessary, and the rapids will be less dangerous. At about 300 c.f.s. it might be possible to get through the Upper Box without a portage.

In the first three miles below the Sheep Crossing Trail, steep, class II to III drops are scattered between tranquil stretches. A powerline crossing high over the canyon marks the first big rapid. This is Upper Powerline Rapid; it's nearly as difficult as its counterpart 30 miles downstream. In the next five miles below Upper Powerline, the channel is beset with some of the most difficult and enchanting rapids anywhere.

Just past Upper Powerline lies N.C.O. Rapid, with a six-foot drop at its entrance, followed by Undercut Falls. Here, the river crashes into an undercut boulder at the base of a steep drop. Undercut Falls is usually the first portage. Note the capaceous lava tube high on the west rim of the canyon at Undercut Falls. A few hundred yards past Undercut Falls lie Long Rapids. These two class IV to V rapids are each 200 yards long and separated by only a short break. The end of Long Rapids brings the first bit of relief in the struggle through Upper Box—a long pool. Ahead the canyon swings sharply to the east.

At the end of the pool the going gets even tougher. The long class V maze ahead was formed by a boulder fan from the side canyon to the west. Boulder Fan Rapid is a mandatory portage above 2,000 c.f.s. Directly beyond the difficult portage at Boulder Fan Rapid, another less difficult rapid leads around the corner toward the east. Below this one, there is another break in the action. The tranquility abruptly ends, however, as the river sweeps into a long, powerful, class IV cataract.

Then come the Falls. This 30-foot falls is almost never navigable. Portage left. Below the Falls the river passes a campground and turns once more to the south. Two difficult rapids remain. The first is a boulder-studded morass, almost always an agonizing portage. Below the second rapid a trail from the east rim meets the river and follows the east bank down to and across the Red River. The difficult rapids and arduous portages are over. Big ponderosa pines

The author about to flip in N.C.O. Rapid, Upper Box Canyon. (Don Grall photo.)

reach down to the river here, and campsite shelters can be seen on the broad flats.

A last crowning rapid sits just above the Red River Confluence. It is less difficult than those upriver, but it's a joyous conundrum, one of the finest of its kind. Just below the Red River a trail leads from the river to Cebolla Mesa Campground on the east rim.

It feels good to reach the Red River with sense of satisfaction engendered by the struggle and accomplishment of negotiating the Upper Box. The Upper Box has neither name nor fame today, but in the future boaters will come here to seek its terrible repose.

Rio Grande: Red River Confluence to Dunn Bridge

This 10-mile novice run is very wild. Tall ponderosas green this section of the otherwise barren Rio Grande Gorge. Slumping of the canyon walls is not as prevalent as upstream.

A trail from the Cebolla Mesa Campground off New Mexico State Highway 3 on the east rim leads down to the Red River confluence put-in. Forested benches provide excellent camping all along this stretch. The fishing is excellent, due to the fact that only a few rough trails reach the river.

A single class III rapid near the end of the run is the only significant whitewater. Take out at Dunn Bridge.

Rio Grande: Dunn Bridge to Taos Junction (Taos Box)

Physical Data: 15 mi; 400-ft drop; 26.6 ft/mi average gradient; 70 ft/mi maximum gradient (for 2 miles above Taos Junction); 416,000 acre-ft average yearly discharge (at Arroyo Hondo).
Maps: Arroyo Hondo, Los Cordovas, and Taos S.W. USGS Quads.
Land Ownership: National Wild and Scenic River.
Information: BLM, Taos, New Mexico.
Flow Information: The U.S. Weather Service in Albuquerque, NM, gives the daily flow at the CO-NM border.

Sometimes called the Taos Box, this run is the most popular in the Rio Grande Gorge. In a good runoff year over 5,000 people make the run on commercial and private trips.

Here the gorge reaches its grandest proportions, over 600 feet deep. The run has some quite difficult class IV drops and boulder fields.

The river volume can reach 7,000 c.f.s. in a heavy runoff year. At levels over 4,000 c.f.s., the rapids become extremely dangerous for rubber rafts. At levels under 500 c.f.s., rafts will have difficulty navigating some of the boulder-choked drops.

Although parties must obtain permits at the Dunn Bridge, there are no restrictions at this time on noncommercial river runners. In the future, however, limits may be set on use and advance permits required.

The put-in at the Dunn Bridge lies three miles west of the town of Arroyo Hondo. Manby Hot Springs, two miles downriver on the left bank, offers a refreshing stop. This is the site of the old stagecoach road across the canyon. The hot springs was a popular stage stop.

Below Manby Hot Springs two class III rapids have been formed by side canyon boulders. The high Rio Grande Gorge Bridge spans the canyon slightly less than halfway down the run (no access to the river). An enjoyable rapid lies just beyond the high bridge. A precipitous class IV drop is found just past the first side canyon on the left, a mile below the high bridge. This drop will require a portage at low water.

From a point one mile below the steep drop, great blocks of the canyonside, miles long, have slumped toward the river, forming a black inner canyon. Here the rapids follow one another in close succession. The biggest drop in the stretch lies just downriver from a high tension powerline crossing over the gorge. Powerline Rapid is a mandatory inspection stop. The river plunges 15 feet among huge boulders. At low levels this rapid will probably have to be portaged.

One mile below Powerline, a three-mile-long series of steep rock gardens begins. Note the vertical columnar basalt towers on the right at the first rock garden. Throughout this long reach, constant attention is required to avoid broaching or dropping into a frothing hole.

Suddenly, around a sharp right curve, the gorge widens ahead, a last big rapid is run at the mouth of Taos Creek, and the Taos Junction Bridge is reached. This marks the end of the Rio Grande Gorge and the Wild and Scenic River area. New Mexico State Highway 96 crosses the river here. A branch of Highway 96 follows the left bank downriver.

Conejos River

The Conejos ("rabbit") River begins in Platoro Reservoir, high in the southern San Juan Mountains below the Continental Divide. Beyond the reservoir, the little river knifes into the volcanic lavas and tuffs of the Hinsdale Epoch. Willows line the watercourse as the river plunges through a narrow canyon before spewing into a broad meadow deposited behind the blockading moraine of the ancient Conejos Glacier. Beyond the Colorado State Highway 17 Bridge, the Conejos meanders through glades of spruce and fir before sallying forth from its canyon recess into the San Luis Valley. Here the river turns northeast, murmuring sluggishly through a forested strip of cottonwoods to meet the Rio Grande below Alamosa.

The endangered peregrine falcon and bald eagle inhabit the river area. Bighorn sheep haunt the high ledges. If the proposed Wild and Scenic River plan is accepted, these and many other species of wildlife will be protected. Part of the Wild and Scenic River will include the section from the town of Platoro to the South Fork Confluence.

An expert kayak run can be found near the headwaters. Below the old mining town of Platoro, where the river turns south, the gradient increases to over 100 feet per mile through three miles of continuous crashing rapids past the Lake Fork Campground. Two miles downriver from the Lake Fork confluence, the Conejos wanders away from the road (County Road 250) and enters a deep, grottolike canyon. In the heart of the gorge, spires of volcanic ash called the Pinnacles stand guard over the river. At the base of the Pinnacles lies difficult Pinnacle Rapid. Here the river takes a hard right turn over a low falls and up against a lava wall. Two miles below Pinnacle Rapid, the gorge opens into a meadowy valley with ranches and pastureland. A bridge at the mouth of the gorge, just above the South Fork confluence off County Road 250, provides a convenient take-out.

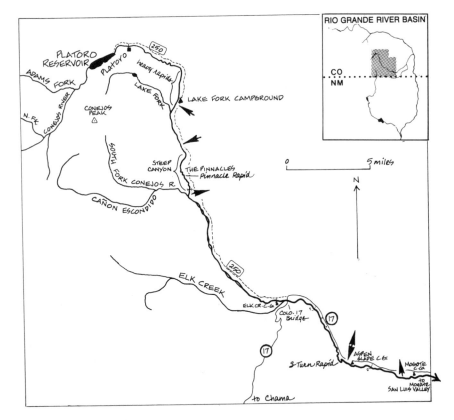

Upper Conejos River.

Conejos River: Highway 17
Bridge to Mogote Campground

After 12 miles of pastureland, the Conejos once again becomes practical for boating. Access is found at the Colorado State Highway 17 Bridge just below the Elk Creek confluence. Elk Creek increases the flow of the small Conejos. Even when the upper section is too low, good boating can often be found below this confluence. Generally, the best floating season is during high water in May and June. After a winter of heavy snowpack, however, the free-flowing Conejos (Platoro Reservoir is presently used chiefly for flood control) holds up well into July.

The river below Elk Creek is relatively gentle (class I and II). Vacation cabins and small resorts along the river indicate private land. Watch for low bridges at high water. Near Aspen Glade Campground, the gradient increases to 40 feet per mile. The most difficult rapids on this section of the Conejos, S-Turn Rapids, are located here. One-half mile above the Aspen Glade Campground the river twists around a sharp left turn through gnarly rapids, then sweeps hard right over a boulder falls.

Below Aspen Glade Campground the river once again enters National Forest land. At least one dangerous barbed wire fence spans the river here. A good take-out is at Mogote Campground near the canyon mouth.

As the Conejos glides out into the San Luis Valley, it becomes undesirable for floating. Nasty barbed wire fences and lots of driftwood clog the channel.

Rio Chama

Years ago, while rafting the Rio Chama in Apache country, we broke camp early, getting on the river as the sun rose. A short way down we saw two Indians, an old man and a boy, riding up the river on stately Appaloosas, their long, black hair draped over their shoulders. They wore no trappings of the white man—no hats, saddles, pendelton shirts, or jeans. We must have looked silly in modern rubber rafts and bright-colored life jackets. I raised my hand in greeting. The old man raised his hand slowly. We floated by. I wondered if they would find any trace of our campsite up the river.

The Chama (Spanish for young girl) is another of the Southwest's little known wilderness rivers. It has hewn an exquisite, remote canyon. Two-day raft or canoe trips through romantic Chama Canyon are growing in popularity.

Like the Dolores, the Chama is best for floating in the spring. Like the Dolores, it carves a scenic canyon through colorful Mesozoic strata. The two rivers are about the same size; both carry a heavy load of suspended sediment; both flow through remote canyons with a few dirt roads, ranches, and dwellings dotting the riverside. Both rivers course through a semi-arid habitat where pinon and juniper trees cling to the canyon walls. But while the Dolores is depleted by trans-basin diversions, the Chama is substantially enhanced by tunnels from the Navajo and Rio Blanco rivers in the San Juan drainage basin. As much as 100,000 additional acre-feet of water swells the Chama from across the Continental Divide.

The Rio Chama is the only major river in the upper Rio Grande Basin to carve a lengthy canyon in sedimentary rocks. Chama Canyon is cut into rocks flanking the eastern edge of the San Juan Basin. The ubiquitous Dakota Sandstone caps the mesas around the canyon. Below it the Morrison Mudstone forms a slope above the orange and white cliffs of Entrada Sandstone. Below, the bright red Chinle Shale slopes down to the river.

The Rio Chama begins in the southern San Juan Range, just north of the Colorado-New Mexico border. It progresses due south through the town of Chama, New Mexico, before it is stilled in the El Vado Reservoir. Below the reservoir it enters scenic Chama Canyon. As the river emerges from the canyon it is once again stilled behind the Abiquiu Dam and Reservoir. Thereafter it proceeds southeast to meet the Rio Grande at Espanola.

Rio Chama: New Mexico Highway 95 Bridge to El Vado Reservoir

The put-in is located half a mile west of U.S. Highway 84 at the confluence of the Rio Brazos and the Rio Chama. Another put-in spot can be found at the gaging station off New Mexico State Highway 112 five miles downstream.

As the river enters its upper canyon, house-sized blocks of Dakota Sandstone, fallen from the rim, obstruct the channel, producing several class III to IV rapids. The canyon, though short, is scenic and wild. A few miles below the Heron Dam, seen north of the river on Willow Creek, boaters reach the

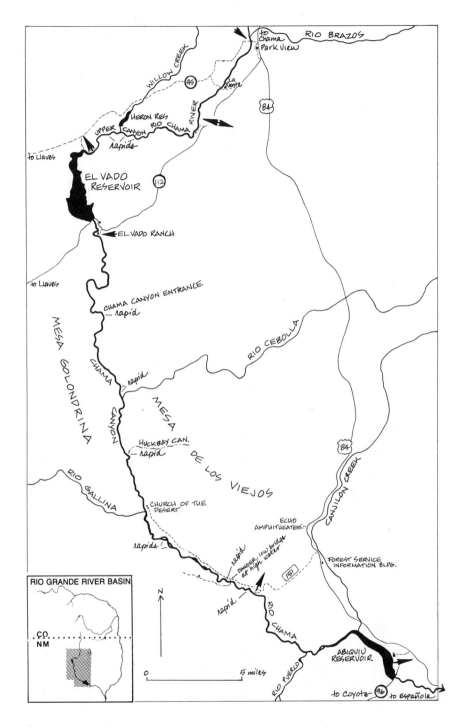

Rio Chama.

backwaters of El Vado Reservoir. A take-out is found on a dirt road leading half a mile south from Highway 95 to the head of the reservoir.

This short section of the Rio Chama, free-flowing, rushes high and strong from late April to mid-June.

Rio Chama: El Vado Dam to Abiquiu Reservoir

Physical Data: 35 mi; 580-ft drop; 16.5 ft/mi average gradient; 177,000 acre-ft average yearly discharge (below El Vado Reservoir).

Maps: Tierra Amarilla, Navajo Peak, Laguna Peak, Echo Amphitheater, and Ghost Ranch USGS Quads.

Land Ownership: Private and BLM land to Chama Canyon entrance. Santa Fe National Forest through Chama Canyon, except for private stretches past the Rio Cebolla confluence and the Church of the Desert.

Information: National Weather Service, Albuquerque, NM.

This is the Chama's prized run. El Vado Ranch, half a mile below the dam, provides a good put-in spot. Automobiles can be left at the ranch for a small fee.

Releases from El Vado Dam range from 1,000 to 2,000 c.f.s. in spring months. This is the most propitious time for a float trip through Chama Canyon.

Flat water in the first five miles leads past weathered ranch buildings to Chama Canyon's imposing entrance. There are three enchanting class II rapids in the first nine miles. The first lies at the canyon entrance, the second just above the Rio Cebolla confluence, and the third at the mouth of Huckaby Canyon. Between the rapids, many riffles too minor to be called rapids

A tense moment. Dr. Cam Berry at the oars.

punctuate the river in this peaceful canyon. The surface is dimpled here and there by a muskrat crossing. Many good campsites in groves of ponderosa pine lie on floodplains above the river. Watch for barbed wire.

Across from the Rio Gallina confluence is the Church of the Desert, a beautiful monastery in the heart of the canyon. The monastery requests that you not stop on church property. They will continue to be gracious about allowing boaters to pass provided it is done quietly and courteously.

Below the monastery the canyon begins to widen. The addition of the Rio Gallina makes the river siltier. A broader floodplain flanks the Rio Chama. The Entrada Sandstone forms a colorful backdrop of white, yellow, and pink on the cliffs to the northeast. In the distance to the southwest, high forested mesas reveal themselves. Cottonwood groves begin to inhabit the riverside.

Beginning two miles below the monastery, the rapids become more difficult. The first two are long class II rapids through channels beside gravel islands. The third, a class II to III rapid, is located on the approach to a dangerously low cement bridge. Watch carefully for this bridge when the level of the Rio Chama exceeds 2,000 c.f.s. A final class II to III rapid tumbles beneath an overhanging ledge river left.

Just beyond this last rapid, a spur off County Road 151 leads to a popular take-out. County Road 151 branches southwest from U.S. Highway 84 between Echo Amphitheater and the U.S. Forest Service information building.

If you continue downriver, all roads leave the riparian vicinity. A shallow mini-canyon holds the river. Soon the Rio Chama dies in the backwaters of the Abiquiu Reservoir, where you'll see groves of ghost cottonwoods that were drowned by the reservoir. Depending on the reservoir's level, up to five miles of dead water must be paddled before reaching the camping area just short of the Abiquiu Dam.

Appendix

Skills Classification

There is no substitute for a boater's own judgement in selecting a stream that is safe for his or her particular skills level.

The following classification of boating skills has been adapted from the A.M.C. Whitewater Handbook and is generally accepted by the American Canoe Association. It is submitted to assist the reader in assessing the skills level required on particular rivers and should be used in connection with the river classification chart which follows.

• *Beginner:* Knows the basic strokes and can handle the raft, canoe, or kayak competently in smooth water.

• *Novice:* Can effectively use all basic whitewater strokes. Can read water and negotiate easy rapids with assurance. Kayakers can attempt eskimo roll with at least partial success in smooth water.

• *Intermediate:* Can negotiate rapids requiring sequential maneuvering and use of eddy turns. Kayakers can use the roll as a means of self-rescue in the river.

• *Advanced:* Has ability to safely run difficult and complex rapids characterized by technical and precise maneuvering. Kayakers can roll on either side in turbulent water.

• *Expert:* In addition to mastery of all whitewater skills, an expert must have wide experience on many rivers and the ability to rescue other rafters or kayakers having difficulty.

River and Rapid Classification

The following International Standard for classifying the difficulty of rivers and rapids is used in this book:

• *Class I:* Suitable for novices. Easy. Waves small and regular; passages clear.

• *Class II:* Suitable for intermediates. Quite easy. Rapids of medium difficulty; passages clear and wide; possible low ledges; occasional boulder in stream.

• *Class III:* Suitable for experienced kayakers, decked canoeists, and rubber rafters; experts only in open canoes. Waves numerous, high, irregular; rocks, narrow passages. Considerable experience in maneuvering required. Advance scouting usually advisable.

• *Class IV:* Suitable for expert kayakers, decked canoeists, and 10-person-size rubber rafts; no open canoes. Long rapids, powerful and irregular waves; dangerous rocks, boiling eddies; passages difficult to reconnoiter; inspection mandatory first time; powerful and precise maneuvering required.

• *Class V:* Suitable for expert paddlers only in kayaks or decked canoes. Extremely difficult, long and very violent rapids following each other almost without interruption. River bed extremely obstructed; big drops; very steep gradient; advance scouting mandatory and usually difficult due to rough terrain.

• *Class VI:* Suitable for teams of expert paddlers only in kayaks and decked canoes at favorable water levels and only after careful study with experienced rescue team in position. Extraordinarily difficult; difficulties of Class V carried to extremes of navigability. Nearly impossible and very dangerous.

The above International Standard can be compared with the American System of Rapid Classification, grades one through 10, in the following manner: Each number on the International Standard is deemed equivalent to two numbers on the American Standard. For example, class I on the International Standard is approximately equivalent to grades one and two on the American Standard. Class II on the International Standard relates approximately to grades three and four on the American Standard, and so forth.

Gradient vs. Difficulty

Information as to a river's gradient can assist the boater in assessing its difficulty and suitability for his craft and experience level.

High volume rivers can be difficult even with low gradients. The Colorado through the Grand Canyon has the highest volume of any southwestern river. Although its gradient averages only 10 feet per mile, it has many class III and a few IV rapids. On the other hand, smaller-volume streams and rivers with steep gradients are often safe to run. The following outline of gradients assumes a moderate volume river of about 1,000 to 2,000 cubic feet per second (c.f.s.):

- *1-10 ft/mi:* Generally flat water with class I rapids. Suitable for novices in kayaks and open canoes.

- *10-50 ft/mi:* Generally class II to III rapids. Suitable for intermediate kayakers, decked canoeists, and rubber rafters.

- *50-100 ft/mi:* Generally class III to V rapids. Suitable for advanced and expert kayakers and decked canoeists only. Control very difficult to maintain in rubber rafts.

- *100-150 ft/mi:* Generally class IV to VI rapids; extraordinarily difficult. Suitable for expert kayakers and decked canoeists at lower water levels only. No rubber rafts.

- *More than 150 ft/mi:* Rarely navigable.

Water Levels

It is important to remember that the difficulty of a rapid varies with the water level. The following classification may aid the beginner in establishing the level of a river he or she might be viewing. It also defines terms relating to water levels used in this book.

- *Flood Stage:* Over banks of lowest floodplain. Water reaches trunks of trees on banks of the river. Debris in water (logs, driftwood, etc.). Small willows and alders along the banks are in water and bent by the current. Current flowing with high velocity.

- *High Water:* Trees on banks barely out of water. Few rocks showing. Alders and willows in water. No sandbars or gravel bars exposed. High-velocity current.

- *Medium Water:* Some rocks exposed. Portions of sandbars and gravel bars exposed. Alders and willows out of water. Trees on banks far out of water. Moderate-velocity current.

- *Low Water:* Large sandbars and gravel bars exposed. Rocky channel. Alders and willows far out of water. Low-velocity current.

A Gallery of River Birds

Rivers are the playgrounds of the birds, who bring the canyons to life with rapturous song and flashing color. They provide unpurchasable relief from our usual background of machines and human chatter.

A few brave birds spend their winters on the mountain rivers. Boaters venturing forth during this season will be rewarded by the canyon wren's ebullient song or by the sight of the dipper flinging itself with heedless abandon into icy waters. Defying snowy blasts, mergansers beat their feverish pace up and down partly frozen watercourses in search of fish. The golden eagle eyes his chilly domain from the canyon rim, the red-shafted flicker drums in a grove of cottonwood on still bottomlands, and the great blue heron lurks in shadowy shallows.

Most birds make their appearance in the spring. In April and May the canyons swarm with industrious activity, their wild inhabitants in full tune. Some, guided in their-northward migration by the river valleys, make only a passing visit. Brightly colored warblers and tanagers, as well as many varieties of ducks, are seen for a few weeks and disappear. The swallows, the osprey, and a few wandering Canada geese nest along the river banks.

As spring is the birds' season, so is morning their time. The earlier the boater rises, the greater the rewards. One must venture to where the birds find peace and solitude on remoter reaches. The gnarled walls of volcanic rock bordering the remote Rio Grande Canyon south of the San Luis Valley is perhaps the best place to see spring birds, both nesting and migrating. The lower Green River provides a major north-south flyway for migrating ducks, geese, and large raptors as well as myriads of tiny warblers. The lower Gunnison and the Dolores are favorite stops for migrating flocks and nesting areas for ducks and herons.

Raptors make their homes on the walls of steeper canyons. In such places many prairie falcons (and occasionally their rare cousins, the peregrine falcons) will be seen, as well as the nesting sites of soaring turkey vultures and golden eagles.

Hummingbirds arrive in great numbers on high, forested rivers about mid-May. Dippers, kingfishers, osprey, jays, chickadees, and mountain bluebirds also prefer the high mountain streams.

The following notes omit many birds seen along the banks of Southern Rocky Mountain rivers. Descriptions have been limited to those indigenous to riparian habitats, those which seldom serenade or play for the city dweller, and those the boater could hardly fail to see and hear while navigating the rivers.

Dipper or Water Ouzel *(Cinclus mexicanus)*

No bird is so wedded to fresh waters or harmonizes so well with clear mountain rivers as the water ouzel. Born in the spray above tumbling cataracts, he never leaves it. He is the only bird to enter foaming whitewater, masterfully capturing and utilizing the river's energy.

Chunky, six to eight inches long, drab grey in color with a short upturned tail, he looks like a large, rather homely wren—a bit out of place in a whitewater habitat. "Find a fall, or cascade or rushing rapid, anywhere upon a clear crystalline stream," said John Muir, "and there you will surely find its complementary ouzel, flitting about in the spray, diving in foaming eddies, whirling like a leaf among beaten foam bells; ever vigorous and enthusiastic, yet self-contained, and neither seeking nor shunning your company."

The dipper is a year-round resident of the Southern Rocky Mountains, ranging from foothills in winter to timberline in summer. He is morphologically unspecialized for an underwater habitat, with the exception of nostril coverings and an enlarged oil gland for waterproofing feathers. Rather than gripping underwater rocks with his feet, the dipper faces the current, tilting his body to a position in which the dynamic force of the current will hold him on the bottom, much like the airfoil on a racing car holds it to the track. In this way he walks, as if on dry ground, picking up larvae and other aquatic insects on the bottom. He can remain underwater for as long as 30 or 40 seconds. Then, using his wings, he "flies" to the surface. Emerging like a cork, he steps out onto a rock and bobs up and down with his entire body—hence the name "dipper."

These birds never leave their stream-side habitat—even in flight. With steady, rapid wingbeats they speed upstream and down, just above the water, trilling *zeetzeet-zeetzeetzeetzeet*. With exuberance and melodious voice they challenge the roar of the whitewater.

A dipper's nest is a globular mass of moss and grass with a small entrance hole, anchored to a vertical rock face or mid-channel boulder, always over the water. Nests on Southern Rocky Mountain rivers are constructed before the late spring runoff. Dippers

Dipper.

possess an uncanny awareness of impending water levels, always building at just the right height and often precariously close to the splash of falls and cataracts.

Common Merganser *(Mergus serrator)*

Many species of ducks stop along Southern Rocky Mountain rivers during their spring migrations. Mallards, greenwinged teal, buffleheads, and pintails are common. But the duck most associated with river habitats is the common merganser. Throughout spring and summer, from whitewater streams at higher elevations to muddy rivers of the Colorado Plateau region, the merganser is a true river duck.

The male sports a diagnostic dark green head that looks black from a distance, while the female's head is rust colored with a slight crest above her neck. Both have a white breast and streamlined body with darker upper parts. Their upper bills, longer and thinner than most ducks, hook slightly at the tip. Unlike most ducks, the merganser is a fisherman. One of its unusual features is a set of small teeth lining the inside of both mandibles for gripping its slippery prey.

As with all ducks, common mergansers are shy. They will swim downriver ahead of you, sometimes through heavy class IV rapids, constantly looking back over their shoulders to see if you are getting too close. When you do, they will crash dive without a ripple, swimming under water, sometimes popping up behind you. In springtime, families of mergansers ply the swift waters, long strings of chicks following faithfully behind their mothers. Occasionally the ducklings perch on her back for an easy ride through whitewater. If a human approaches her brood, the mother raises a squawking fit. She flops downriver, feigning injury, drawing attention from her babies, who hide in alder patches along the shore. Then, around a bend, after she has led the intruder for a quarter of a mile or more, she rises and haughtily races back upriver to her waiting youngsters.

Osprey or Fish Hawk *(Pandion haliaetus)*

The osprey is one of the few large raptors still frequently seen along Southern Rocky Mountain rivers, although its numbers have decreased in recent years. Its appearance and flight characteristics are akin to those of other large hawks, although it is easily distinguished by an underside of white plumage. Also unmistakable is the osprey's call, a series of loud, clear whistles. Its nest consists of huge piles of sticks, usually sitting atop a dead tree, always near to or overhanging the water.

Pesticides and habitat destruction seem to have been the cause of the ospreys' decline. "Their eggs are just not hatching." explains a Colorado Division of Wildlife official. A fledging osprey banded in Colorado in 1976 was found the next fall in El Salvador, where large amounts of U.S. manufactured dieldrin and DDT are used.

A fishing osprey is a thrilling sight. It cruises at about a hundred feet above the river. Suddenly it plunges in a bent-wing dive, extending its legs forward at the last moment to strike its prey. Often disappearing underwater for a few seconds, it emerges, shakes the water from its plumage like a wet dog, and carries its fish into the air. An osprey sometimes shows off its catch by swooping up and down the river screaming *hee-hee-hee* for several minutes, the hapless fish dangling in the death-grip of the bird's grappling hook talons.

Canyon Wren *(Catherpes mexicanus)*

The person who has never heard the canyon wren's decending call has missed some of the world's best music. Any deep canyon in the semi-arid part of the rocky Mountain region is this bird's year-around concert hall. Each of its eight to ten notes *peeup, peeup, peeup* is sung lower on the chromatic scale and is more delayed than the last. For this reason he is sometimes called the "scale bird." Mates sometimes sing duets, one beginning the tumbling song and the other finishing it.

Like all wrens, the canyon wren is a small, brownish bird with the curious habit of cocking his tail skyward. With sharp claws he climbs up and down canyon walls hunting

Osprey.

Canyon Wren.

insects and spiders. The canyon wren is difficult to spot unless he decides to expose himself. At these times he will usually choose the top of a riverside boulder, where he will expand his white breast and astound the listener that such a booming voice could gush from such a tiny creature. The call can carry up and down a canyon for half a mile or more.

American Avocet *(Recurvirostra americana)*

The American avocet is another shorebird that migrates through Southern Rocky Mountain river valleys in spring.

His stilt legs; upcurving, needlelike bill; and long orange neck provide the primary identitying markings.

We once surprised a group of avocets on the White River. They released loud *wheet* calls and flew down river. We were surprised when they landed in a small rapid ahead. "That's the wrong place for a frail shorebird," I thought. But they swam through the whitewater with the aplomb of ducks. With his webbed toes, the avocet, it turns out, is as well equipped for swimming as for wading.

These stately birds provide graceful and endearing additions to Rocky Mountain rivers during their short visit in early spring.

Killdeer *(Charadrius vociferus)*

Killdeer are the only common plovers on Southern Rocky Mountain rivers. They remain year-round at all but the highest elevations and are not usually observed in the water. Instead, they inhabit open sandbars, mud flats, and pastures along the water's edge. Here they feed on grasshoppers, ticks, flies, and mosquitos. They are solitary birds, seldom gathering in flocks.

Killdeer are most readily identified by two dark neck bands and a snowy white breast. They perform amusing histrionics when approached too closely, especially near their nesting sites. They feign injury in a most convincing manner, crawling, fluttering, and dragging themselves along as if horribly wounded.

These delightful birds can also be recognized by their vociferous call: a single, loud *killdeer.*

Cliff Swallow *(Petrochelidon pyrrhonota)*

Cliff swallows arrive by the millions on our western rivers when mosquito larvae begin hatching in May. Their cheerful presence is welcomed by all river runners who are plagued by those syringed fiends.

These small, industrious birds immediately begin building colonies of bulbous mud nests on overhanging or vertical cliffs next to the water. The young usually hatch by mid-June. When this occurs, the squeaking melee of feeding provides endless entertainment. I enjoy picking out a single swallow in the midst of the fracas and watching it feed its young. Remarkably, it returns to the nest with a fresh mouthful of insects about every 30 seconds. Clusters of the swallows gourd-shaped nests dot riverside cliffs from the mountains to the desert.

Swallows claim the prize as nature's most adroit flyers. Cliff swallows spend most of their time flying over water. All their activities are done on the wing—feeding, drinking, playing, preening and, some say, even mating. In a brash gesture, one will occasionally fly directly at you and bank away at the last second.

Violet green swallows and white-throated swifts often fly with the cliff swallows. Violet greens are distingushed by their green color and moderately forked tails. Black and white colored swifts, slightly larger than the swallows, appear to be wearing tuxedos because of their black and white markings.

Cliff Swallows.

Canada Goose *(Branta canadensis)*

Canadas are the only geese commonly found on Southern Rocky Mountain rivers. Beginning in late March or early April, the familiar honking echos over the canyons as their flying wedges follow watercourses northward to breeding grounds in Canada. On the way they stop to feed on aquatic plants along the water's edge.

Canadas are large-bodied birds; on these rivers they are second in size only to great blue herons and eagles. Boldly patterned, they are characterized by a black head and neck with a prominant white cheek.

These birds rarely feed alone. One sees them in pairs or occasionally in flocks. They mate for life. If a Canada goose loses its mate, it will not take another. The sight of a lone goose brings a twinge of sadness as will as speculation: Could its mate have flown in front of a shotgun muzzle?

Some of these faithful birds stop to breed on Southern Rocky Mountain rivers. They build nests of grass and twigs close to the water's edge. Only the most remote areas are selected, where grassy banks provide abundant food and nesting places. Portions of the Rio Grande, Green, and lower Gunnison come alive with families of geese in early May. Raucous parents honk continuously as river runners approach, leading them downriver away from their downy yellow goslings, who dive when humans get too near.

Whether stopping here only to feed or staying to breed, these stately geese disappear by late July.

Belted Kingfisher *(Megacerle alcyon)*

Dropping headfirst from an overhanging ledge or limb, the kingfisher strikes the water with a splash, grasps a fish in his heavy beak, and surges into the air. With an ir-regular wingbeat reminiscent of a woodpecker, he carries his prey to an isolated perch where he stuns it with a sharp blow on the head and swallows it whole. Larger fish take several minutes to disappear, tail-last down the bird's gullet. Later the undigestible bones, bleached white by stomach acid, are regurgitated.

Belted kingfishers are common along Southern Rocky Mountain rivers. Although preferring clear, mountain streams, they are occasionally seen on siltier lower reaches. Singly or sometimes in pairs they patrol a stretch of riverside territory up to a mile long, advertising their presence with a loud, rattling call.

The kingfisher is a stocky bird with a large, grey-blue, crested head, long, straight beak; blue breast band (the "belt") below a thick white neck; white and brown under-parts; and slate blue wings. The female has a second breast band of reddish brown color.

Although their features stand out distinctly, kingfishers are shy. They seldom get close enough for a clear view. Instead they are recognized by their unmistakable, ir-regular wingbeat while dashing low, up and down watercourses. With its shyness and streamside habitat, the belted kingfisher stands as a symbol of riverine wilderness.

Spotted Sandpiper *Actitus macularia)*

The spotted sandpiper is the most common small wading bird on the Southern Rocky Mountain rivers. Its habitat ranges from large desert rivers to the forested streams at high elevations.

The sandpiper is difficult to recognize by markings, but its habits are unmistakable. Its back and head are brown, with a white strip from bill through eye to neck. Darker spots on a white breast—from which the name was derived—do not always stand out clearly, due to its shy nature and small size. It is best recognized by unique flight characteristics and the habit of tilting its body forward, continously bobbing the tail up and down. It teeters, hence the nickname "teetertail." During flight, the wings don't flap or beat. Instead they are held stiffly to the side and vibrated in short spurts between glides.

This endearing bird's habitat is restricted to the riverbank and narrow margin of shallow water near the bank. It rarely swims. It is a loner and, despite its abundance, is never seen in flocks. However, you might pass a dozen of these solitary chaps along one mile of water, each patrolling its hundred-yard stretch of the bank.

Spotted Sandpiper.

Sandpipers arrive on the lower reaches of the rivers by early May. They spend the entire summer moving to higher streams as the weather warms. Then, usually in August or early September, they depart for their wintering grounds on the rivers and shores of Mexico.

Spotted sandpipers are sometimes seen with their cousins, solitary sandpipers. The two are difficult to distinguish. The solitary, however, makes only a short stop in the Southern Rocky Mountains on his migration to breeding ranges in northern Canada.

Great Blue Heron *(Ardea herodias)*

The great blue heron, elusive spirit of the watercourses, is the most common large wading bird on Southern Rocky Mountain rivers below 8,000 feet. It stands four or five feet in height, often with a wingspan of six feet. The great blue is not only big, but superbly statuesque, with long legs, soft gray and blue plummage, and a largely white head.

Shy and difficult to approach, the great blue will often lead you on down the river. It waits patiently until you get to within about 50 yards, then lifts off downriver in strong and gracefully animated flight, its long neck kinked in an "S" shape, its feet projecting behind like a rudder.

The great blue is often seen standing patiently on a sandbar in slack water, waiting for some luckless frog, fish, or insect to come within range. Its crooked neck acts like a taught bow. When the bow is released, the head and daggerlike bill are thrust forward toward its prey with the speed of an arrow.

Great blue herons live solitary lives except during nesting season. In April they gather in rookeries (or heronies) along the Colorado, Rio Grande, Green, Yampa, Gunnison, and San Juan rivers. Nests, commonly in groups of two or three dozen, are situated in cottonwood trees, often on mid-river islands. Passing an active rookery is one of the joys of an early season trip. But boaters should proceed quietly and respectfully, remembering these great birds are upset by intruders. They have not yet come to realize that most river runners are their friends.

Wilson's Phalarope *(Steganopus tricolor)*

Wilson's phalarope, another passing visitor to Southern Rocky Mountain streams, often intermingles with willets and sandpipers in open valleys where rivers creep through willow flats.

Its name is derived from the Greek words *phalarus pous* or "coot footed." This refers to the bird's lobate toes, similar to those of the common coot. He is a beautiful shorebird with a small head, long neck, straight and slender beak. Phalaropes reverse the sex stereotypes of most species. The female is larger than the male and bears the more brightly colored plumage. A bright russet band extends from the female's eye down the neck and across the back. The male is the drab sex, with a grey back and plain white breast.

Phalaropes are exceptionally bouyant. They float high in the water like ducks and have the unusual habit of spinning in circles, often for several minutes, to stir up food in the slack water. They are voracious consumers of mosquito larvae and tadpoles. Due to their unique motions they have often been called "whirligigs."

Snowy Egret *(Leucophoyx thula)*

One of the most agreeable, albeit rare, sights on the rivers is the elegant snowy egret. His appearance conjures up the image of a sparkling diamond in the rough of the river's edge. Pure white except for a daggerlike black beak and long black legs, he stands out

Snowy Egret.

sharply against darker backgrounds. These stately birds are close relatives to great blue herons although smaller and less common on Southern Rocky Mountain rivers. The name egret is often given to herons of white coloration.

Snowy egrets feed singly, but where one is seen others will probably appear in the miles ahead. Boaters on the river in April might see a pair performing their graceful mating dance. The male spreads the feathers on his head, neck, and back peacocklike and jumps gaily around the female.

Snowy egrets fly slowly and casually with a heavy, arrested wingbeat. The head is tucked back almost to the leading edge of the wings, with the feet trailing behind. The egret is not a particularly shy bird. He will probably let you pass without springing into flight.

Willet *(Catoptrophorus semipalmatus)*

Willets standing in flocks along the river banks may hardly seem to notice your passing. You, in turn, may hardly notice them, for these small, plump, nondescript waders have a dull grey color. Only when they flash into flight do they display their striking markings. Unmistakable black and white stripes color the undersides of their wings. Two black bands with a white one between extend from the body to the outer edge of the wing. Willets almost always fly in tight diving and dipping formations resembling an Air Force aerobatic team.

Willets gather on Southern Rocky Mountain rivers during spring migration to breeding grounds on lakes and streams of North Dakota, eastern Montana, and southern Saskatchewan. On the way they feed on mollusks and small fish where the water is quiet. By late May they are gone.

The unusual whistle of this delightful shore bird is the source of its name—a rapid *pill-will-willet, pill-will-willet.*

Willets.

Afterword

You can feel the anger in water behind a dam.
—Barry Holstun Lopez, *River Notes*

Before the Last Dam

I am reminded of a night around the campfire in 1976 on our final float trip through the upper Black Canyon between Cimarron and the East Portal before the completion of Crystal Dam. We pitched our camp on a bench high above the junction of Crystal Creek and the Gunnison.

Enveloped within the canyon walls, listening to the roar of Crystal Creek Rapid, we soon forgot those nearby monuments to man's ability to pour concrete which stood both upriver and downriver from our campsite. Hidden from cultural intrusions, a canyon transmits a feeling of tranquil solitude and closeness to eternal forces. The dark gray walls of black Canyon Schist turned burgundy with evening light.

We were lifted from the hypnotizing campfire by the outline of four beavers swimming side by side down the middle of the river. "Mom, dad, and the kids," said Joan. "Beavers exhibit many of the traits we humans admire: life-long marriage, family groups, hard work, the building of functional and aesthetic structures."

"Right," replied Walt, "but those beavers are wiser than we are." Taking a gulp of his favorite concoction, Wyler's lemondade with grain alcohol, Walt launched into an unexpected monologue. "Trapping the sediment behind their dams," he observed, "beavers build and open up valley floors, slow the annual spring meltwater flooding, and change the face of this country more than we could ever do. The riparian environment is enhanced by beaver dams. Open meadows push back the dense woodland, providing habitat for sun-loving plants which in turn provide food for many animals. The beaver provides a habitat for the pond fish. Its open meadows give the large, soaring raptors space to hunt. Each species provides not only for itself but also for its living brethren. The beaver does much more than its share. How do we provide for our wild brethren, we who hold the power of the sun?" Another gulp goes down Walt's inexhaustable gullet.

"The beaver isn't aware of the environmental changes he is creating," responded Joan.

"Neither are we," answered Walt, listing dangerously close to the fire. "We build as the beaver does, oblivious to the intrinsic changes we are making, in a drunken desire for more and more comfort."

"Speaking of drunken," commented Bill, slightly perturbed at Walt's sermonizing.

Walt's head was drooping. "This living canyon will soon be drowned and dead, all for the sake of a few air conditioners, 'foot fixers,' and hair dryers."

"In addition to necessities like heat and light," retorted Bill.

"No," Walt slurred, "we are not as wise as the beaver. We have forgotten our compact with the green world from which we emerged, and the green world will have the last laugh." He rose to his feet and, like a wounded soldier standing defiantly in the path of the onrushing enemy, raised his cup over the crackling fire and boomed: "A toast to the beaver; a toast to the river!" Then he stumbled into the darkness toward his sleeping bag.

Bibliography

The Birth of Rivers: A Geologic Odyssey

Blackwelder, Eliot. *Origin of the Colorado River*. Bulletin of Geological Society of America, vol. 45, 1934.

Curtis, Bruce. *Cenozoic History of the Southern Rocky Mountains*. Geological Society of America, Memoir 144, 1975.

Fenneman, N.M. *Physiography of Western U.S.* New York: 1931.

Follansbee, Robert. *Some Characteristics of Run-Off in the Rocky Mountain Region*. USGS Water Supply Paper 500-C, 1922.

Hunt, C.B. *Cenozoic Geology of the Colorado Plateau*. USGS Professional Paper 279, 1956.

Powell, J.W. *Exploration of the Colorado River of the West and Its Tributaries*. Washington D.C.: 1875.

Rabbitt, McKee, Hunt, and Leopold. *The Colorado River Region and John Wesley Powell*. USGS Professional Paper 669, 1969.

Shelton, John. *Geology Illustrated*. San Fransisco: Freeman and Co., 1966.

Of Dams and Diversions

Berkman and Viscusi. *Damming the West*. N.Y.: Grossman, 1973.

Bingham, Jay. "Reclamation and the Colorado." *Utah Historical Quarterly, July, 1960*.

Chiras, Jay. *"Colorado Water Decisions." Spray Newsletter, 1978.*

Milliken, J. Gordon. *Water and Energy in Colorado's Future*. Boulder: Westview Press, 1981.

National Research Council, Committee on Water, National Academy of Science. *Water and Choice in the Colorado Basin*. 1968.

Shelton, John. *Geology Illustrated*. San Fransisco: Freeman and Co., 1966.

U.S. Dept. of Interior. *Colorado Bureau of Reclamation Projects. 1978.*

U.S. Dept. of Interior. *The Story of the Colorado Big Thompson Project*. 1968.

Upper and Lower Colorado River Basins

Adams, Samuel. Reports and Letters to 42nd Congress, U.S. House of Representatives, Misc. Documents #37, 1871.

Dellenbaugh, Frederick S. *The Romance of the Colorado*. N.Y.: Putman's Sons, 1902 (also "Upper Green River Basin").

Kendrick, Frank C. "Notebook of Colorado River Survey, 1889." Manuscript files of State Historical Society of Colorado.

Marston, Otis. "River Runners: Fast Water Navigation." *Utah Historical Quarterly,* July 1960 (also White, Yampa, Upper and Lower Green river basins).

Stegner, Wallace. *Beyond the Hundredth Meridian*. Boston: Haughton Mifflin, 1954.

Stiles, Helen. "Down the Colorado in 1889." *Colorado Magazine*, XLI/3, 1964.

Waters, Frank. *The Colorado*. N.Y.: Rinehart, 1946.

Gunnison River Basin

Hunt, C.B. "Geologic History of the Colorado River," USGS Prof. Paper 669-C, 1969(also Dolores and Yampa river basins).

Kolb, Ellsworth, *Railroad Red Book,* vol. 33 #95, 1916.

Marsh, Barton W. *The Uncompahgre Valley and the Gunnison Tunnel,* Montrose, Colorado, 1980.

Mason, Ron. Letter to Mr. Kastellic of Black Canyon National Monument, 1975.

Rennebaum, Fritz, et. al. *Gunnison Wild and Scenic River Study,* U.S. Bureau of Land Management, Montrose, Colorado, 1980.

Sprague, Marshall. *Colorado,* W.W. Norton and Cox: N.Y., 1976.

Warner, Mark and Walker, Dexter. *Through the Black Canyon,* Black Canyon of the Gunnison National Monument, Colorado, 1967.

"The Gunnison Gorge, the Forgotten Black Canyon," *Denver Post Empire Magazine,* Sept. 1976.

Dolores River Basin

Atwood, Wallace and Mather, Kirtley. *Physiography and Quarternary Geology of the San Juan Mountains, Colorado.* USGS Prof. Paper 166, 1932 (also San Juan and Rio Grande river basins).

Cater, Fred. *Geology of the Salt Anticline Region.* USGS Prof. Paper 637 1970.

Lavender, David. *One Man's West.* Doubleday, 1945.

Marston, Otis. "Running the Dolores River." *Colorado Magazine,* Oct. 1949.

O'Rourke, Paul. *Frontier in Transition, A History of Southwest Colorado.* Bureau of Land Management, 1980.

Sumner, David. "What Fate for the Beleagured Dolores?" *Living Wilderness,* 1977.

Toll, Henry. "The River of Sorrows." *Trail and Timberline,* May 1973.

Toll, Henry W. III. *Dolores River Archeology: Canyon Adaptations.* Bureau of Land Management, 1971.

USGS. *Geologic History of the Slick Rock District.* Professional Paper 576, 1969.

Wild and Scenic River Report, Dolores River. House of Rep. Document 164, 95th Congress, March 1976.

San Juan River Basin

Baars, D.L. *Geology of the Canyons of the San Juan River.* Four Corners Geological Society, 1973.

Bolton, Herbert. *Pageant in the Wilderness.* Salt Lake City: Utah State Historical Society, 1950 (also Dolores and White river basins).

Frost, John. "Canyons, Mystery and Solitude." *Guidebook to the Geology of the Paradox Basin.* Intermountain Assoc. of Petroleum Geologists, 1958.

Hafen, Leroy. "Dominiguez and Escalante Expedition of 1776." *Hispanic Contributions to the State of Colorado.* 1976.

Miser, Hugh. *The San Juan Canyon, Southeastern Utah.* USGS Water Supply Paper 538, 1924.

Rigby, Keith. *Southern Colorado Plateau.* Dubuque: Kendall/Hunt, 1977.

Silver, Caswell. "Railroad Log, The Den. and Rio Grande West. R.R., Silverton to Durango." *Guidebook of Southwestern San Juan Mountains, Colorado.* New Mexico Geological Society, 1957.

Upper and Lower Green River Basins

Bonner, T.D. *The Life and Adventures of James P. Beckwourth.* N.Y.: Knopf and Co., 1931.

Bradley, W.H.: *Geomorphology of the North Flank of the Uinta Mountains."* USGS Prof. Paper 185-I, 1936.

Dale, Harrison Clifford. The Ashley-Smith Explorations and Discovery of a Central Route to the Pacific—1822-1829. Cleveland: Authur Clark Co., 1918.

Fremont, John Charles. *Narrative of Exploring Expedition to the Rocky Mountains in the Year 1842.* D. Appleton & Co., 1846.

Mahoney and Grant. "Are You For or Against the Echo Park Dam?" *Collier's,* February 1955.

Manly, W.L. *Death Valley in Forty-Nine.* San Jose: 1894.

Untermann and Untermann. *Geology of Dinosaur National Monument.* Dinosaur National Monument, 1969 (also "Yampa River Basin").

Yampa River Basin

Athern, Frederic J. *An Isolated Empire—History of Northwest Colorado.* Denver: Bureau of Land Management, 1976.

Burroughs, John Rolf. *Where the West Stayed Young.* N.Y.: Morrow & Co., 1962.

Intermountain Assoc. of Petroleum Geologists. *Guidebook to the Geology of Northwest Colorado.* 1955.

Sears, J.D. "Relations of the Browns Park Formation, Etc." Bulletin of Geological Society of America, vol. 35, 1924.

Wise, Rob. "Working notes for Cross Mountain Run." 1974.

White River Basin

Bureau of Land Management. *White River Dam Project: Final Environmental Impact Statement.* 1982.

Dawson, Thomas. *The Ute War: A History of the White River Massacre.* Boulder: Johnson Publishing Co., 1964.

Egan, Ferol. Fremont. N.Y.: Doubleday, 1977 (also "Rio Grande River Basin").

Sprague, Marshall. *Massacre: The Tragedy at White River.* Boston: Little, Brown, 1957.

North And South Platte River Basins

Crofutt, George. *Crofutt's Guide to Colorado.* 1885.

Fry, Norman. *Cache la Poudre, the River as Seen From 1889.* 1954.

Grand Encampment Herald, 1889 to 1910.

Grand Encampment Museum, Encampment, Wyoming.

Kindley, Mark. "Behind the Lines in the Water War." *Denver Magazine,* August 1978.

McCoy, Tom. "Waterton Canyon, A Lovely Site for a Battle." *Colorado Magazine,* July-August 1978.

Smith, Bud. "The South Platte." *Colorado Outdoors,* September-October 1980.

Arkansas River Basin

Campbell, Marius. *Guidebook of the Western U.S., Part E, The Denver and Rio Grande Western Route.* USGS Bulletin 707, 1922.

Davis, Clyde. *The Arkansas.* N.Y.: Farrar and Rinehart, 1940.

"Late Cenozoic Events in the Leadville District and Upper Arkansas Valley, Colorado." USGS Prof. Paper 424-B, 1961.

Pike, Zebulon Montgomery. *An Account of the Expedition to the Sources of the Mississippi and Through the Western Parts of Louisiana.* Philadelphia: 1810.

Powers, William. "Physiographic History of the Upper Arkansas River Valley and the Royal Gorge, Colorado." *Journal of Geology,* vol. 43, 1935.

Taylor, Ralph. *Colorado South of the Border.* Denver: Sage Books, 1963.

Thwaites, Reuben. *A Brief History of Rocky Mountain Exploration.* N.Y.: D. Appleton & Co., 1904.

Tweto, Ogden. "Rio Grande Rift System in Colorado." *Rio Grande Rift.* American Geophysical Union, Washington, D.C., 1979 (also "Rio Grande River Basin").

U.S. Bureau of Reclamation. *Fryingpan-Arkansas Project: Final Environmental Impact Statement.* 1975.

Van Alstine, R.E. "Allochthonous Paleozoic Blocks in the Tertiary San Luis-Upper Arkansas Graben." USGS Prof. Paper 700-B, 1970 (also "Rio Grande River Basin").

Rio Grande River Basin

Belcher, Robert. *The Geomorphic Evolution of the Rio Grande.* Baylor University, 1975.

Dellenbaugh, Frederick. *Fremont in '49.* N.Y.: Putnam's Sons, 1914.

Hawley, J.W. *Guidebook to the Rio Grande Rift in New Mexico and Colorado.* New Mexico Bureau of Mines and Mineral Resources, 1978.

Siebenthal, C.E. *Geology and Water Resources of the San Luis Valley, Colorado.* USGS Water Supply Paper 240, 1910.

Simmons, Virginia McConnell. *The San Luis Valley.* Boulder: Pruett Publishing, 1979.

Spencer, Frank. *The Story of the San Luis Valley.* San Luis Valley Historical Society, 1975.

Wolle, Muriel. *Stampede to Timberline.* Sage Books, 1949.

Index